Coming Home to the Self through Freeing the Singing Voice

Joan Dosso

Coming Home to the Self through Freeing the Singing Voice

A Qualitative Study of the Psycho-emotional Experience of Singers, Focusing on the Mind-body Connection, Identity Development, and Shame

VDM Verlag Dr. Müller

Imprint

Bibliographic information by the German National Library: The German National Library lists this publication at the German National Bibliography; detailed bibliographic information is available on the Internet at http://dnb.d-nb.de.

Cover image: www.purestockx.com

Published 2008 Saarbrücken

Publisher:
VDM Verlag Dr. Müller Aktiengesellschaft & Co. KG , Dudweiler Landstr. 125 a,
66123 Saarbrücken, Germany,
Phone +49 681 9100-698, Fax +49 681 9100-988,
Email: info@vdm-verlag.de

Produced in Germany by:
Reha GmbH, Dudweilerstrasse 72, D-66111 Saarbrücken
Schaltungsdienst Lange o.H.G., Zehrensdorfer Str. 11, 12277 Berlin, Germany
Books on Demand GmbH, Gutenbergring 53, 22848 Norderstedt, Germany

Impressum

Bibliografische Information der Deutschen Nationalbibliothek: Die Deutsche Nationalbibliothek verzeichnet diese Publikation in der Deutschen Nationalbibliografie; detaillierte bibliografische Daten sind im Internet über http://dnb.d-nb.de abrufbar.

Coverbild: www.purestockx.com

Erscheinungsjahr: 2008
Erscheinungsort: Saarbrücken

Verlag: VDM Verlag Dr. Müller Aktiengesellschaft & Co. KG , Dudweiler Landstr. 125 a,
D- 66123 Saarbrücken,
Telefon +49 681 9100-698, Telefax +49 681 9100-988,
Email: info@vdm-verlag.de

Herstellung in Deutschland:
Schaltungsdienst Lange o.H.G., Zehrensdorfer Str. 11, D-12277 Berlin
Books on Demand GmbH, Gutenbergring 53, D-22848 Norderstedt
Reha GmbH, Dudweilerstrasse 72, D-66111 Saarbrücken

ISBN: 978-3-639-04284-9

This thesis is dedicated to my authentic self, whose voice I can finally hear and am learning to trust and use more freely.

I wish I could speak like music.

I wish I could put the swaying splendor
Of the fields into words

So that you could hold Truth
Against your body
And dance.

I am trying the best I can
With this crude brush, the tongue,

To cover you with light.

I wish I could speak like divine music.

I want to give you the sublime rhythms
Of this earth and the sky's limbs

As they joyously spin and surrender,
Surrender
Against God's luminous breath.

(Hafiz)

ACKNOWLEDGEMENTS

Writing this thesis has been a journey home to myself. I am deeply grateful to the following travel companions who guided, encouraged, listened, and provided practical support, patience, and humour along the way.

To Annika, the primary co-researcher, and her partner Maureen—who opened their lives so honestly to me, sharing their wisdom and music. My profound thanks. Your skill and vulnerability have made this thesis a transformative journey and created a safe place for me to begin opening my own voice.

To the three Deborahs: Deborah Barrett, my supervisor who believed I had a voice worth finding and making heard, who was enthusiastic about my work when I was exhausted, worked diligently on my many drafts, and encouraged me to be faithful to my own process; Deborah Garrick, who read my writings out of faithful friendship and interest, and provided feedback and stimulating discussion; Deborah Lawson, who shared her writer's wisdom and listened to much of my journey.

To Molly MacIsaac, who shared in symbolizing my learnings at the river.

To Sara Jo Pipher, who reminded me in the difficult times that there would be life beyond the thesis, and that the ocean was waiting for me.

To Jenn Timm, who applied her analytical skills to clarify my muddled musings.

To Judy Simpson, who helped me process the process, and pointed me towards research methods and people who could best draw out my voice.

To Jill Dosso, my grammatically astute niece, who creatively shared her wisdom with me.

To the gracious music therapists, Susan Summers and Kirsten Davis, who shared their personal and professional work.

To Dr. Elizabeth Bolger, who accompanied me through my therapeutic voice lessons, helped me begin the work of freeing my authentic self, and gave me the permission to run right through the middle of emotional mud puddles.

To my parents, who made it possible for me to undertake this degree and have stood solid and supportive through so many life changes.

My warmest thanks and appreciation to all of you. I hope you will find your own voices becoming freer through what you read here.

TABLE OF CONTENTS

CHAPTER ONE

INTRODUCTION

Setting the Scene: My Early Vocal Experience

During my Master's programme in choral conducting several years ago, I had my first formal voice lessons. I had been a flutist for many years and had been teaching high school choir and band but had never studied voice. It was, in fact, not my choice to study voice but a requirement of the program. My audition for acceptance into the choral conducting program included singing, which made me far more nervous than any of the other components (i.e. conducting!). I sang with a clear, straight tone (no vibrato)—the type of voice I had used since I was a young girl singing hymns in church. It was a pleasant enough sound, in time and tune, but I chose a song with a small range so I didn't have to go uncomfortably high, and I avoided fast notes.

My first voice lessons were with Michael (pseudonym). He assessed my voice quite matter-of-factly after the first lesson. He said I had a few distinct breaks—one around middle c, the other around the e an octave above that. I had a lot of tension in my throat and tongue, and I wasn't moving the air freely. I wasn't staying in contact with the lower resonances as I went higher, and I didn't know how to get into my head voice. I found this very discouraging and saw little point in continuing if there were that many problems to overcome. I was also paralyzed by the frankness of his criticism and withdrew vocally and emotionally, feeling that I needed to avoid further exposure of my inadequacies.

That was the beginning of two semesters of personal and vocal turmoil. I was very guarded in all that I said and did in voice lessons which further constricted my voice. Michael tried to trick me into opening up through vocal games, such as lip trills (vibrating the lips by blowing a lot of air through them while vocalizing, as a child does when imitating a motor boat), the siren, and high pitched giggling. I struggled to participate in these vocal games, fearing I would be criticized for looking silly, and needing to stay in control of my voice to protect myself.

In voice lessons I was paralyzed but I was actually longing to sing the beautiful music we were rehearsing in choir, and wishing I could have the freedom I heard in other voices around me. I also knew that there was another voice inside of me, my "fake opera voice" that I had played with since childhood. It was somewhat unwieldy, harsh, and loud, but it was full, supple, alive with vibrato, and effortless in the upper register. As a child I burst into this voice spontaneously at the sound of classical music, and shrieked at the top of my lungs pretending to be an opera singer. I had a feeling real singing should have the ease of my fake opera voice rather than the tiny, controlled sound I was cautiously squeaking out in voice lessons but I never felt safe enough to use it in front of Michael.

I was always well prepared for my lessons, with words memorized, text translated, and notes learned, but I was making no progress with vocal production. Michael coaxed and prodded, trying to distract and trick me into loosening my vocal control, but I could not. I felt as if there was a door inside of me that I needed to open, but I couldn't find the door knob. The more pressure I felt to hurry up and open it, the less chance I had of finding it. I also feared that if I did open the door, horrible things would pour out—dark, painful, uncontrollable emotions that would completely engulf and annihilate me. I couldn't let myself feel those things, and certainly not in the presence of Michael, whom I respected, and whose approval I very much wanted. That was part of the problem. I felt so much pressure to be perfect that I couldn't let any uncontrolled and possibly ugly or undignified sounds out. He told me to just experiment with my voice but I couldn't trust that he wouldn't judge and reject me for being less than perfect in the experimentation process. Once during a lesson when he'd tried all his tricks and I was still closed tight, he blurted out, "You've just got to trust me!" I surprised myself by replying, "That's what I can't do," and I walked out of the lesson in tears.

Sometimes I managed to take a tiny step forward if I blocked him out by staring at the wall and imitating the sound of another singer. This short lived risk of vocal openness was soon choked off by fear and a flood of embarrassment. Opening my voice felt like being naked, unprotected, with nowhere to hide myself or my shame. I couldn't look him in the eye. I couldn't always hold back the tears. I felt the door within had cracked open for a few seconds and he'd seen more of me than was safe to show anyone, even myself.

I was as surprised as he was that I was reacting this way to voice lessons, particularly because in every other way I was eager to learn. As a young person I had struggled with self-acceptance in a number of areas, being particularly rejecting of my body and sexuality, but I thought I had largely resolved these issues in therapy some years earlier. Voice work dramatically unearthed feelings of shame, not being good enough, and fear in a way that cognitive therapy never had. Music had been an important part of my life for years, and I had met my drive for perfection and experienced feelings of failure as a flutist no matter how successful the performance. But this feeling of exposure, vulnerability, and fear of being rejected if my true self were uncovered had never paralyzed my music making like this before.

Voice lessons with Michael were not the context in which to deal with these deep emotions, yet I found it impossible to open my singing voice without opening everything else. Since neither Michael nor I was equipped to deal with "everything else," I held my voice and emotions under tight control, consequently making little vocal progress. If I was going to find my voice, I was going to have to find myself and I wasn't able to face her yet.

Several years later I entered therapy again, and because voice had brought me in touch with my emotions in the past, I chose to take voice lessons as part of my therapeutic process.

I chose Kate (pseudonym), a female voice teacher who was recommended for being frank but gentle, and open about having lived through her own difficulties. There was a chance she would understand my process, which I hoped would make it easier for me to trust and open up to her. I was up front with her from the beginning. I was not taking voice lessons to become a singer, although I hoped that some of what I learned would help me work with the voices in my choir. I didn't want any pressure to perform or sing heavy repertoire, just help producing the sound and getting comfortable with opening myself vocally.

Kate worked a great deal with my breathing and with helping me relax throat tension so that the breath could sigh out without me pushing from my abdominal muscles as I was in the habit of doing from flute playing. She asked me to feel my ribs, abdomen, and chest with my hands while singing, and to make gestures with my arms to release some of the tension in my body while I walked around the room vocalizing. Although I felt embarrassed and self-conscious at times, I wasn't choked up with tears or blocked with fear and shame. That lasted until about the fourth lesson when she tried to move me out of the safety of the low register into vocalizing at the top of my range. As I ascended my throat tightened involuntarily and my face blushed hot and red. I turned away from her eyes. She continued the piano accompaniment and encouraged me to keep singing. Very soon I couldn't make any sound over the lump in my throat and the tears. We stopped and I told her that I was just too embarrassed; I couldn't do this. I'd had this problem before and I had never been able to get through it. Kate sat down with me and we talked honestly about what I was feeling. She was understanding, humorous, and honest about some of her own life struggles, and said the only thing to do was be kind to myself, be courageous, and get through any way I could, a bit at a time. I trusted her more after that lesson. Although I still ran into shame and tears at times, it was less paralyzing and I was able to inch my way along.

Kate repeatedly told me not to judge what I sounded like, to trust her ears and match the sensations I felt in my body with what she told me she heard. I constantly had to remind myself to stay in the process. Just listen, imitate, and not evaluate. Just let it be. At the time I wrote in my journal:

> Interesting voice lesson—very open from the beginning and a few notes really wiggled and vibrated. I felt I could push all the air I wanted. The voice wants to get free and so does the Joan. I wasn't nervous. I wasn't much of anything (I was so tired and fed up with everything that day). Just stay in the process and sing.

I was trying to do the same thing in psychotherapy at the time. Stay in the process of life. Don't judge myself so harshly. Don't project ahead in anxiety. Just let myself be. I often used metaphors from one process to the other. My vocal process helped me find an experiential way of connecting with my psychotherapy, and my therapeutic process helped me work through the fears that came up in voice lessons. My journal reflects this dual process:

I wish I could let myself "stay inside hugs." I'm afraid. I don't feel them because I'm holding myself in a tight little ball inside… I hate it that I can't take in the warmth I need, even when it's offered to me. It makes me hopeless.

It's like voice lessons. I want to learn with my volitional mind and will. I pay money and work hard to learn, but there is a part of me that is shut tightly on the inside—a part that I don't seem to have conscious control of. It is in control of itself, and refuses to open. This year of lessons has been "beating a path"—not just to God, but to gain access to my inner self which needs to be released, discovered, validated, and celebrated. I only get tiny glimpses of that self when I least expect her to show, and then she disappears again. When I was studying with Michael I used to come home to my safe little room, wrap myself tightly in blankets, and rock myself calm as I cried into my stuffed hedgehog. Something about trying to open that part of myself through singing in front of him felt terrifying and violating. I remember thinking that if I let him hear my real voice then he would realize I was a woman. That would be the ultimate exposure—so unsafe and shameful. I realized I couldn't let myself know that I was a woman—that was too scary and shameful for me, let alone in front of him. Bit by bit I have come to accept more of myself as a woman but it is horribly painful for me at times, and feels like the thing that will seal my fate if discovered.

After another voice lesson that same spring I wrote:

My voice teacher says my voice wants to get free—that it has been so tight—held on like hell for so long. It's weak and vulnerable when it tries to get free. It doesn't know who it is. It doesn't want to accept what it is. It's afraid to be fully female. It's afraid to be seen for what it is in case it is judged harshly. You don't deserve that title—female—you are a horrible excuse of it.

…I wasn't supposed to have a body—that was the problem (or so I thought). I used to pray every day that I wouldn't grow up in those ways, but I couldn't stop it. How could God damn me for something I couldn't change? I tried to obliterate my femaleness in numerous ways—how I dressed, talked, by acting like a tom-boy, not letting myself feel or express anything that seemed "girlish." I couldn't be gentle or nurturing, I didn't hug things, like stuffed animals (I got my hedge hog when I was 26!) or people. I wasn't supposed to need or feel anything that put me in the "female camp". Now I see that you can't chop off your femaleness like a finger. It's a thread woven through your whole being. If you try to shut it off then you actually tear up the fabric of your being.

I had intuitively combined voice work and psychotherapy to access my inner self, but why did it work? I chose to combine the two partly because I needed to go back and try to conquer the past failure of not being able to free my voice. I also wanted to know how much the dynamics of the teacher-student relationship with Michael had contributed to my strong reaction and if it was easier to free my voice in a different context. But a much greater reason was that voice work put me in touch with buried feelings that I needed to release and therapy didn't do that for me. Why did this happen with voice and not other instruments I'd studied, like flute or piano? Why did voice work point so specifically to body image and sexuality issues?

I knew I was not alone in my experience. While I was in the choral conducting program I had seen other singers run out of their voice lessons in tears. I'd listened to the personal problems of several choir students whose emotional issues were triggered by singing. I'd sadly watched a very talented female singer in my choir develop a debilitating voice disorder and quit singing. She had bitterly quoted the voice specialist who had been treating her, saying, "It's all in my head." I had a close friend who was studying to be a singer and struggled for years to open her voice with little success. After being out of touch with her for some years, she popped back into my life and proudly played me a recording of her transformed voice. She told me it wasn't until she had done body work and psychotherapy to release childhood loss and wounding that she had been able to free her voice.

Now as I am studying pastoral counseling and seeing clients in my practicum, I often feel frustrated that "talking therapy" allows them to remain in their heads, analyzing issues without releasing the feelings that are holding them stuck. I know that voice was an important part of my therapeutic process, particularly helping me to integrate mind, body and emotions. What is it about working with the voice that facilitates this integration? Can the link between a person's voice and their psycho-emotional self be accessed in pastoral counseling? How?

The Research Question

It is these questions, born out of my personal experience, which I am attempting to answer through this qualitative case study of a female singer in the process of freeing her voice. I am interested in the experience of a singer freeing her voice, how she feels physically and emotionally, how she thinks about the process, and if it has broader effects on her person beyond opening her singing voice.

I decided that I would limit the study to one female singer who was seriously pursuing vocal training with the goal of freeing her voice for public performance. This would ensure the singer was committed enough to the process to have persevered through blocks and had been in the process long enough to have reflected on how she was able to make progress. My primary focus began, and has remained, the process of freeing the singing voice which includes releasing restrictions, obstructions, interfering tensions, and inhibitions which encumber the voice. My understanding of what must be released has expanded as I have discovered the singing voice can not be easily separated from the rest of a person's identity and physical self. However, I did not set out to explore "finding one's voice" in the metaphorical sense that is common in feminist literature. There is some overlap of these meanings of "voice" which enter into the discussion, but it is not the main focus of this study. Therefore, the research question I am investigating is: What is the experience of a female singer in the process of freeing her voice?

About the Study

My preliminary exploration of this question was to reflect on my own experience. Moustakas (1990) describes heuristic methods of research that resonate with my natural approach to this study. "I begin the heuristic journey with something that has called to me from within my life experience . . . The initial 'data' is within me; the challenge is to discover and explicate its nature" (p.13). I have always been a person who engages intensely and personally in whatever I study, seeing it as a journey towards self-growth. I was drawn to the question of freeing the voice because it was an unanswered question in my own life which I hoped I could grow into answering through the study. Heuristic discovery claims to be a process of transforming one's own self that includes self-understanding and self-growth, and is self-directed and self-motivated (Moustakas, 1990, p.13), and therefore appeared to suit my purposes.

In addition to the personal interest and hope for growth I invested in the question of freeing the voice, I believed that it was significant for others and could shed light on both the teaching of voice, and the use of voice in pastoral counseling. Moustakas (1990) says that every question that matters personally also has a social, if not universal, significance (p.15) and Van Manen (1997) agrees saying "whatever are *my* experiences could be *our* experiences" (p.57).

I began an heuristic inquiry by looking back on journal entries from the time of my vocal experiences, talking with musician friends who were with me during that time and heard my struggles, and journaling again about my experience. Through these activities I was able to get in touch with the thoughts and feelings I experienced at that time. From this material I drew up a set of topics I needed to investigate to further unravel the mystery of how and why the attempt to free my singing voice accessed deep emotional and psychological issues. I knew I could not answer these questions solely from my experience, so I sought out other singers for discussion. From these informal interviews, I decided that I needed to go outside of my own experience and observe singers in the process of freeing their voices, and hear them talk about their experiences. I also realized that to have an in-depth understanding of the inhibitions, emotional issues, and tensions which blocked a singer's voice, I would need to spend a good deal of time with a single singer. Therefore, I decided to structure my research as a qualitative case study of one female singer whom I could interview a number of times and observe singing and teaching singing.

Annika (pseudonym), the singer I chose, invited me to attend a week of voice master classes she was teaching with her partner Maureen (pseudonym). I observed classes for six days, as well as the private lessons and concerts of their 12 voice students. I interviewed Annika and her partner extensively, and had one hour interviews with five of the 12 master class students about their experiences in the classes and of their process of freeing the voice. During the six months after the master classes I transcribed the interviews, analyzed for themes, and correlated the information from the interviews with what I observed in classes and lessons. I then sent my findings to all co-researchers to check for accuracy and obtain further input. I had four lengthy telephone conversations with Annika clarifying and deepening the material from her interviews, and then integrated all of my data with the literature and concluded my study.

Even though I chose case study as my primary research method, I was not able, nor did I want to stop reflecting on my own experience or using it as a way of knowing what the next step should be. This in itself was a learning process for me because there is a good deal of academic pressure to make "rational" outlines and plans at the beginning of the study which can take on prison-like rigidity and keep one from the deepest, most personal learning. Therefore, I decided to incorporate some heuristic elements into the case study and trust the heuristic process that:

> ... requires a return to the self, a recognition of self-awareness, and a valuing of one's own experience. The heuristic process challenges me to rely on my own resources, and to gather within myself the full scope of my observations, thoughts, feelings, senses, and intuitions; to accept as authentic and valid whatever will open new channels for clarifying a topic, question, problem, or puzzlement. (Moustakas, 1990, p.13)

The decision to allow myself the freedom to follow this flexible, intuitive research format was a step towards finding my own research and writing voice, the beginning of the growth I was seeking.

Outline of the Thesis

Having discussed the personal underpinnings of this study in Chapter One, Chapter Two goes on to outline the method I used—case study with some heuristic activities used to examine my personal experience. Chapter Three is an interdisciplinary literature review covering material from vocal pedagogy, body work, music therapy, shame and identity development from a self-psychology and object relations perspective, and the psycho-spiritual roots of shame. Chapter Four is a presentation of the data discovered in the study. This includes the life history of Annika (the main co-researcher) as it pertains to her vocal journey, my experience of a voice lesson with Annika and her partner Maureen, the main themes from interviews with five of the master class students, and an in-depth examination of breathing. Chapter Five is a synthesis of my analysis of the data, including the process of moving towards freedom, the effects of the teacher-student relationship on the vocal process, and the benefits of "staying home" to sing. Chapter Six presents conclusions drawn from the study, contributions to knowledge and literature, suggested topics for further study, applications for voice teachers and pastoral counselors, and a summary of my personal learnings and how the study transformed me personally.

CHAPTER TWO

METHOD

Choice of Research Design: Case Study

I knew when I chose the research question, "What is the experience of a female singer in the process of freeing her voice?" that I was choosing a topic that would allow me to reflect deeply on my personal experience, and hopefully grow through the study into a new experience. Because of this desire for personal involvement, I was drawn to heuristic inquiry as described by Moustakas (1990), "Heuristic inquiry is a process that begins with a question . . .that has been a personal challenge and puzzlement in the search to understand one's self and the world in which one lives" (p.15). Heuristic inquiry asks the researcher to "enter fully" and personally into the study, and encourages "self-search, self-dialogue, and self-discovery; the research question and the methodology flow out of inner awareness, meaning, and inspiration" (p.11).

Heuristic inquiry is a very appealing approach to me, a person who is naturally given to deep introspection. However, I knew that I had already ruminated over my own experience of attempting to free my voice for several years and not come to any new conclusions, so I needed to go outside of myself in my research. I wanted to use my experience as a guide, and continue working out my personal questions as part of the meaning making and inspiration, but I agreed with Van Manen (1997) that personal experience is a starting point for qualitative research (p.54) since "one's own experiences are the possible experiences of others" (p.57).

I decided to explore the "experiences of others" as well as my own, and hopefully through integrating them I would come to a new self-understanding, and find "universal significance" in my personal question (Moustakas, 1990, p.15). Therefore, it will become apparent that although I did not choose heuristic inquiry as the method for this study, there are elements of the heuristic approach and activities present throughout.

One of the first things I did in exploring possibilities of how to bring other singers into the study was to have informal interviews with three singers to whom I had easy access. I wanted to know if other singers had similar experiences of emotional and psychological blocks inhibiting their vocal freedom. Male and female singers alike responded with great interest to my question. They said that to varying degrees they had experiences similar to mine, and they had observed and attempted to help their students through such blocks as well. Each one asked if they could read my study when it was finished because they wanted to know more about what it was in voice work that brought up deep personal issues, and how to handle them appropriately in their teaching studios. I also noticed that when I asked about vocal blocks they began talking more about their personal lives—stories of divorce, loss of loved ones, life threatening traumas and injuries, and struggles with sexual identity, than they did about their voices. The connection I heard them making was that the struggles they encountered in the process of freeing their voices were directly related to their life contexts and emotional experiences.

Realizing this connection between life context and vocal freedom, I began exploring case study as a possible methodological approach since case studies "focus on a contemporary phenomenon within some real-life context," especially when "the boundaries between phenomenon and context are not clearly evident" (Yin, 2003, p.13). These boundaries are not clear in the case of a singer in the process of freeing her voice because the context has an effect on the phenomenon, and the context is part of the phenomenon. By context I mean not only the singer's physical surroundings, such as the room where she is singing, and the presence or absence of an audience or other musicians, but also her day to day fluctuating psycho-emotional, physical, and spiritual states, as well as long term habitual ways of being. Her life context influences her starting point, approach towards, and experience of the process of freeing her voice. In order to understand her way of being and its influence on her process I needed to trace the significant life events and influences that shaped her as a person. I concluded that I needed a research design that allowed a holistic approach, which according to Merriam (2001) is characteristic of a qualitative case study. "A case study is an intensive, holistic description and analysis of a single instance, phenomenon, or social unit" (p.27).

Robert Yin (2003) states, "case studies are the preferred strategy when 'how' or 'why' questions are being posed" (p.1). Even though my question was posed in a "What is the experience?" form, I knew that within this "what" question there were many "how" and "why" questions that needed exploring about how these life experiences related to the journey towards vocal freedom. I wanted to do more than just describe the experience, I wanted to understand, explain, and interpret. In order to do that, "how" and "why" questions would be a large part of my process of investigation. Yin (2003) again recommends case study. "'How' and 'why' questions deal with operational links needing to be traced over time" (p.6). Using a case study design allows me to ask detailed, specific questions that examine my proposition that a relationship exists between life context and vocal freedom. Within some methods, such as phenomenology, such a proposition would have to be bracketed out and questions could not be posed which directed the participant towards enforcing this proposition. However, according to Yin (2003), "In a case study there are benefits from the prior development of theoretical propositions to guide data collection and analysis" (p.14). In the analysis of the data, a case study will allow me to describe, interpret the meaning, and mention "lessons learned" from the case (Cresswell, 1998, p.63).

Another significant reason that led me to choose case study is "its ability to deal with a full variety of evidence—documents, artifacts, interviews, and observations" (Yin, 1984, p.20). The experience of the process of freeing one's voice has public, observable components such as live performances, recordings of singers at various points in their development, and teaching situations such as voice lessons and master classes where singers are in an obvious learning phase of their vocal journey. One can also collect data from documents such as reviews from music critics, and correspondence and journal entries from the singers themselves. All these forms of data can be used in triangulation with the more standard form of data collection—interviewing singers directly about their experience. Yin (2003) states, "Case study relies on multiple sources of evidence, with data needing to converge in a triangulating fashion" (Yin, 2003, p.13-14). Therefore, I concluded that the most thorough way to investigate and portray the experience of a singer in the process of freeing her voice was to use a case study approach.

Case Study Further Defined

A significant question raised by most case study authors, particularly Yin (2003), Stake (1995), and Merriam (2001) is how to define the case. Yin (1994) defines case study in terms of research process, Stake (1995) focuses on trying to pinpoint the unit of study, and Merriam (1988) originally defined it in terms of end product. Merriam (2001) has recently re-defined her position:

> The single most defining characteristic of case study research lies in delimiting the object of study, the case. Smith's (1978) notion of the case as a bounded system comes the closest . . . Stake (1978) adds that "the case is an integrated system" (p.2). Both definitions allow me to see the case as a thing, a single entity, and unit around which there are boundaries. I can "fence in" what I am going to study. (p.27)

The "integrated system" under examination in this study is the process of working towards vocal freedom as experienced by the singer. In some ways the singer is the boundary of the system because it is her experience I am most interested in, even though I refer to my own and other people's experiences and generalize beyond the main co-researcher in this study. In other ways the vocal experience is the boundary of the system because I am not studying every detail of the singer's life, but only those that she describes as being relevant to her vocal experience. Whether one thinks of it as "the unit of study" or the "bounded-system," the "thing" I am studying is the integrated system of a female singer in the process of freeing her voice.

Stake (2000) makes distinctions between intrinsic and instrumental case studies, although the boundaries between them are flexible and overlapping. Stake (2000) states, "Intrinsic case study is undertaken because . . . the researcher wants better understanding of this particular case . . . Because in all its particularity and ordinariness, the case itself is of interest" (p.437). The bulk of case study work is done by individuals who have an intrinsic interest in the case and little interest in the advance of science. "Their designs aim the inquiry toward understanding of what is important about that case within its own world, which is seldom the same as the worlds of researchers and theorists. Those designs develop what is perceived to be the case's own issues, contexts, and interpretations, its thick description" (p.439). In contrast, instrumental case study is described by Stake (2000):

> A particular case is examined mainly to provide insight into an issue or to redraw a generalization. The case is of secondary interest, it plays a supportive role, and it facilitates our understanding of something else. The case still is looked at in depth, its contexts scrutinized, its ordinary activities detailed, but all because this helps the researcher to pursue the external interest . . . the choice of case is made to advance understanding of the other interest. (p.437)

Although I had an intrinsic interest in the case to begin with, and it deepened as I got to know the co-researcher through observation, interviews, and member checking, I set out initially to understand the experiences of freeing the voice and its generalizability to the use of voice in therapy, and therapeutic issues facing singers. Therefore, in aid of focusing my research, I viewed it as an instrumental case study but recognized its intrinsic value and the uniqueness of this case.

Yin (2003) makes a distinction between exploratory, explanatory, and descriptive case studies, again with overlap and flexibility between the categories (p.5). Exploratory case studies answer "what" questions, with few pre-study propositions, wondering "what" they will find. Explanatory case studies answer more of the "how" and "why" questions, showing operational links which usually have propositional roots. Descriptive studies more simply describe the case, using thick description and possibly experiential vignettes, allowing readers to vicariously experience the case and come to their own conclusions. This case study has elements of all three of these categories, but because of my interest in the "how" and "why" questions about the relationship between the life context and how the process of freeing the voice is experienced, I would say that it leans most strongly towards being an explanatory case study. Merriam (2001) refers to this type of study as interpretive or analytical because of its complexity, depth, and theoretical orientation (p.39).

Single or Multiple Case Studies

In designing the method I was faced with the question of whether to study single or multiple cases. I knew it would take a number of interviews with a singer to come to a deep understanding of her life context, personality, and the beliefs which shaped her approach to and experience of freeing her voice. In addition to interviewing the case, I wanted to observe her singing and teaching, interview students about their experience of her teaching, and listen to recordings of her past performances to hear her vocal process for myself. This was a rich and varied way of collecting data. However, given the limits of time and resources available for this project, it seemed better to invest myself deeply into a single case than study multiple cases at a more superficial level.

Strengths and Weaknesses of Case Study

One of the major strengths of case study is its flexibility (Sprenkle & Moon, 1996). It offered me a wide variety of data collection methods and flexibility in integrating and presenting data in a creative, intuitive way that suits the creative nature of the process of freeing the voice. A case study anchored in a real life situation, as this study is, "can result in a rich and holistic account of a phenomenon. It offers insights and illuminates meanings that expand its readers' experiences" (Merriam, 1998, p.41).

Yin (2003), Stake (2000), and Merriam (2001) discuss the strengths and limitations of using a single case as opposed to multiple cases. "How can you generalize from a single case?" is a frequent criticism (Yin, 2003, p.10). This criticism is often made of multiple case studies as well since a small number of cases, although having more generalizability, are still not a representative sample. Yin (2003) answers the question by saying:

> Case studies, like experiments, are generalizable to theoretical propositions and not to populations or universes . . . the case study, like doing an experiment, does not represent a "sample" and in doing case study, your goal will be to expand and generalize theories (analytic generalization) and not to enumerate frequencies (statistical generalization). (p.11)

Stake (1995) strengthens this point by simply stating, "We do not study a case primarily to understand other cases. Our first obligation is to understand this one case" (p.4). In studying this particular single case, I was in the unique position to also interview her life-partner, who is also a singer and co-teacher. I also interviewed five of the master class students to obtain supporting data about the main co-researcher, asking them to reflect on how they experienced her as a teacher, singer, and the leader of the master classes they were involved in. Much of their interview data verified the data I received from the main co-researcher and therefore expanded the generalizability of the study beyond that of a single case study.

Sprenkle & Moon (1996) say that single-case study is a particularly suitable method in situations where one has access to a unique case and there has been little written on the topic. Since I have not found any other in-depth studies in the literature on the experience of freeing the voice, I see this study as an opportunity to "learn more about the case, generating hypotheses about the case, and serving as a first step for future research on the topic" (Sprenkle & Moon, 1996, p.393).

Case studies, single or multiple-case, have often been criticized as having "insufficient precision (i.e. quantification), objectivity, or rigor" (Yin, 2003). Although this stereotype exists, it is not necessarily accurate, particularly since case study continues to be used extensively in social science research in a variety of traditional disciplines (psychology, sociology, political science, anthropology, history, and economics) as well as practice oriented fields (Yin, 2003, p.xiii). Case study has been thought of by some as appropriate only for the exploratory or descriptive phase of research and not suitable for experiments and explanatory inquiries. There are explanatory case studies, and exploratory experiments—the distinction is more about when to use each strategy based on the type of research question being asked, and how much control one has over behavioral events, rather than there being a hierarchy of methods with case study on the bottom (Yin, 2003, p.4-5).

Another criticism of case study is that "they take too long and result in massive, unreadable documents" (Yin, 2003, p.11). This might be true with the way some case studies are conducted, but it doesn't have to be, particularly if one leaves out a lengthy narrative (which is possible in Yin's strategy) and doesn't confuse case study method with the method of data collection.

In Merriam's (2001) discussion of the strengths and limitations of case study, she cites Lincoln and Guba's (1981, p.77) argument that, "case studies can oversimplify or exaggerate a situation, leading the reader to erroneous conclusions about the actual state of affairs . . . they masquerade as a whole when in fact they are but a part—a slice of life" (p.42). This danger could be avoided or greatly lessened by a careful definition of the parameters of the study and statements of what it is not trying to accomplish as well as what it is.

Merriam (2001) also makes the point that "qualitative research is limited by the sensitivity and integrity of the investigator. The researcher is the primary instrument of data collection and analysis . . . the investigator is left to rely on his or her own instincts and abilities throughout most of this research effort" (p.43). This problem of bias is true for other qualitative research methods as well, but case study researchers are seen as particularly susceptible to the unusual problems of ethics that they "could so select from among available data that virtually anything he wished could be illustrated" (Lincoln & Guba, 1981, p.378).

This is a significant concern, not entirely unique to case study, but nevertheless necessary to take into account. Taylor & Bogdan (1998) speak to this issue:

> Within the researcher's theoretical perspective, stock of cultural knowledge, and particular vantage point, findings can more or less accurately reflect the nature of the world. As Richardson (1990) writes, "... because all knowledge is partial and situated, it does not mean that there is no knowledge or that situated knowledge is bad." (p.160)

After all, if we discarded all reports "merely because of biases or flaws... there would be no history" (Taylor & Bogdan, 1998).

Through member checking, triangulation, peer debriefing, and other methods of ensuring validity and reliability, the bias of the researcher can be minimized to an acceptable level. Even with these limitations:

> Case study is a means of investigating complex social units consisting of multiple variables... it offers insights and illuminates meanings that expand its readers' experience... These insights can be construed as tentative hypotheses that help structure future research: hence, case study plays an important role in advancing a field's knowledge base. (Merriam, 2001, p.41)

Choosing a Co-researcher

My choice to invite Annika (pseudonym) to be the focus of this case study was purposeful and convenient. I had unique access to this case, having been a friend of the family for many years and a close friend and musical colleague of her sister. Yet I did not have a close friendship at any point with Annika so I didn't feel there was a problem with dual role relationships. My choice might be questioned because of the possibility of sharing confidential information from interviews with Annika with other family members. I have ensured that this does not happen since I am only in contact with Annika's sister at this point in my life, and she and I have purposefully set up boundaries in our conversations to avoid problematic discussion.

My previous history with the family gave me an advantage in the research in that I had a sense of the family dynamics, culture, and belief system that had shaped Annika and her vocal journey. Although she was respectful of those who had influenced her, she trusted me with a great deal of personal detail which was sometimes painful and she probably would not have shared as openly with a stranger.

Having been in contact with the family for many years also gave me the opportunity to hear Annika perform at various points in her development, beginning at age 16. From the vantage point of being a friend of her sister, I had been aware of major developments in Annika's career and personal life as they unfolded, and this prior knowledge guided some of my questioning in the interview process. Some might question my choice of Annika because my previous knowledge could cloud my objectivity and bias my interviewing. Holstein and Gubrium (1997) see background knowledge of a case as an advantage in the interviewing process of data collection. "Background knowledge of circumstances relevant to the research topic and/or the respondent's experience can be an invaluable resource for the interviewer." The benefits they cite are:

> being familiar with the material, cultural, and interpretive circumstances to which respondents might orient, and with the vocabulary through which experience will be conveyed... means better understanding respondents' perspectives and interpretation... and a way of cultivating shared awareness and experiences that might be referenced as basis for interview questions... and allows the interviewer to move from the hypothetical or abstract to the very concrete by asking questions about relevant aspects of the respondents' lives and experience... promoting circumstantially rich description, accounts, and explanations. (p.77)

Annika was also an excellent choice for this study because she has had extensive experience as a singer in the process of freeing her voice, having worked with her own voice for over 30 years through voice lessons, opera school, and a variety of therapies to address psycho-emotional, physical, and spiritual issues which arose. She is a singer who has come far enough on the vocal journey to be able to reflect from a point of relative resolution and freedom, although she herself would say that freeing the voice is always in process and never finished. Many singers have a successful sound in the early stages of their careers but discover, once they have been singing for ten years, that they have been producing their voices with a great deal of tension and their voices are wearing out. Annika is committed to the process of discovering true vocal freedom rather than the "quick fix" of producing a sellable sound regardless of the price to vocal health. This commitment and sensitive work has her now reaping the benefits in her early 40's as she is settling into the full resonance of a mature, free voice.

Since I am interested in how the relationship between voice student and teacher affects the process towards vocal freedom, it was important that I choose a co-researcher who had experienced the teacher-student relationship from both sides. Annika fits this criterion well since she is a dedicated voice teacher, and applies the same intuitive, attentive observation of her students' vocal process as she does to her own.

Choosing Student Participants

I wanted to obtain data from the student perspective on Annika as a teacher, and to explore how students perceived the teacher-student relationship affecting their vocal process. To do this I selected five female students from the master class for one hour interviews. The first day of class I introduced myself and my research project briefly and asked any students who would like to be interviewed to see me after class. Two students immediately presented themselves to me and I arranged interview times for them during the week. I wanted to talk with more than two students, so I watched carefully during the first few master classes, kept notes on each singer and pinpointed two others who showed openness to examining the process of learning to sing, and showed some interesting vocal mannerisms. I approached these two singers, arranged appointments with them, obtained written, informed consent and interviewed them. Later in the week I noticed another student with a particularly obvious vocal problem make a huge vocal breakthrough, beginning in her lesson and continuing in the master class the next day. I asked her if she would be willing to describe what the breakthrough process was like for her and she happily agreed to an interview.

Of the five student singers, three were in their mid-twenties and two were in their early 40's. Two of the young singers were quite advanced and on the verge of promising careers while the third, who was having the breakthrough, was probably the least experienced of the whole class. The two older singers were both career women in non-music professions, but dedicated to the vocal journey to enrich their lives, and to release a creative part of themselves that had no outlet in their careers or family life. Four of the singers were white North Americans, while the fifth was a Jamaican who had been raised in Canada. I was satisfied from the interviews with these five singers that there was some variety of stages of vocal process, diversity of goals and motivations, and at least some representation of ethnic diversity.

Observation

Being a musician and a teacher myself, it was important for me to hear my co-researcher in action, making music and teaching, so that I could experience her as a musician and not just interview her about it. Annika was an excellent choice because she was teaching a week long voice master class in the summer of 2003, and that fit into my data collection time frame and was affordable to attend. Since the class was held over a seven day period, I had the opportunity to observe and interview each day and could ask about my observations of both Annika's teaching and her students' progress as it unfolded. I was able to hear live examples of voice students in various stages of the process of freeing their voices, make my own observations, discuss with Annika what she saw and heard, and interview the students themselves and hear about their experience of the process.

The Choice to Study Only Female Singers

In choosing a single case study, I had to choose between examining the experience of a male or a female singer. Part of my preparation for the study was to interview three singers/voice teachers—two male and one female—to whom I had easy access. I found that, in general, the males were more technical in their answers, and less willing to discuss emotional or psychological issues related to voice. Both the male and female teachers said that they found their male voice students to be less expressive of, or in touch with, their emotional and psychological experience, and that many more female students than males would break down in tears in their lessons and want to discuss personal issues. Since life context and psycho-emotional issues which affect the process towards vocal freedom are crucial to my study, I thought that it would be easier to collect this type of data from women, who are generally more expressive of it. I knew that there was also the possibility that interviews would include discussion of very personal issues such as sexual identity, shame, and self-worth, so I thought it would be easier to establish trust and collect more in depth and honest data if I was working with females.

My most natural way of learning is through experience and identification, and since I am the primary data collection instrument in this study, it is important that I take my learning strengths into account. I realized that it could be much harder for me to get an experiential sense through working with a male co-researcher since there are significant physiological differences between how males and females experience breathing and opening the body— fundamental components of singing freely. A female co-researcher would most likely describe the experience in a way with which I would more easily identify. I would feel freer asking her questions, and experimenting with her responses, in my own body.

Limitations of Working with Only Female Singers

I realize that working solely with females is a limitation of this study, but in a single case I could examine only one gender's experience. Although I have not seen any studies examining the process of freeing the voice with either men or women, Sandgren (2002) did a qualitative and quantitative study of 15 male and female opera singers. His purpose was to determine what factors affected their ability to perform, and how they felt about performing. This study showed significant differences between males and females in their motivation for singing, the meaning they attached to singing, and their feelings about themselves related to their tone quality and the successfulness of their performances, as seen in the following findings from Sandgren (2002):

> For the women, to sing on stage was an important source of self-expression, and they often expressed idealistic views about relations between singer and audience, body and psyche, giving and receiving. The men stressed great satisfaction coming from perfect mastery and control of the instrument, the voice, and enjoying its plasticity. The audience was regarded more as spectators to their great vocal performance. (p.18)

Men feared losing their voices and associated this fear with being potent or impotent, and therefore were constantly testing to see if their voices were in good shape. When they weren't they felt shame, incompetence, and decreased self esteem (p.13). Women also tested their voices often, but their focus was to determine vocal quality. If the quality was impaired they experienced guilt over having done something incorrectly, such as not caring for their health. They also experienced guilt over:

> … behaviours and attitudes, such as self-assertiveness, which were enhancing their professional ambitions. The guilt seemed to arise from the conflict between their own individualistic striving and the traditional role of women as being less achievement-oriented and taking more responsibility for relations in work places, in the family, and with their partner. (Sandgren, 2002, p.13)

This study shows some differences between men and women in their attitudes towards singing, and raises questions about many more differences that must exist. The fact that women could be experiencing guilt because of "the conflict between their own individualistic striving and the traditional role of women," (p.13) points to a vast area of difference—gender roles in society and their effects on the vocal journey. I examine the effects of shame on a singer's ability to free her voice in this study but I can see from the findings of Sandgren (2002) that what causes shame in women is quite likely different from what causes shame in men. Dale Throness, voice instructor at the University of British Columbia, and one of the male singers I interviewed as part of the pilot study, commented that men face a different type of shame on the vocal journey. Singing is stereotypically seen as a feminine profession, and males often face ridicule for their vocal pursuits, a factor that creates its own pressures and reasons to resist vocal vulnerability (personal interview, June 20, 2003).

17

Another element of this study is the examination of the voice teacher-student relationship and its effects on the student's vocal progress. The few differences already seen between males and females could contribute to communication problems, and differing goals and expectations between teachers and students of opposite genders.

One can see that the few differences between male and female vocal experiences cited here are only the "tip of the iceberg." There is clearly a need to explore the male experience of freeing the voice. However, there was also a need to explore the female experience, which is what I have attempted to do. I hope that future research is done that not only explores the male experience, but also compares the two in order to deepen the understanding of both in their interactions.

Ethical Considerations

To ensure that my study would follow ethical guidelines I submitted my research proposal to the St. Stephen's ethics committee and received approval before I began collecting data. I designed consent forms for all participants—Annika my main co-researcher, her partner Maureen, whom I observed co-teaching with Annika and who was involved in some of Annika's interviews, and the five voice students whom I interviewed at the master class (Appendix A). Before interviewing I explained the parameters of the study, the forms, confidentiality protocol, and potential benefits and risks to each individual. I told them I was audio taping the interview and would be transcribing it, and I received their written consent. I made it clear to all participants that they were in no way obligated to be involved in the study, and that they were free to withdraw at any time. The student interviews were conducted in a sound proof room in the church where the master classes were being held, with the exception of one that was held on a park bench because of scheduling difficulties with meeting places. Interviews with Annika and Maureen were either held in the room at the church, or in their personal accommodations at their request.

I contacted the organization sponsoring the master class several weeks before the class began and received permission to observe classes and lessons, and to interview the students and the teachers. The identities of all the participants have been kept anonymous and confidential at all points during the study. Pseudonyms are used and other identifying information has been altered to protect the identities and privacy of all involved. The tapes from the interviews and transcripts are kept in a locked cabinet in my home, and are coded to ensure anonymity. The tapes and transcripts will be destroyed at a later point when the study has been processed and accepted by St. Stephen's College.

Data Collection

In preparation for field work I used some heuristic methods to reflect on my own experience of attempting to free my voice through writing and re-reading journal entries, poetry, and letters from the time of my experience studying voice some years ago. I also tape-recorded a "self-interview" in which I explained some of the more emotional aspects of my experience studying voice with my first teacher. I spoke as if I were talking to that voice teacher for part of the interview, which put me back in touch with some of the emotional issues. For a second part of the taped interview I spoke as if talking to a semi-informed friend. I transcribed these tapes and included them in my self-data for analysis.

I analyzed my experience into themes, and then integrated those themes with the themes I saw emerging in my preliminary literature review and developed a set of interview questions. I did an informal pilot study by interviewing three singer-voice teachers to whom I had easy access. Through these pilot interviews I determined that some questions were not useful and that others needed to be added. I then took my revised interview questions and began my field work. (Questions are listed in Appendix B.)

My field work consisted of being an "observer as participant" (Glesne, 1992, p.40) in a voice master class taught by Annika and her partner Maureen for three hours each morning of a seven day voice workshop. I was an observer in the classes in the sense that I never performed as a singer, which was required of all other class members. This prevented me from being perceived as part of the "competition" amongst the singers and helped build trust with them. However, I was involved as a participant in every other way, taking part in all other group activities—Tai Chi, breathing and vocalization exercises, and discussions about musical interpretation and the performances of the students. I was involved musically as a flutist, accompanying one singer during a master class, a private lesson, and in the final concert. This involvement won me respect as a fellow musician with the other students, established that I had the musical experience to hear and understand what was happening in class, and raised the level of discussion in which I was included.

After master class each day I observed two 45 minute private lessons of students with Annika, and a half hour ensemble rehearsal which Annika coached. I also had the opportunity to have my own one hour private voice lesson (which I tape recorded with permission) with Annika and Maureen after the classes were finished at the end of the week. This put me in the role of full participant of one part of the vocal experience. I kept a project journal (Sprenkle & Moon, 1996, p.397) of detailed notes during all observations and experiences. At the end of each day I reviewed my notes and added personal reflections about what I had seen, heard, and experienced. I wrote about how the overall experience was affecting me—my emotional reactions to interviews and personal conversations, technical questions I wanted answered, singers who had caught my attention for indefinable reasons who I wanted to watch more closely the next day, and the social patterns that were developing in class. I also explored my own biases and reactions (Glesne, 1992, p.45) particularly to specific people and views they embodied, and was able to work out some issues there which helped me remain appropriately but pleasantly detached from my research participants.

Interviewing

During the week of classes I interviewed Annika six times—three individual interviews of one hour duration each, and three additional interviews including her partner Maureen, each of which took an hour and a half. I also interviewed five students for one hour each. All interviews were tape recorded with the consent of the participants, and because of the value of immersing oneself in the data through the transcription process, I chose to transcribe them all myself. As I worked through the transcriptions and the preliminary analysis of the data, I kept a log of questions that emerged and used e-mail and telephone calls to seek clarification from Annika and to expand and deepen data on significant themes. To a lesser degree I also had e-mail contact, for clarification and expansion, with the students I had interviewed.

Although I had a list of questions going into my interviews (Appendix B), I used a conversational interviewing style which Bender and Jordan in Van de Creek (1994), describe as:

> ... discourse in which the meaning of an experience is constructed jointly by the interviewer and the respondent within the conversation itself. Meaning emerges between the two, dialogical. The interviewer continually reformulates the questions in light of the respondent's answers and the respondent continually reframes the answers in terms understood by the interviewer. Both work together to more accurately and more fully articulate the experience of the respondent for their mutual understanding. (p.102)

I was drawn to this method of interviewing Annika because it allowed me to share some of my own experience and encouraged a natural give and take of ideas between us as a partnership. I had prepared an interview guide for use within a conversational-style interview. Since I interviewed Annika six times within the course of a week, I took time each day after the interview to review the material we had covered and to decide what direction the next interview should take. I usually began the next interview with asking a few questions to clarify concepts from the day before, and then suggested a direction for the present interview. However, in a conversational partnership style, Annika often brought up topics that she wanted to talk about or thought were relevant as she reflected on the previous day's interview, so we chose the direction of each interview together and were flexible in re-visiting topics as the conversation flowed naturally.

As part of the interview process with Annika I listened to recordings of her at various stages of her vocal development, and heard her live "commentary" on her vocal and personal experience at the times of the recordings. She and Maureen also provided a critical analysis of what they perceived as the vocal issues demonstrated in the recordings and guided my ears to hear her vocal development for myself.

The student interviews were also in a semi-structured format with a relaxed conversational nature. However, I did not share as much of myself with the students, since we had much less time and I was less interested in the details of their life stories and more interested in specific information about their experience of voice with Annika as the teacher.

I made sure to ask the question, "What does the phrase 'freeing your voice' mean to you?" at some point near the beginning of the interview, but beyond that the interview was fairly flexible. I had an interview guide prepared with possible questions (Appendix B) but I often revised my questions as I went along, not asking all questions and adding others as seemed appropriate. I followed Holstein & Gubrium's (1995) advice: "A rule of thumb for using an interview guide is to let the respondent's responses determine whether particular questions are necessary or appropriate as leading frames of reference for the interview conversation" (p.77).

The interviews with the students were originally intended as another way of gathering data about Annika as a teacher through the eyes of her students. The interviews provided some data about Annika, and about voice teacher-student relationships in general, but it also provided data on the process towards vocal freedom of each of the students. To keep the study manageable I maintained my focus on the single-case of Annika and didn't do a full analysis of each of the student interviews. However, I have included the data from the students as it pertains to Annika and the master class and when it provided enriching examples of themes common to Annika's experience.

Another decision I faced in the interviewing process was whether or not to include Maureen, Annika's life partner, in the interviews. The advantages of including her in the interviews seemed to outweigh the disadvantages so I decided to include her in half of the interviews. Maureen holds a valuable perspective on Annika's journey, having been with her for the last 19 years (most of Annika's adult life). They have studied with many of the same voice teachers, gone to the same osteopath, craniosacral specialist, and psychotherapist, and have made many vocal discoveries together. They speak in the "we" form when teaching together because they share a vocal philosophy and method that they have developed together. Maureen is a successful singer who can hear and analyze Annika's voice from a professional standpoint and remember significant life events and struggles that affected Annika's voice at various points in her career. She remembers, and was willing to share, some of the more painful aspects of Annika's journey which Annika had blocked out. As is the case with most long term couples, one must really know both partners to fully understand the one partner.

However, there were some disadvantages in interviewing Annika and Maureen together. Being that close and emotionally involved can cloud objectivity and heighten bias and protectiveness. Patterns inherent in their relationship showed up in interviewing which sometimes made it hard to hear Annika's view without it being altered by Maureen, or without deferring to Maureen as holding a more accurate view. However, interviewing Annika alone half of the time allowed me to hear her speak for herself and include the richness of Maureen's experience of Annika. Interviewing Maureen also provided some interesting data about her vocal journey as a fellow singer.

Analysis

As I stated at the beginning of this chapter, I resonate strongly with the heuristic activities "self-search, self-dialogue, and self-discovery," and have therefore incorporated some of these activities into this case study. My first analysis was of my vocal experience of several years ago as seen in the introductory chapter, and my second analysis was of my voice lesson with Annika and Maureen.

To analyze the data from my lesson, I listened to the tape a number of times and transcribed all that was possible (some of it was vocalizing or physical exercises that could only be described and not transcribed). I then worked my way through the transcription and the tape, re-imagining the physical sensations, emotions, questions, and facial expressions that accompanied the text of the experience. By feeling my way back into the experience and listening to the tape I was able to determine where the "aha" moments took place, vocally, emotionally, physically and, in one place, spiritually. I wrote the analysis chronologically as a thorough account of what took place in the lesson, highlighting the "aha" moments and offering brief explanations of the issues that were being touched upon in these moments.

Next I transcribed all of Annika's interviews. I chose to transcribe them myself as a way of beginning the analysis, since hearing the fluctuations of her voice, the pauses, laughter, and occasional tightness, told me something about the feelings behind the words and helped me interpret the words. There is also the fact that having to discern every word a person says and translate it into writing is a good way to become intimately acquainted with what they are actually saying and to begin to see themes that recur and are linked to other themes and developed in subsequent interviews. After transcribing each interview I wrote summary notes of the main themes that stood out in my memory and gave the interview a title based on either the main topic of the interview or a very striking idea that had been discussed. After transcribing all the interviews I returned to the first interview and began working through it, summarizing the main idea of each paragraph of text in a few words in the margin, and highlighting key phrases that stood out. At the end of each interview I again reviewed the whole interview and wrote notes about the main themes across all interviews. After doing this with all of Annika's interviews I began a page on each theme I had extracted and listed quotes and page numbers every time the theme was mentioned. I divided the themes up into categories—those that were information about Annika's life context, and those that related to her philosophy of singing and teaching. I constructed a life story, "Coming Home to Myself," out of the first category of themes. I told the story in Annika's words as closely as possible, and if I added any explanation or commentary it was acknowledged by Annika to be accurate to her meaning. In the synthesis chapter I organized the data related to Annika's philosophy of singing and teaching into the themes "breathing," "moving towards freedom," and "the student/teacher relationship." In these sections I integrated her words with my observations of master classes and private lessons, literature which spoke to the same issues, and data from the student interviews.

I analyzed the student interviews in much the same way, listening and transcribing the tapes, re-reading the transcripts a number of times, highlighting themes, and then writing summaries of each interview. I did not present the life stories of each student as I did with Annika, but if there were significant life events which affected a student's vocal progress I included them.

As I learned more about the emerging themes, I expanded the literature I researched (see the interdisciplinary literature review). When I analyzed my own experience of voice lessons and realized that shame was at the core of my vocal block, I studied literature on shame. When I realized from Annika's interviews that the Alexander Technique and other types of body work were important to her process of freeing her voice, I studied literature in that area. This reflects another aspect of the influence of heuristic inquiry on my approach:

> Learning that proceeds heuristically has a path of its own. It is self-directed, self-motivated, and open to spontaneous shift (p.17)... The research question and the methodology flow out of inner awareness, meaning, and inspiration (p.11)... The one who searches heuristically may draw upon the perceptual powers afforded by... direct experience. (Douglass and Moustakas, 1995, p.44 cited in Moustakas, p.17).

Validity and Reliability

Moustakas (1990) says that ultimately the judgment of a study's validity rests on the shoulders of the primary researcher:

> There are no rules that can be relied on in the last resort; the scientist must make the ultimate judgment. The synthesis of essences and meanings inherent in any human experience is a reflection and outcome of the researcher's pursuit of knowledge. What is presented as truth and what is removed as implausible or idiosyncratic ultimately can be accredited only on the grounds of personal knowledge and judgment. (Polyanyi, 1969, p.120, cited in Moustakas, 1990, p.33).

Researchers do the best they can to "constantly appraise significance" (p.33) and put in as many internal and external checks as possible, but ultimately they must present the reader with the truth as they see it and the reader must decide if it rings true. If one can provide evidence from multiple sources that point to the same conclusions within a qualitative study, the credibility of the research is increased.

One of the external checks I used to ensure credibility was peer debriefing which is "the extended discussion with a disinterested peer of findings, conclusions, analysis and hypothesis" (Mertons, 1998, p.182). I had regular telephone and e-mail conversations with fellow qualitative researchers, musicians, and music therapists to help me identify my biases, re-define my direction, and question my conclusions. The feedback I have received has been that the parts of the study I shared shed light on related areas of the readers' lives and rang true. One woman to whom I e-mailed the description of my own experience of voice and the explanation of shame, wrote back that she experienced a similar emergence of deep emotions at the hands of her acupuncturist. For her, the explanation of shame brought buckets of tears, release, and ultimately hope, because my words had given her a way of understanding her experience. Mertons (1998) says, "The credibility test asks if there is a correspondence between the way the respondents actually perceive social constructs and the way the researcher portrays viewpoints" (Mertons, 1998, p.181). It appears from the responses of those who have read my work to this point that they are perceiving credibility in this study. The term *credibility* is used by Mertons (1998) instead of validity and I use it from here on since it seems more suitable to the experiential nature of qualitative research.

I used member checking (Mertons, 1998, p.182) as another means of ensuring credibility by having regular e-mail contact and phone conversations with Annika, the main co-researcher of the case study. I had several conversations in which I asked for clarification and further explanation of the data I was analyzing from our interviews. I sent her drafts of the interview material as well as my analysis. We discussed her suggestions for changes and I implemented them until she felt I had accurately represented her in the finished text. I also e-mailed each of the student participants with a draft of the material pertaining to their interviews and worked with them on revisions until they were satisfied it was accurate. Two of the students accepted the text on the first draft as accurate, and the other three suggested very minor corrections of factual details including, in one case, changes centered around the student's desire to express her ideas more succinctly than she had in the verbal interview.

Triangulation of multiple sources of evidence is a strategy used to establish both credibility and reliability (Merriam, 1988; Mertons, 1998). Some authors use the term *trustworthiness* to encompass both the concept of credibility and reliability and accept triangulation as a suitable strategy of establishing both. Triangulation can be achieved by the use of multiple methods or by utilizing divergent sources of data. I collected data from Annika herself, from her partner regarding her perceptions of Annika as a singer, and from her students regarding Annika as a teacher. I observed Annika in master class and teaching private lessons, and experienced her as a teacher for myself in my own private lesson. I listened to tape recordings of her vocal development as audio evidence of her description of her process of freeing her voice and correlated some of her previous performances with written assessments from music critics who heard her at the time and published reviews in local papers. I also drew on my memory of having heard her perform live on a number of occasions in the last 20 years and heard her live performances at the master class and at a recent competition.

Another means of establishing trustworthiness is interdisciplinary triangulation. Denzin & Lincoln (1994) suggest that "we may broaden our understanding of method and substance" by using information from a variety of sources and experiences. I have explored the literature of various disciplines—vocal pedagogy, therapeutic voice work, bodywork, Alexander Technique, and music therapy.

Transition to Chapter Three

As we will see in the literature review in the next chapter, these disciplines reinforce one of the main findings of this study: there is a connection between breath, body, and emotions.

CHAPTER THREE

LITERATURE REVIEW

An Interdisciplinary Approach

"The voice is the combination of all of our emotions and feelings, as well as our physical, psychological and mental abilities. It combines all our capabilities and asks us to bring them to life in the most natural and uninhibited manner" (Arman, 1999, p.23).

The human voice is complex. Unlike a toe or elbow that you can observe with the naked eye, the vocal organ is mysteriously concealed. It always retains a certain level of mystery because we can't just roll up our sleeves and poke it out for inspection like a knobby elbow. We choose what we want to show of our emotional, psychological, and spiritual self when we use our voices. Physically we would be far less debilitated if we lost our voices than if we lost an arm, but emotionally and psychologically we would be intensely challenged. How would we communicate our needs, feelings, desires, and thoughts? Losing a voice would be like losing a self.

Therefore, researching the process of a female singer freeing her voice is a complex task that requires an interdisciplinary approach. In order to explore the physical, psychological, spiritual, and mental components of freeing the voice, I researched literature in a number of areas as my experience, the data from Annika, and the literature led me. Since my own vocal experience began by taking voice lessons, with one of the goals being that I would be more qualified to teach voice to choirs, I began my literature review in the area of vocal pedagogy.

Vocal Pedagogy

Richard Miller has written several volumes on the singing voice and is a highly respected scholar and pedagogue. *The Structure of Singing* (1986) is Miller's complete guide to the physiological systems related to singing—the breathing mechanism, vocal tract and folds, the mouth, the throat, the cavities in the head, the tongue, and the jaw. Miller methodically works through the technical problems particular to male and female voices and registers, and issues such as diction, resonance, agility, and healthy singing habits, and provides practical exercises to improve in each area. Miller takes a very strong stance on the necessity of anatomically correct teaching, making sure concepts are grounded in physiological knowledge and not based on imagery (1986, p.213).

In *On the Art of Singing*, Miller (1996) develops the argument that teachers need to inform themselves of correct physiology, particularly with the plethora of scientific and acoustical information available today, which "verifies many empirical notions found in historic vocal pedagogy" (p.244). He explains that some teachers avoid factual information because it proves some pedagogical concepts wrong that have been accepted historically. Even more prohibitive to some is the false assumption that "artistic, instinctive singing and factual information are irreconcilable" (p. 246). Miller recognizes that a singer who never moves out of strictly technical thinking will be hampered in performance and that the artistry of singing goes beyond technique. However, no amount of artistry can assist in certain types of technical problems.

English, French, German and Italian Techniques of Singing, one of Miller's (1977) earliest works, explores how national temperament and vocal ideals relate to ideals of emotional expression in the singing voice. He begins by explaining and comparing what each of the four main European schools of vocal technique have to say regarding the main vocal issues of breathing, attack, vowel formation, vibrato, registration, and voice categorization. He acknowledges the limits of national stereotypes but proceeds to build profiles of the national vocal ideals, describing how they correlate with national values and ways of expressing emotion:

> Any practicing artist is encircled by a psychological web of nationalism; his vocalism has been formed by the sounds which surround him... Perhaps because of the immediacy of that unique emotive power which resides in the human voice, the essence of national temperament may be most manifest in singing. Certainly, tonal concepts indicate temperamental proclivities as emphatically as do the fields of literature, architecture and painting. (p.190)

Miller (1977) characterizes Italian singers as having a "joyous lyricism" because of their "natural physical vitality" and the national tendency to project emotion outward (p.192). Germans tend to have a philosophical, romantic nature that can enrich the colour of the voice. However, in communicating their inner, intimate emotional lives they might tend to internalize the sound, making it darker and more covered, and keeping them from strong outward projection (p.192). The French, according to Miller, have "a typical commitment to proper proportions and balanced perspective on aesthetic and practical matters, thus presenting a mannered vocalism, without over emotional or bodily involvement" (p.193). He characterized the French sound as subtle and poetic, with a controlled profundity, neither displaying the naked sentiment of the Italians, or the introspection of the Germans. The English, who display little emotion in life or vocally, are chiefly concerned with the skill and craft of singing.

Miller's (1977) characterizations of national tendencies are contentious now, over 25 years after they were originally written, but the principle behind the characterizations is relevant to our discussion—vocal expression is affected by one's beliefs and habits of emotional expression, and those beliefs and habits are shaped by one's social environment.

Reid's (1983) *Dictionary of Vocal Terminology* defines and analyzes terms and expressions that have been in use by the vocal profession from the early seventeenth century till the present. Reid covers anatomical terms, vocal techniques from a wide variety of pedagogical and national perspectives, and psychological issues such as inhibitions and stage fright that affect vocal freedom. Reid is particularly helpful for understanding the terms of this study and for providing an overview of many vocal issues.

Principles of Voice Production, by Ingo Titze (1994), could double as a medical textbook of the vocal tract and folds and the breathing apparatus. The text contains photographs of vocal folds vibrating and in various states of disease. The introduction, however, situates it very nicely in the field of singing and makes some important points about the voice being a primary mode of communicating emotion, making our needs known, and significantly reflecting our personalities. "Voice is a 'window' to the health of the body, and to mood and personality"(p.xxi).

Meribeth Bunch's (1993) *Dynamics of the Singing Voice,* and Bunch's (2000) *Condensed Handbook of Singing,* are "user friendly" guides to vocal pedagogy. Bunch (2000) describes the anatomical structures of the vocal mechanism and how they function in normal singing. She emphasizes "the balance of the whole body and understanding its co-ordination for optimal vocal health and quality" (preface). She understands the physical aspects of vocal production in the context of the singing voice "as a combination of mind, body, imagination, and spirit" (p.1). She encourages singers to "observe the body as a newcomer, not through the myths of singing but through reality" and to realize "your body is your greatest anatomy textbook of all" (p.1). Bunch (1993) bridges the communication gap between artists, teachers, therapists, and doctors, creating "common ground" for communication; thus, the imagery and sensory descriptions of singers, and the obscure and frightening medical terms of physicians, can be encompassed in simple, clear terms. She draws heavily on the concepts of the Alexander Technique, as described in de Alcantara's (1997) *Indirect Procedures: A Musician's Guide to the Alexander Technique.* Bunch's work has deeply affected the views and teaching style of Annika, the main participant of this study. Annika has taken anatomy classes with Bunch, and has co-taught voice master classes with her.

Bunch was a student of Vennard, (1968) author of *Singing: the Mechanism and the Technic,* and clearly drew from him the philosophy of teaching the anatomy and physical functioning of the vocal apparatus. Vennard (1968) explains the functioning of the individual parts, such as the breathing and the vocal folds, but stresses not focusing on any one part or method. He says "a knowledge of the various processes involved in singing is like a disjointed skeleton until their interrelation is understood… The one thing that all must achieve is coordination… [A teacher's] analytical knowledge of the mechanism is like the sub-basements of a skyscraper; there may never be occasion for it to be displayed, but it is a necessary foundation" (p.191). A teacher must be versatile in discovering the approach that works for each student and once he [*sic*] has interested the student in one area he can usually work in the other areas to achieve this coordination of the entire instrument, and the entire personality (p.191).

Vocal Wisdom: Maxims of Giovanni Battista Lamperti, edited and translated by William Earl Brown (1957), is not the typical vocal pedagogy method and contains no anatomical diagrams of the breathing apparatus or the vocal chords. Lamperti's father heard these maxims of Italian singing from great composers and singers such as Rossini, Donizetti, and Bellini who were from the "Golden Age of Song" (mid-to-late 1800s in Italy). Father and son passed these maxims down to William Brown who kept them in a notebook that was edited and published after his death by one of his students. The maxims cover a wide variety of technical and expressive vocal issues, as well as pedagogical advice for teachers, encouragement to students, and philosophical musings about "the soul of a singer" and what it means to be an artist. Lamperti's views on "letting go" and relaxation are described in the discussion, later in the chapter, on control and letting go.

Freeing the Natural Voice by Kristin Linklater (1976) is largely a vocal pedagogy text. However, Linklater also includes information on the link between mind and body that is relevant to singers. "To free the voice is to free the person, and each person is indivisibly mind and body... The natural voice is most perceptibly blocked and distorted by physical tension but it also suffers from emotional blocks, intellectual blocks, aural blocks, spiritual blocks" (p.2). Linklater recognizes the growing interest of singers, and society in general, in psychotherapeutic practices such as Alexander Technique, Rolfing, T'ai Chi and Yoga "to help free the emotional and psychological self by ridding the body of habitual tension" (p.4). Her recognition of these psycho-body therapies is significant to this study because Annika, the main participant, has practiced the Alexander Technique throughout her career and many aspects of Alexander philosophy affected her teaching, her beliefs about the unity of body, mind and spirit, and her principles of control and release. She has also used craniosacral therapy and osteopathy, practices based on principles similar to those of the Alexander Technique, which have benefited her physical, emotional, and vocal health. Therefore, we now examine the literature on these body therapies in order that we might understand the philosophy behind them and the effects they can have on a singer in the process of freeing her voice.

Related Body Work—Alexander Technique, Osteopathy, Craniosacral Therapy

"The Alexander Technique is a subtle method for changing habits and attitudes, which releases the body and mind, enhances body awareness and functioning, and gives the body new freedom, coordination, and energy" (Leibowitz & Connington, 1990, p.xv). People in a wide variety of professions use the Alexander Technique, but of most interest to us is its use by performers who use their voices—singers, actors, and public speakers. Rosenthal (1987) claims that it is particularly useful for "performers whose minds and bodies are their instruments" (p.53). Many people think it is a physical set of habits aimed at improving posture and alleviating muscle pain and tension (which it does), but it goes beyond these physical benefits and trains one in a philosophy of healthy use of the self in all aspects of life.

Frederick Matthias Alexander, the progenitor of the Technique, was a Shakespearian actor living in Australia at the end of the 1800s. He struggled with chronic hoarseness, sometimes losing his voice completely, and was unable to find any medical cure. Doctors advised him to rest his voice completely for periods of time, which improved his voice temporarily, but as soon as he began using it again the hoarseness returned. He decided to try to treat himself through months of careful self-observation with the aid of a three-way mirror. Here is what he discovered:

> The hoarseness was a result of vocal misuse but that the vocal misuse was not an isolated phenomenon. It was only one aspect of an overall pattern of poor functioning in his entire body... He discovered that every time he opened his mouth to speak he gasped for air, pressed his head down onto the back of his neck and compressed his spine, which produced tensions throughout his entire body. His hoarseness was a result of this excessive tension. (Leibowitz & Connington, 1990, p. xvii)

Nine years of experimentation and careful self-observation led Alexander to discoveries about his physical, intellectual and emotional self, which he developed into a number of principles pertaining to the "use of the self." These are now referred to as the Alexander Technique.

When Annika first began using the Alexander Technique in her late teens as part of her process of freeing her voice, her Alexander teacher put her hand on her back and, without having any prior knowledge of Annika, commented, "You have been taught to be a good girl, haven't you?" She could feel the physical holding pattern that was firmly established in Annika, and intuitively connected it with her attitude of pleasing by being a "good girl." Alexander teachers are trained to be very attentive to the holding patterns and tensions in a person's body and part of their work is gently guiding a person's body into the most efficient "use of self" to release these tensions. Alexander did not divide the self into mind and body, as the commonly used metaphor of "the body as the car and the brain as its driver" (Alcantara, 1997, p.10). Instead he described the self as follows:

> Talk about a man's [sic] individuality and character: it's the way he uses himself. The self does not consist of two halves (body and mind) or three thirds (body, mind, and spirit) that work together; it consists of a whole, so unified in its workings that no separate part (body, mind, spirit) can be said to exist independently of the others.... . You are one and you work as one, and you cannot examine, change, or control one of your parts separately from the whole. (p.12)

Based on this premise of a unified self, Alexander stated the following:

> We translate everything physical, mental or spiritual into muscular tension, and therefore the mental stress we experience can affect our physical body in a variety of ways... If this inappropriate muscle tension persists over a long period of time, it can affect every other system in the body. (Brennen, 1998, p.52)

An Alexander Technique "convert" describes her experience of being cut off from her body, in much the same way that Annika was at the beginning of her vocal journey:

> My self-image was that everything I needed was in my head—my life was taking place mainly in my head. I was afraid of my body and of moving it, and that shut my

body down. I needed to have my fear worked on in an indirect way. The Alexander Technique provided that way. (Leibowitz & Connington, 1990, p.81)

Another person who benefited greatly from the Alexander Technique explained as follows:

The Alexander Technique provided an enormous opening for me to begin to deal with my emotional habits. My body was very tight and by releasing it, I became more open to my tensions. My emotional issues were locked into my body. That's one reason my body was so rigid. (p.80)

These Alexander Technique converts were on a journey of self discovery similar to Annika's journey. They were coming to the same understanding of the integration of body, mind and spirit and the realization that tension in one area affects all the other areas. In Annika's case, that tension and disconnection from her body was showing in her voice because that was the specific area she wanted to free, but her whole body and self needed to be "used" differently to achieve this freedom. Rosenthal (1987) clarifies the concept of "use of self" with the following anecdote: "Imagine a man in handcuffs. He tries to play a musical instrument and tries to prepare an omelet—and certainly does neither very well. You remove his handcuffs and both his playing and his cooking improve" (p.53).

As Alexander set about developing a method of change towards a healthier use of self, he distilled a set of ten principles. The first principle, as we have just explained, is that body, mind and spirit are an inseparable unit. The second principle is Primary Control, the concept that there is a dynamic relationship between the head, neck, and back. This relationship governs the workings of all mechanisms of postural reflexes and constantly reassesses our balance. Primary control must be allowed to work without restriction or muscle tension if we are to have freedom of movement (Brennan, 1998, p.37).

In the master class, Annika and Maureen introduced us to the basics of Primary Control by analyzing the relationship between head, neck, and back in each of us through the use of "the plumb line." They asked each of us stand naturally, then hung a cord with a weight on the end of it along the side of our bodies, running from the top of our heads to our feet. A person who stood with the ideal relationship between head, neck, and back would find the cord running through the center of her ear, shoulder, hip, knee, and the arch of her foot. When the cord did not fall through these midpoints it showed that people stuck their heads forward (a very common breaking of the ideal relationship of head and neck), or locked their knees back, or thrust their hips forward, or caved their shoulders inwards. Once the "diagnosis" was made through the use of the plumb line, Annika gently guided the person's body into a different way of being which was closer to the ideal. Ironically, the person who was being adjusted often felt very off balance or out of alignment even though the observers said that the posture looked much improved after the adjustment.

This leads us to the third principle of Alexander Technique, Faulty Sensory Perception, which says, "A person cannot rely on his [sic] sensory feelings to tell him where his body is in space or even what he is doing with different parts of his body" (Brennan, 1998, p.40).

Alexander realized through his work with a three-way mirror that what felt "natural" to him was not necessarily a tension-free, natural state; it was just what he had become used to.

Principle Four, Holistic Discovery, states that the parts of the body do not function as separate entities, but work as a whole unit with each part affecting all the other parts (p.41). This explains Alexander's experience of pressing his head down on his spine, contributing to tension in his whole body system that resulted in his voice going hoarse.

Principle Five, Stimuli and Reactions, is an expansion of principle three, addressing our lack of accurate sensory perception. Principle Five states that a given stimulus produces the same reaction over and over again. If the reaction goes unchecked it turns into habitual behavior and will eventually feel normal and natural to us no matter how detrimental this habit is to our health. This principle helps to explain how stress builds up in our bodies through the tension of daily activities we perceive as normal, but which take their toll on our bodies over years of repetition (Brennan, 1998, p.41).

The first five principles outline the existing state of affairs in one's use of self, and Principles Six through Ten look towards bringing about change. Principle Six, Changing the Pattern of Thought, states that the release of tension comes not from doing something differently, but from changing the way one thinks. Principle Seven describes the Primary Directions which are: allow for freedom of your neck, allow your head to go forward and up, and allow your back to lengthen and widen. A direction is a process that involves projecting messages from the brain to the body's mechanisms, and conducting the energy necessary for the use of these mechanisms. Primary directions involve the freedom of the head in relationship to the neck and spine—the primary relationship within the body which must be maintained in a healthy way in order to have freedom anywhere else in the body (Brennan, 1998, p.44). Principle Eight, Secondary Directions, supplements the primary directions and helps release tension in localized areas of the body including shoulders, hands, feet, pelvis, jaw, and knees (p.45).

Principle Nine is about Goal Orientation, or what Alexander called "end gaining." Alexander believed that the cause of our troubles is not in what is done to us but in what we do to ourselves. "He saw that the problem was not in the stimulation of modern life, but in our response to it; not in the stress, but in the straining. The straining he called the misuse of the self; its cause not human design, but end-gaining... End gaining causes misuse" (Alcantara, 1997, p.5). End gaining can actually prevent us from obtaining our objective (Brennan, 1998, p.45) because we aren't paying attention to how we are getting there, which causes unnecessary tension and strain. A key aspect of pulling ourselves out of an end-gaining attitude is giving up judging ourselves. Alcantara (1997) uses the example of a pianist who, while end-gaining, will focus only on hitting the right chord and, in doing that, will tense his arm to achieve his goal. That tensing might be the very thing that causes him to miss the chord and if not that chord, then the habit of tension he has introduced to achieve his goal will have long-term effects on his overall playing and tension levels. The pianist has to be willing to miss the chord and free his arm. This, in turn, will help him find the chord:

Alexander pointed out that, if you are really paying attention to the means and not to the ends, then you must be willing to act "irrespective of whether, during the progress of the activities concerned, the performance is correct or incorrect." Suspend your judgment of right and wrong and act with indifference to the end result of your actions. (Alcantara, 1997, p.73)

The solution to End Gaining is Principle Ten, Inhibition, which is "deliberate restraint in order to make a more conscious choice. Through stopping and consciously choosing a different way of reacting or acting, one can gain control over one's habits and prevent automatic reactions" (Brennan, 1998, p. 46). Alcantara (1997) points out that inhibition is not about doing something new but about not doing something old, which is itself an activity:

Inhibition, or non-doing, means not using wrong tensions (such as the contraction of an antagonistic muscle in a pair)... Our non-doing simply means not doing anything that is not right and desirable. Under ideal conditions—when inhibition precedes and accompanies every action—activity becomes free from excessive tension, thereby appearing effortless to the doer and to the observer... In doing you do it whereas in non-doing, it does you. (Alcantara, 1997, p.51)

Part of Inhibition is giving up judging. One often hears a teacher instruct a student to "relax and try it again, this time with less tension," which Alcantara (1997) says is futile because "if the intention and the desire behind an unsuccessful gesture remain the same, the gesture itself will remain unsuccessful, regardless of the amount of tension involved. A better directive, then, is 'don't try again; do something else altogether'" (p.73). It's very much like an adage a friend of mine reminds me of when I'm stuck in a problem that I've met many times before: "If you always do what you've always done, you'll always get what you always got!"

Osteopathy and craniosacral therapy are based on the same foundational principle of Alexander Technique, that body, mind and spirit are an inseparable unit and that if you affect one part you affect the whole. Dr. Still, founder of osteopathy, believed "the human body should be studied as a whole, and that all the elements of a person's body, mind and spirit had to be incorporated into the total care of that person" (Hurby, 1995, p.49). He also believed that the body contained all the elements required to maintain good health and to recover from illness if it was treated properly (p.49). Dr. Still believed that there was a relationship between structure and function in the body and "the musculo-skeletal system can reflect and produce changes in other body systems." He saw a correlation between abnormalities in the structural system of the body and symptoms of various diseases (p. 50). He developed "manipulative methods," now known as osteopathic manipulative treatment, which removed the structural abnormalities and alleviated the patient's illness. He concluded that diseases were not the cause of bodily malfunctions but the result of them. He considered bodily malfunctions to be musculo-skeletal abnormalities that decreased the ability of the nervous and/or circulatory systems to function properly and lowered the body's resistance, resulting in illness. Therefore, if the musculo-skeletal system was returned to proper relationship the body would be able to heal itself and return to a healthy state (p. 50). He saw his role as an osteopathic physician being to "help the body utilize its own self-healing mechanisms to overcome disease and maintain health" (p.50).

The general public today knows osteopathy as "a system of manipulation to treat aches and pains in the spine, muscles and joints—the framework of the body known as the musculoskeletal system" (Masters, 1988, p.11). Osteopathy can also release muscles, soft tissue, and joint casualties, and have far-reaching effects on the whole body through gentle manipulative techniques (p.11).

Osteopathic medicine today has not strayed far from Still's original discoveries, and continues to be based on the "structural-integrity" or the harmonious balance of the musculo-skeletal system. It recognizes the body's ability to be self-regulating and self-healing, and treats the individual as a whole—mind, body, and spirit, in prevention, diagnosis, and treatment of illness. Osteopathic medicine uses gentle manipulative treatment to address the structural dysfunction as well as the somatic component of illness and can help patients recover without medication or surgery. Osteopaths emphasize the need for a close personal relationship between physician and patient, and realize it must be an intelligent collaboration in order to effectively treat the complaint (Masters, 1988, p.64). Osteopathy has become accepted within the medical profession today. Osteopaths have equal status with medical doctors, and are required to take the same exams as the orthodox doctor, with additional training in manipulative therapy (p.30).

Craniosacral therapy is not as well accepted by mainline scientific and medical practices as is osteopathy. However, patients have reported positive results subjectively, and postural changes can be attributed directly to the treatment (Manheim & Lavett, 1989, p.4-5).

Craniosacral therapy, like Alexander Technique and osteopathy, is founded on the principle of the inseparable unity of mind, body, and spirit. Whether a person is subjected to physical stress or mental stress, craniosacral therapists believe it will be felt in the body as twisting. Manheim & Lavett (1989) describe the effects:

> When twisting occurs in the periphery of the body, the resulting stress will ultimately affect the dural tube that surrounds the spinal cord. Because the dural tube is continuous with the menninges enclosing the brain, stress on the dural tube is transmitted up the spinal cord to the brain and cerebral structures. (p.3)

This twisting results in pain and restricted movement, which can only be eliminated by eliminating the twisting. The body can "heal itself" if it knows what positions to assume to relieve the twisting and realign the body. Most people don't know how to realign their bodies on their own, but with the gentle soft tissue mobilization techniques of craniosacral therapy, the individual can be shown how to move into realignment. A craniosacral therapist is:

> the ultimate biofeedback machine. Connected to the patient's nervous and muscular systems through touch, responding to signals so faint that the patient is unaware of himself as the source, amplifying those signals to bring them into the conscious

awareness of the patient, the therapist makes manifest the self-healing organism. (Manheim & Lavett, 1989, p.4)

Annika mentioned several times how intuitive her body workers were, whether they were craniosacral therapists, osteopaths, Alexander Technique teachers, or voice teachers. Voice teachers are a kind of body worker if they work holistically with their students, paying attention to the body, mind, and spirit and realizing that the voice reflects the state of all these components. Voice teachers also work with breathing and posture, key issues in the therapies we have examined, and at times will use gentle physical touch to guide a student into a different posture or help them sense their breathing.

Singing is Physical

The fact that virtually all vocal pedagogy texts include anatomical diagrams and discussions about how to manipulate the breathing apparatus, open the throat, shape the mouth, and correct the posture should have been my first clue that singing is a physical activity. However, because of my own sense of being cut off from my body and denying the physical, it took me a long time to fully grasp this truth. I had always thought of music, particularly singing, as predominantly intellectual, artistic, emotional and, at times, spiritual, but not physical. This was partly due to the fact that I was unaware that emotions are felt in our bodies. Annika asked me during one of our interviews whether "you could feel an emotion in your head." This made me realize that I had always assumed I "thought" my emotions.

It wasn't until I attended a piano competition in November of 2003, and watched pianist after pianist with fingers flying, arms raised above their heads and crashing down on the keys—with some players even standing up to get better leverage for producing bass fortissimo chords—that I came to grips with the physicality of music. I attended the competition primarily to listen to Annika, who was the invited soloist that each pianist was required to accompany to show their abilities in musical collaboration. I was thinking about all I had seen Annika teach and demonstrate in the master classes about body awareness, alignment, and breathing—knowing that singing must be physical, but not seeing the physicality externally in the obvious way I observed in the pianists. As I watched the pianists I felt more like I was watching a sport than listening to music, because I wasn't connecting with their sounds internally. However, when Annika sang I felt the sound in my body, along with the desire to breathe with her, as I'd often found myself doing when I listened to a good flutist. I could relate to her sound through the breath much more viscerally than I could with the pianists who appeared to be so much more physically engaged. Or were they? From my voice lesson with Annika and Maureen I knew that without doing anything as obvious as flailing my arms or moving my fingers like a pianist, I had been very focused on my physical experience. The breath, the support of the abdominal muscles, the struggle to hold my throat open while the soft palate tried to close in resistance—those were physical happenings even though they weren't visible. I realized I had been stuck in the childhood belief that if I couldn't see it, it wasn't happening or didn't count.

One often hears piano teachers tell their students to "make the piano sing." This is a great challenge, since pianists don't need the breath to make a sound as a singer or a flutist does. They can hold their breath and still strike the keys with their fingers to produce sound. However, making an instrument "sing" is used as a metaphor for producing a connected melody that flows with the expressive qualities of the human voice—the ultimate ideal. To do this, pianists need to connect with their breath to feel the musical phrase.

I noticed it was far easier to feel this flow with one particular pianist in the competition than with any of the others. First I watched. Then, when I listened with my eyes closed, I felt the sound coming from low in his abdomen, as it would come from a singer. It felt different to me physically to listen to him and to watch him—he seemed centered in his breath. I talked with Annika after her day of performing with a variety of pianists and asked if she noticed anything different about this one pianist who had stood out to me. Immediately she said she had felt the same thing while working with him—that he was breathing low in his body—and she found it delightful to make music with him. His breath wasn't visible, like his fingers running up and down the keyboard, but it was the physical factor that brought his music to life and gave it the "singing" quality I was missing in others.

I thought back to my earliest experience of music, beginning piano lessons at age six and not being particularly interested. When I was 12 I started playing the flute in the school band and music came alive for me. I felt connected to it much more intimately than I had to the piano, where music happened at the tips of my fingers instead of at my lips, close to my ears, and on my breath. Singing held that same connection with the breath, and had exhilarated me as I jokingly sang opera around the house. Why then, had it been such a disturbing emotional experience for me to attempt to free my voice through voice lessons? I had worked with breath on the flute before and had never been strangled by shame or frozen in fear. What was so different? What was it about opening the voice that exposed my inner self so vulnerably that my body involuntarily constricted my throat in its efforts to protect me? These personal questions, along with Annika's description of voice being a "coming home to herself," which was based in coming home to her body, led me to search the literature for the connection between body, voice, and psyche.

Your Body is Your Instrument

You, singer, are the instrument. Therein lies much of the mystery and the folderol that surrounds the art of singing and the art of the teaching of singing. (Miller, 1996, p.88).

… Unlike the case with other musicians, on whose very visible instruments motor skills can be superimposed through finger or arm movements, or by the measuring of intervallic distances, the singer's own body must experience the kinds of coordination that produce ideal tone. (Miller, 1986, p.209)

I asked Susan Summers, voice instructor and professor of music therapy at Capilano College in Vancouver, B.C., why I felt so much more vulnerable and emotionally exposed trying to sing than I did playing the flute. Her explanation was as follows:

> The voice is so intimate. If I put a guitar in front of me there is something between me and the world. There is something additional that's an extension of me that I can say, "The instrument is really cold today" [which can affect the pitch].There's something other than me that is the reason for something not being right. But when it's your voice and you're standing up there with your body, your whole personae and your emotional life, you just can't fake it. (Personal interview, Jan. 24, 2004)

When playing an instrument there is something to hide behind and blame for any imperfections. It feels less personal to admit that you have not quite mastered the flute than that you have not mastered your voice, which is essentially your self. Playing an instrument introduces one layer of translation in the communication between the raw you and the listener. Martin Howard (2003) describes the difference between playing an instrument and singing:

> With instrumentalists, the musical expression originates from an interplay between the instrument and the musician which is to say that although a player's musical/emotional intention originates within, it is brought to life through their instrument. In the case of the vocalist, the singer is the instrument in which the musical/emotional intention comes to fruition. The voice is literally within, and hence is particularly equated with the self of the singer. (p.20)

Summers says "voice is an embodiment of our energy. It's the audible manifestation of our being-ness" (Personal interview, Jan.24, 2004). "Our voice is our own. It is as unique to each of us as our fingerprints. It is as unchanging as our DNA" (Martin, 1996, p.265). "Voice is a 'window' to many functions (normal and abnormal) performed by the body" (Titze, 1994, p.xxi). Our voice is like a barometer of what's going on inside us. Our health, our mood, our emotions, our motivations—all affect our instrument. "Everything you do, your voice does; everywhere you go, it goes; how you treat yourself has a direct bearing on the voice" (Arman, 1999, p.114).

Think of answering the telephone. Within a two second greeting you can usually recognize the caller, and hear that they have a cold, or are in a hurry, or are upset. Newham (1999) says "the ever shifting collage of emotions… infiltrate the voice with tones of happiness, excitement, depression and grief… The physical condition of the body is also reflected in the vitality of vocal expression" (p.14). It is difficult to separate our voices from the rest of ourselves because "the impulse to communicate vocally comes from and uses your whole person, not merely the vocal organs" (McCallion, 1998, p.3). Your environment, relationship with yourself and other people, and your intention of the moment all affect your whole person, including your voice, "which is an expression of yourself and what all of that self is doing" (p.3).

The Gift of Voice, The Loss of Voice

As human beings, the first musical instrument we play is our own voice. The breath stream is to the vocal cords as the bow is to the violin strings (Martin, 1996, p.262). The voice is an instrument apart from the rest. We are not born with a violin in our hands or a piano to play. We are born with a voice with which to sing (Oddy, 2002, p.68).

When a baby first arrives in the world, she spontaneously lets out a cry, or the doctor gives her a gentle slap to help her. If the mother doesn't hear the cry within a minute of the birth she anxiously asks, "It's too quiet, what's wrong with my baby?" That cry lets her know the baby has taken that first life giving breath on her own. According to Martin (1996) it also holds the significance of the child claiming her existence:

> Our first intentional voiced sound comes not as a statement of our needs, not as an attempt to persuade those around us to act, not as a reaction to the birth trauma, but as an assurance of our very existence—tactile and auditory proof via vibration and sound that we have arrived in a new environment and we are now an entity all on our own. (p.261)

Babies calm themselves from the fear of disappearing or ceasing to exist by voicing. Projecting themselves through voicing, they are engaged in a process of claiming their power (Martin, 1996, p.264). Campbell (2001) says, "A baby can bawl and whine for hours, and its cries convey the incredible power that it knows to be its self. Utterance then becomes the pathway to self-knowledge, self-naming, and self-respect—as well as self-hatred. The voice, in many ways, is the most exposed 'organ' of the body" (p.87).

As babies we are born with natural, free voices, with no useless tensions and a wide vocal range of pitch and rhythm. Our breath is free, as demonstrated by a baby's ability to scream for hours without going hoarse, and the visibly free involvement of abdomen and chest in the breathing process. We are born with the knowledge of how to breathe and vocalize freely. However, as life's pressures and expectations infiltrate, we develop habits that take control and "the natural voice begins to slip away" (Rodenburg, 1992, p.23). Instead of developing our natural vocal equipment into a powerful instrument of self-expression, "life batters and restricts us in such ways that most of us settle into what I term an habitual voice; a voice encrusted with restrictive tendencies that only awareness and exercise can undo and counteract. The natural voice (or what others term a 'free' or 'centered' voice) is quite simply an unblocked voice that is unhampered by debilitating habits" (Rodenburg, 1992, p.19). Most of us only re-discover this voice when "We really need emotional release or when our need to speak overrides our restrictions or self-consciousness" (p.23). Arman (1999) describes the process of freeing the voice as "rediscovering the original blue print" of the inborn perfect instrument "that was mistaken or forgotten" (p.43). In order to rediscover that perfect instrument, we must work through the "restrictive tendencies" and "debilitating habits" that not only affect our vocal apparatus, but that have become part of our identity and self-image.

Titze (1994) says, "We use our voice, in combination with our face and hands, to communicate who we are, what we want, and how we feel. We can 'let our voice be heard' to gain acceptance or communicate ideas… it gives instantaneous clues to vitality and personality" (p.xvii). But what if we have learned, through upbringing, traumatic experiences, and/or socialization, that, as a woman or a member of a minority group, it isn't safe to "let our voice be heard?" What if we have been rejected, ignored, or ridiculed for freely expressing our feelings or needs? Most likely those experiences will be reflected in our voices as "restrictive tendencies" or inhibitions. To free the voice we will have to deal with the emotional and psychological reasons for the restrictions.

Ann Patteson (1999), author of *Singing a Woman's Life: How Singing Lessons Transformed the Lives of Nine Women*, did a qualitative study of eight women to whom she was teaching voice. In this qualitative study Patteson (1999) reviews literature about the psychological development of women, feminist theory, and feminist pedagogy. She establishes that the field of music has been male dominated throughout western history and that there are few feminist music educators, which has affected the experience of women studying voice (p.22). She explores metaphors of "silence" and "voice" and cites a study of seven facilitators of women's' singing by Joyce (1993), who found that her participants spoke of the voice as representing "women's power to be seen and heard in order to survive" (Joyce, 1993, p.120 as cited in Patteson,1999, p.51). Participants in a study by Lamb (1999) on mentoring in music education students linked voice to "positive power, empowerment, self-esteem, and a functioning mentor relationship, and the absence of voice to negative experiences with power or lack of self-esteem" (Lamb, 1999, p.224 cited in Patteson,1999, p.51).

Patteson (1999) looks at how the family, sexual abuse, the church, the educational system, society, and cultural norms silence women's voices. Each of the participants articulated to Patteson that, when she came to voice lessons, she knew "the development of her singing voice would involve confrontation with issues that had caused her pain… which was part of the process of reclaiming power, authority, and joy in her life" (p.77).

Although I see the obvious connection with the discussion of being silenced and finding one's voice in feminist literature and the impact societal forces have on the voice, I purposely did not focus my research in that direction. We will see, through analysis of the data from interviews with Annika, the master class students, and my own experience, that feeling a lack of power is definitely a factor in the process of coming to vocal freedom. However, I didn't want to start with a preconceived notion that read all experience through the feminist lens of power imbalance and oppression. I wanted to hear what emerged naturally. I was also interested in exploring, in-depth, Annika's experiences and my own, so as to identify the very personal factors that had affected our vocal process. I wanted to understand the physiological, emotional, and psychological inter-related workings of the process and move outwards towards generalizations, rather than to work the other direction from the broad philosophy inward.

In Patteson's (1999) study, her participants talked about "owning your voice" as being a way to "be more present to yourself" and said that "lack of trust in your own voice shows up in a weak voice or in a voice that is halted or constricted" (p.52). Another participant talked of "retrieving lost parts of herself through singing," saying, "My voice is a way of externalizing what I feel is unique inside of myself... my uniqueness as a woman... Singing allows me to take the lid off a beautiful box (inside myself) and to allow the beauty out ... I don't connect with it until I sing" (p.53).

Well-Tuned Women: Growing Strong through Voice Work, edited by Frankie and Jenny Armstrong (2000), is a collection of essays about women finding their voices after having "lost" them through pressure from society, family, or abuse. "Finding one's voice" is becoming a common metaphor for "finding oneself" and having the courage to express one's true thoughts and feelings. "Standing up for yourself" or "making your voice heard" are similar metaphors that go one step further—projecting oneself out to be seen and heard. "Finding one's voice" implies that it can be lost. Cameron (1998), in *The Right to Write*, argues that we do not "lose our voice" but only the use of it:

> When we are less than well physically we sometimes "lose our voice." In truth we haven't lost it. We have lost the use of it... When we are psychologically unwell, we often "lose" our inner voice. Again what we have lost is really the use of it. The Inner Voice is still there, waiting to be rediscovered and re-connected to. (p.160)

Cameron is using the term "the Inner Voice" as a metaphor for that core of absolute self inside us which can never be completely lost.

Rodenburg's (1992) *The Right to Speak: Working with the Voice* defines emotional, physical, psychological, cultural, and social forces that impinge on our freedom of vocal expression and ultimately limit and shape the way we use our voices. Rodenburg (1992) discusses the vocal and breath related habits we develop to compensate for physical injuries and trauma and to protect ourselves emotionally by holding painful experiences out of our consciousness. The deep breath work necessary for singing and good vocal production often unlocks these protected areas and retrieves painful memories. According to Rodenburg (1992):

> If the breath is affected and altered by even a quiver of emotion... then it must follow that more powerful violations or grievings which are not immediately purged will penetrate deep into the breathing mechanism and lodge there... By keeping silent at key moments of our life we lay the sort of unexploded mines that will tick away just waiting to be triggered. That trigger can easily be squeezed if we are encouraged to breathe deeply or voice fully. (p.86)

Re-claiming Voice through Therapeutic Voicework

Paul Newham (1998, 1999) believes "the human voice is one way in which we preserve our identity... The voice is an expression of psychological state, a physiological operation and the means by which a person asserts his or her rights within the social order" (Newham,

1999, p.13). In Newham's books, *Using Voice and Song in Therapy* (1999) and *Therapeutic Voicework: Principles and Practice for the Use of Singing as a Therapy* (1998), he describes Voice Movement Therapy. This is a therapeutic approach that he has designed to work with the psychological, physiological and social pressures that have restrained, inhibited, or depleted a person's "capacity for unencumbered expression." Through the use of movement, breathing exercises, and various kinds of vocalization, Newham helps a person "overcome difficulties which hinder the acoustic and kinetic expression of Self" (Newham, 1999, p.13).

Carolyn Braddock's (1995) *Body Voices* describes a very similar technique to Newham's (1999) *Therapeutic Voicework*. She draws on her experience working with clients, most of whom have been sexually abused, to tell the stories of three women (composites) who move through therapeutic voicework to resolve emotional issues and somatic symptoms. She examines the use of breath, sound (any form of vocalization), and body movements in unlocking, re-experiencing, and releasing the emotions, belief systems, and memories of clients who are trying to overcome the crippling effects of trauma and abuse.

Carmen Berry (1993), author of *The Body Never Lies,* was a client of Braddock's (1995) as she sought healing from her own abusive past and rejection of her body. She writes of her struggle to validate anything non-intellectual such as feelings:

> Foolishly I believed I could control my feelings by ignoring them, hiding them or pretending they just didn't exist at all. But feelings do not evaporate simply because they are unwelcome. Rather, emotions that are not allowed authentic expression can be stored in the body evidenced by an achy shoulder, repetitive clenching of the toes, or an overwhelming sense of fatigue. Like a beach ball pushed underwater, popping up in unexpected places, my emotions found a home in my body and erupted in unpredictable and often distressing ways. (p.9)

Berry (1993) illustrates the connections between our bodies and emotion and establishes that feelings are real events carrying physical energy that must be released for us to remain healthy. Much of this release began for her through the Body Voice work she did with Braddock, and was a clue to me that attempting to open one's voice in voice lessons could have a similar therapeutic affect.

Music therapist Nicola Oddy (2002) says that not only is singing a form of "body work" that allows clients to "see into parts of her or his self that were hidden away," but it allows them to express themselves as spiritual beings (p.70). "The process of 'giving voice' is sacred work… It connects us to our humanity and to our sacredness; it grounds us and centres us in our power" (Joyce Moon, 1999, p.249 cited in Oddy, 2002, p.70). Gardner-Gordon (1990) in *The Healing Voice*, and James D'Angelo (2000) in *Healing with the Voice,* also explore the voice as spiritual. They base their work on the same premise—that the voice connects us to the body and psyche and provides a release for emotions. They employ all kinds of natural vocal sounds such as humming, groaning, and yawning for cathartic release, and work with chanting, mantras, and sustained toning to get in touch with the spiritual and for use in religious rituals.

Identity and Self-Esteem Reflected in the Voice

> Our vocal image is one that we choose for ourselves to a large extent, sometimes
> consciously and sometimes unconsciously, to represent us in the world. The quality of
> our voice directly reflects what is going on inside us. We need to ask ourselves why
> we choose the quality we choose… especially if that quality is weak, overly strong or
> excessively irritable. (Martin, 1996, p.263)

Our identity is reflected in our voice, yet we have some control over what parts of that
identity we choose to display. However, the parts we feel we need to hide still show up under
careful scrutiny as tensions, facades, somatic symptoms, or audible abnormalities. Summers
illustrated this poignantly in a story she related about one of her voice students:

> I was working with a voice student who struggles with ownership of her voice. She
> makes herself very small, has low energy, low vibration in her voice and body. When
> she sings her voice is quiet and breathy—I can hardly hear her. Being a girl is not
> something she identifies with, she's gay. Yesterday in the lesson there was a little
> more pure, higher pitch. We were working with technique—breathing and resonance.
> I said to her, "What does that feel like to you? What do you know about that for
> yourself?"
>
> The student answered, "I sound like a girl!"
>
> Now that's a whole identity that she's never taken on, in fact shunned for whatever
> reasons, but I could tell, and she could tell by her voice, that that's not what she's
> sounded like for 40 years. (Personal interview, Jan.24, 2004)

The voice student Summers described was uncomfortable with her identity as a female
and had therefore down played the feminine characteristics of her voice for years. She
discovered them inadvertently through singing, illustrating Bunch's (1993) belief, "Singing is
a powerful tool for self-realization" (p.22). Summers says:

> We can put on all kinds of affects and airs with our speaking voice, but it's much
> harder to do with your singing voice. You can't fake it with your singing voice
> because it comes from so deep down inside—my sense of it is that it comes from a
> place that is autonomic—it's like our heart rate, or breath. (Summers, personal
> interview Jan. 24, 2004)

Some singers do "fake it" by disconnecting emotionally and hiding behind perfecting
technique, and focusing on making beautiful sounds instead of communicating from the
heart. However, one can sense the detachment in the singer and it leaves one "cold" and
untouched by the performance, not to mention questioning how "free" the voice is (Summers,
personal interview, Jan. 24, 2004).

Both instrumentalists and singers are tempted to make music from behind a "technical
screen" for a variety of protective reasons. Dorita Berger (1999) in *Toward the Zen of
Performance,* explores the experience of instrumental musicians who are learning to
improvise in the context of being treated with music therapy. She realized that one of her

clients, instead of getting in touch with her emotions and expressing them in her music, was actually using the music as a screen to hide behind. She had been culturally conditioned to repress the expression of emotion and her playing was an extension of that repression in that she played rigidly from her left brain, perfecting her technique, following the rules, and glued to the music written on the page. Berger (1999) describes this client's process of stepping out from behind the screen.

> As she began to open herself up to the various improvisation tasks I directed her to undertake, she began to see her inner self—the person forbidden by cultural mores, to emerge. There were no more excuses. She had a right to her opinions, angers, passions, and individuality. These were imperative requirements for honest musical expression. (p.31)

The improvisational tasks coaxed this musician to come out from behind her technical screen and trust her intuitive right brain to guide her, which helped her discover her self and re-connect with her feelings. Improvisational music is particularly useful in music therapy because it "offers an holistic form of assessment that is relational, non-invasive, and nonverbal, and that allows the identity of the patient to be revealed" (Aldridge, 1989, p.96). Bunch (1993) says that a person's voice "can give you some clues as to a person's self-esteem and a façade they might be attempting to hide behind" (p.7). A technically driven singer (or instrumentalist) might be hiding behind a façade "to avoid judgments and self-rejection, [performers] erect barriers of defense, perhaps [invent] blame and get angry, or bury themselves in perfectionistic work" (McKay & Fanning, 1992, p.2 cited in Emmons & Thomas, 1998, p.57).

Sandgren (2002) conducted a qualitative and quantitative study of the problems in the professional and personal lives of 15 opera singers; they found somatic symptoms were another "screen" or façade employed to protect a singer's self esteem. A singer might complain of a cold or allergies to excuse them "from present or potential failure," saying the illness—real or imagined—was the "cause for poor achievement" (p.19). Summers commented on this all-too-common habit of singers, saying, "there might be a physical reason for a slight change in the voice, but what is the deeper reason? There is always a psychological reason" (Personal interview, Jan. 24, 2004). Arman (1999) maintains, "If you are having trouble with the voice, I believe there is something wrong with the connection to your heart" (p.111).

Andrews & Schmidt (1996) examined an interesting example of somatic symptoms pointing to a deeper problem in a case study of an 18-year-old female singer who was in her first year of university as a voice major. She complained initially of feeling a "lump in her throat" (globus hystericus) while singing and sometimes in every-day life. Both her physician and a specialist at the Speech and Hearing Centre to which she was referred found no physiological evidence for her condition. She was referred for ten voice therapy sessions, and counseling that focused on psychosocial factors and cognitive restructuring associated with her transition from a small high school to a large university as a voice major. The researchers followed her over the two semesters of her first year. They interviewed her counselor, voice therapist, voice teacher, parents, and the singer herself. The "lump in her throat" ceased to be the focus of her problems but it emerged that she was very dependent on her family, was homesick, doubted her commitment to music, and had a high external locus of control. Her relationship with her voice teacher had begun fairly well but deteriorated throughout the year to the point that the teacher had "withdrawn all emotional support" and said, "There is something wrong somewhere… she is a very weird girl." The student withdrew from the voice major program at the end of her first year but decided to continue taking lessons out of personal interest while pursuing another major at University. The study concluded, "music teachers should be more cognizant of the physical manifestations of psychological problems," familiarize themselves with medical and psychological services, and refer without hesitation (p.242).

"Psyching" Yourself Out

The Inner Game of Music by Barry Green (1987) is a guide to overcoming mental obstacles and achieving maximum performance. It is based on Timothy Gallwey's principles of "getting out of one's way" as described in his books, *The Inner Game of Tennis* and *The Inner Game of Golf*. The idea behind "the inner game" is that there are always two games going on when we play sports—or music. There is the outer game, where we manipulate golf clubs or piano keys, and there is the inner game in our minds, where we encounter mental obstacles such as "lapses of concentration, nervousness, and self-doubt" (p.22). Gallwey's goal was to devise principles and exercises to reduce mental interference and inhibitions, and free a person to fulfill his or her full potential. Green's (1987) application of these principles to the game of music begins with an explanation that we also have two selves. Self #1 is the talking we hear in our heads about things we "should" or "shouldn't" do, and judgments about how we are doing—in other words, the inner critic, often fueled by a sense of shame. Self #2 is "the vast reservoir of potential within each of us" which contains our natural talents and abilities, and can perform with grace and ease if we keep Self #1 from inhibiting it. The inner game basics are awareness (without judgment), will (the direction and intensity of intention), and trust (in our inner resources). If we develop and balance these skills we will be in a state of "relaxed concentration" where we have the potential of optimum performance. Green (1987) supports the idea of trusting "body wisdom" and needing to release control on the level of Self #1 to let Self #2 be in more control, even though it feels like a very different kind of control. The obstacles to trust, according to Green, are self-image, feeling things are out of control, and doubts and fears about one's ability. These concepts are relevant to the later discussion in chapter five of control, trust, and letting go, and more specifics of Green's (1987) theory are included there. The metaphor of two games and two selves is a simple way to understand that singing is about far more than pursuing correct technique, and reinforces the premise of this study that freeing the voice is connected to freeing the self. However, Green's argument is written on a popular level, offering quick fixes and not exploring any of the underlying issues of where a person's inhibitions and fears come from, or the need for re-integration of the self.

Eloise Ristad's (1982) *A Soprano on Her Head* is a humorous, metaphorical, lightly philosophical look at inner issues that block a performer. Ristad "gives people permission to discover moment by moment awareness and 'trick our old stuffy know-it-all chattering self out of the way'" (p.8). Ristad reinforces and illustrates the roles self-image, inhibitions, and bad experiences from the past—and the faulty conclusions we draw from them—have in keeping us from performing freely and reaching our potential as people.

Power Performance for Singers by Emmons & Thomas (1998) is designed to help singers learn how to perform vocally to the best of their ability. It gives strategies for dealing with many mental issues involved in performing such as distractions, anxiety, memory, setting goals, physical well-being and relaxation, developing self-confidence, and designing performance plans and routines. Its most relevant chapter is on "the self and performance" which examines the effect that rejection, self-judgment, hunger for approval, failure, lack of self-worth, and identity problems have on a performer:

> Life itself mandates that human beings have an awareness of self, that is, the ability to form an identity and then attach worth to it. So performers must define themselves as persons and then decide whether they like those identities or not... (p.57) You must understand how you perceive yourself and what consequent effects this perception has on your behavior. (p.58)

Your self-esteem is a "platform" for you as a performer, and if you don't feel worthy, or you condemn and reject yourself and have a negative self-evaluation, you are singing from a very unstable platform (p.60).

I was aware, from my first experience of voice lessons with Michael, that my self-esteem platform was shaky. However, the "holes" in the platform into which I was falling felt deeper and more specific than my usual feelings of "I'm not talented enough musically." The "I'm not good enough" feeling that I carried as generally poor self-esteem slowed my progress down at times in many aspects of life. It robbed me of feeling fulfillment and satisfaction when I performed well as a flutist and kept me seeking approval, but it had never stopped me short before. The feelings that erupted when trying to open my voice were much more piercing and paralyzing, with an overwhelming power that I could not will myself over or around. I tried to push these feelings back down, or sing around them, but such attempts only constricted my voice further.

The literature on vocal pedagogy acknowledges the possibility of psychological issues affecting a singer's vocal progress, but goes no further. Green (1987), Ristad (1992), and Emmons & Thomas (1998) suggest strategies for dealing with the effects of common mind games while performing, but none of them go deep enough into the psychological roots of the problems or explain the connection between mind and body. Newham (1998, 1999) and Braddock (1995) work on a deeper psychological level with people through voice/body work, and reinforced my belief that voice lessons were unintentionally unlocking emotional and psychological issues for me. However, I wanted to understand the psychological roots of those emotions and decided I would have to go to the psychological literature to do that. I listened to the clues my feelings were giving me during voice lessons and let them guide me into an exploration of shame and identity.

Shame

It's All in the Eyes

As I analyzed my experiences in voice lessons, I realized that I often avoided eye contact, looking at the ceiling or the floor, or anywhere but at the teacher. I felt exposed, as if I was standing there with no clothes on, and I didn't want to be seen so I hid by averting my eyes. Averting the eyes and turning the face away are the most common physical indicators observed in people experiencing shame. The words and images I used to describe my experience—naked, exposed, vulnerable, wanting to hide or escape—are the language of shame. The word shame is "derived from an Indo-European root *skam* or *skem* which meant 'to hide,' from which we derive our words skin and hide" (Nathanson, 1987, p.8, cited in Albers, 1995, p.33). "The English word *shame* shares the same root with the word *chemise*— a shirt or slip that covers us. With us, as with Adam and Eve in the garden, the experience of shame is one of exposure and our immediate response is to cover ourselves, even to hide" (Whitehead & Whitehead, 1995, p.94).

Mary Ayers (2003), in *Mother-Infant Attachment and Psychoanalysis: The Eyes of Shame,* examines the perceptual element of shame, verifying what I experienced—that shame manifests itself most through the eye. "In shame, we meet eyes and avoid eyes; the solitary, scrutinizing eye of our inner selves or the collective eyes of the world that will bear witness to our state of self-worthlessness, impotence, undesirability, ugliness, incompetence, filth, or damage" (Ayers, 2003, p.2). Kaufman (1985) explains that we feel others are watching us, but in fact we are watching ourselves; the exposure in front of another heightens our awareness of our inner scrutiny (p.9). Albers (1995) says that by hiding our eyes we are attempting to escape from the experience, but this hiding also represents a desire to shut out the other person's discovery of our true selves. "The eyes are the window of the brain, and in the language of primary process, we may feel people can look in on our thoughts almost as well as we can see out. It is as if, when we avert our eyes, we hope to prevent the other person from knowing what we are thinking" (Nathanson, 1987, p.252, cited in Albers, 1995).

Ayers (2003) explains that because our own internal eye is critical, it "makes it hard to realize oneself mirrored through another's eyes. The only reflection one gets back is one's own vision of oneself staring back" (p.11).

Capps (1993) speaks of shame as "a sense of self-estrangement, a wave of self-rejection, even of self-revulsion" (p.76). At least when another person is involved we can deflect our feelings of shame outward by blaming the other for humiliating us. Facing self-exposure is much more painful because there is no one to blame but ourselves. "Self-exposure is at the heart of shame," according to Lynd (1958), and even though we might perceive the disapproving gaze of another as the cause, when we feel extreme shame "we are unable to look at ourselves in the mirror, the self-recognition would be too difficult to bear"(p.31).

Lynd (1958) describes shame as being totally self-involving:

> It tends to involve one's body as well as one's mind. Whereas guilt is usually described as felt in the conscience (i.e. the mind), shame is deeply visceral and gut-wrenching; it is usually felt in the pit of the stomach. Shame involves the bodily self, not just the thinking self but also the feeling self, and this is perhaps why shame experiences often have debilitating physical effects. (p.27-34)

Kaufman (1985) describes the inner scrutiny being so excruciating that, "the torment of self-consciousness becomes so acute as to create a binding, almost paralyzing effect upon the self" (p.8).

As much as the scrutinizing "internal eye" must exist for us to experience shame, feelings of shame are often triggered by the real experience of being in the presence of an external eye whose opinion we value highly. Kaufman (1985) explains as follows:

> Whenever someone becomes significant to us, whenever another's caring, respect or valuing matters, the possibility for generating shame emerges (p.13) ... Whenever we openly admire someone and hence more willingly surrender to their guidance or influence, we have also surrendered power. Whenever we permit ourselves the vulnerability of needing something emotionally from someone regarded as significant, we inevitably give that special person also a measure of power which can either be respected or abused. (p.77)

On the one hand we are at risk of being shamed when we are in the presence of someone we have allowed to become significant to us. On the other hand, when we are in roles of significance (as parents, teachers, therapists, and even as spouses or friends) we must realize the power we hold to induce shame in another person (p.13). Shame comes into these relationships as perceived or actual expectations that are not being met. Sometimes the expectations are actually imposed by the other and the shamed victim realizes his or her inadequacy to meet them and feels ashamed. At other times, the expectations originate from the victim of shame who has unrealistic expectations of him/herself and projects them outwards on the respected other, feeling that they have disappointed that other. "Disabling expectations," according to Kaufman (1995), can be generated either internally or externally, but they have the same "disabling" effect of binding one with excessive self-consciousness at the prospect of not being able to fulfill them (p.23).

Shame-bound individuals defend against their feelings of inadequacy through perfectionism, rage, contempt, striving for power, transfer of blame, withdrawal (Kaufman, 1995, p.71), arrogance, judgmentalness and moralizing, patronization, caretaking and helping, envy, people-pleasing, and being nice (Bradshaw, 1988, p.88). Each of these strategies is employed to deflect scrutiny from the person's perceived flaws or to prove that they do not exist. Perfectionism is a particularly common shame defense among musicians, who, consciously or sub-consciously, believe that if they can become perfect they are no longer vulnerable to shame. Their quest after perfection "is a striving against shame and attempts to compensate for an underlying sense of defectiveness" (Kaufman, 1995, p.78). Kaufman (1985) comments on shame-driven perfectionism as follows:

> It is as though one sees the only means of escaping from the prison that is shame is to erase all signs that might point to its presence. Thus it is that an individual already burdened by a deep, abiding sense of defectiveness will strive to erase every blemish of the self and experiences an inordinate pressure to excel in an ever-widening circle of activities. Since one already knows that one is inherently not good enough as a person, nothing one does is ever seen as sufficient, adequate, or good enough. No matter how well one actually does, it could have been better. (p.78)

Unfortunately, perfectionists are robbed of the joy of their achievements, which are often outstanding, because of the feeling that it is "never good enough." The drive to do better is never satisfied because the expectation of "perfection" sets them up for constant failure.

Development of Shame

Despite the inhibition and pain often caused by shame (in my case, causing vocal constriction), Whitehead & Whitehead (1995) point out, "At the heart of shame and guilt are benefits—gifts that hinder mortals but help them too" (p.91). What can be the benefits of feeling that horrible? One significant benefit is the motivation to change or curb behaviors that result in a negative response from others, and which threaten to alienate us:

> Humans have an insatiable desire to be part of the group. We long to belong... Shame and guilt are social dynamics monitoring our lifelong efforts to belong. Often working together, these painful emotions guard our social identity by warning us of personal transgressions that threaten to exclude us from "our kind." (p.91)

Shame, guilt, and embarrassment are considered "social emotions" because socialization influences their development, society is affected by them, and another person or perceived person is involved in the generation of these emotions (Barrett, 1995, p.5). Societies must have a way of enforcing standards of human interaction (guilt) and maintaining the respect and affection of others (shame). They do so by the use of social emotions that highlight society's rules and standards and motivate people to keep them (p.28). Shame and guilt regulate a person's behavior, both intrapersonally (internal regulation) and interpersonally (social regulation). When people feel shame they avoid contact (avert the eyes, hide the face, slump the body) to distance themselves from those they perceive to be evaluating them. This regulates the evaluator's response to them because they are presenting themselves in a "low" position. They will also be motivated not to "do wrong," both morally and in the sense of not meeting standards, because of the pain of shame. Guilt differs from shame in that it serves to repair the damage of wrong-doing, often prompting the guilty one to pursue rather than withdraw from contact in order to confess wrong-doing and set it right. Guilt highlights moral/behavioral standards but it teaches one about oneself as an agent rather than an object, helping one learn about one's capabilities and deficiencies (Barrett, 1995, p.41). This is because guilt involves the appreciation of oneself as having done something contrary to one's standards and consequently injuring someone. Shame, on the other hand, involves the sense that one is being viewed as a bad person, even if there is no other person present.

The difference between guilt and shame is often described in English as being the difference between "doing" something bad (guilt) and "being" bad (shame). In German this concept is reflected more clearly in the sentence structure as well as in the difference in the words themselves. In German, shame (*scham*) is used in a self-referential, *Ich schame mich,* or *I shame myself.* However, when guilt (*schuldig*) is expressed, the construction used is, *Ich bin Schuldig,* I am guilty (of owing a debt, duty, or obligation) (Lynd, 1958, p.24).

The actions associated with guilt are different than those associated with shame. This makes sense, since they spring out of different appraisals of oneself. Someone who feels guilty and sees themself as having committed a specific wrong, or as being obligated or indebted in a specific way, will be motivated to make contact with the other person involved to confess and make reparation. However, someone feeling shame, sensing that they are evaluated by others as bad or diminished, "cannot remake the self then and there… the only recourse is to die, disappear, or withdraw from evaluating others" (Barrett, 1995, p.44).

All of us will have isolated incidents throughout life that are humiliating, embarrassing, guilt-inducing, and yes, even shameful. This is the reality of life and, as seen in the previous discussion, may even be necessary to help us learn to regulate ourselves internally and externally in our interactions with others in society. Shame and guilt also aid in the development of the self, acting as a mirror for us to see ourselves as others see us. "It causes one to step back from the self as agent and to evaluate that self, and thus helps one elaborate and/or modify one's view of the self" (Barrett, 1995, p.47). Yet how is it that some people internalize a basic appraisal of themselves as bad, diminished, and unworthy and have a pervasive sense of shame about their being? To understand how such a shame-based identity can develop, we need to understand identity development.

Developmental psychologist and theorist Erik Erikson claimed that identity formation was a social process. He defined identity as "an inner sense of sameness and continuity which is matched by the mirroring eyes of at least one significant other" (Bradshaw, 1988, p.118). Bradshaw expands this definition and goes one step further, saying, "if our core identity comes from the mirroring eyes of our primary caretakers," then " our destiny depended to a large extent on the health of our caretakers" (p.29). I will now unpack this claim of Bradshaw's by looking at identity development from a self-psychology and object relations perspective.

Self Development from a Self-Psychology/Object Relations Perspective

Psychoanalyst Heinz Kohut (1977, 1978) theorized that people need two things to develop and maintain a cohesive self-identity. The first is mirroring, and the second is merging with an ideal selfobject (parent/caregiver) (Kohut, 1977, cited in St. Claire, 2000, p.146):

> The child establishes her cohesive, grandiose-exhibitionistic self by the relation to the selfobject, which mirrors and approvingly responds to the child. On the other hand the child establishes her cohesive, idealized parent imago by the relation to the selfobject parent, who responds empathically and permits and enjoys the child's idealization and merger. (Kohut, 1977, p.185, cited in St. Claire, 2000, p.146.)

Consider the mirroring experience of a developing child. A baby looks into her mother's smiling face and feels she is safe and admired. A toddler takes her first steps and her parents cheer. A child cries over a skinned knee and her pain is acknowledged and she is physically comforted. A teen tries on a new dress and is complimented by her father as having become a young lady. These are ways in which our caregivers mirror back to us who we are, which helps us interpret our feelings and build our identities. Our caregivers are our first psychological, emotional, and physical mirrors. They reflect back to us what we look like to the outside world and give us a sense of being accepted or judged for what they see. The need to be mirrored is most intense in our early years of building our identity. However, it continues throughout life to a greater or lesser degree, helping a person maintain cohesion of identity and preventing fragmentation (Wolf, 1988, p.39).

Many times I have said, or heard counseling clients or friends lament, "If my spouse/parent/significant other could only see me for who I really am, and accept me." The longing to be deeply seen, known, and accepted is a universal desire and in our formative years it is crucial to the development of a healthy sense of identity:

> If a child is lucky enough to grow up with a mirroring, available mother who is at the child's disposal—that is, a mother who allows herself to be made use of as a function of the child's development—then a healthy self-feeling can gradually develop in the growing child. Ideally, this mother should also provide the necessary emotional climate and understanding for the child's needs. (Miller, 1981, p.53)

Pediatric Psychiatrist and Object Relations theorist Donald Winnicott (1971) uses the term "good-enough" mothering to describe a mother who, despite her flaws as a human, offers "good-enough" maternal care to facilitate the maturational processes of the infant (St. Claire, 2000, p.65). A "good-enough" mother is at first totally given over to the infant's care, highly attending, and adaptive to the infant's needs. Gradually she moves towards less adaptation and reasserts her own independence as the growing child's dependence decreases. The mother provides a "holding environment" in which the infant is contained and experienced, serving to organize the child's perception of herself through the mother's organization and collecting up the bits and pieces of the child's experience to help her to become self-integrating (Greenberg & Mitchell, 1983, p.191).

In the early stages of growth, the infant has no relation to reality and creates its world through subjective hallucination. The mother "brings the world to the child" by presenting her with an object that suits her needs at precisely the moment she is hallucinating an object to meet her needs. For example, when the child is hungry and ready to believe that something could exist to ease her hunger, the mother presents her breast; this allows the baby the illusion that what is there, easing her hunger, is the thing she created through hallucination (St. Claire, 2000, p.66). The infant will experience herself as omnipotent when the hallucination and the object presented by the mother are subjectively experienced by the infant as identical. This experience of omnipotence is the basis for healthy development and self-cohesion. If the mother empathically anticipates her baby's needs and presents herself to fill them simultaneously with the infantile hallucination, it will have the effect of the mother mirroring to the child her own experience and gestures, and will help the baby become attuned to her own bodily functions and impulses, which is the basis for her evolving sense of self (Greenberg & Mitchell, 1983, p.192).

Our caregivers are humans with their own needs and desires, other demands on their time and energy, and values about what are acceptable behaviours and likeable characteristics in their children. For all their good intentions, they cannot be completely objective, accurate mirrors of their children, and the flaws, inconsistencies, and unmet needs that exist in them will distort the image they mirror back to their children. Winnicott (1971) uses the term "good-enough" because no parent can perfectly mirror and attune to their child's needs, yet "good-enough" mothering will fill enough needs, enough of the time, so that the child matures in a basically healthy way. Nevertheless, there are a number of ways in which mothering that is not "good enough" can negatively affect the child's emerging identity. We will focus now on how mothering that is not quite "good enough" can plant the seeds of a shame-based identity in a developing child.

Take, for example, a parent who repeatedly disregards the child's needs for affection, perhaps because she is uncomfortable with it from her own experience of not receiving affection as a child. It doesn't take long for the child to stop asking for affection, not wanting to risk the pain of being rejected or to feel her impotence in getting her need met. She cannot control the caregiver into giving her the affection she needs, but she can control herself by rejecting the part of herself that needs affection and repressing it out of consciousness. The child essentially binds the need with shame, convincing herself that she shouldn't need affection, and that her parent's denial of affection is based on her "badness" or the badness of the need itself. This protects her from feeling the pain and helplessness of not having her needs met and of feeling rejected by the parent. However, it builds into her identity a sense of shame about her needs—an inescapable part of herself that she holds in contempt. Kaufman (1985) states that a child eventually "silences her awareness of deprivation itself" (p.68).

Unless there is a conscious effort to heal the wounding that caused the sense of shame to develop in the first place, this self-judgment will be carried forward into adulthood where it can paralyze her in contexts that unearth her buried needs for affection, such as intimate relationships. If the significant other in the intimate relationship offers her affection, her own desire for affection could be unearthed. But along with the desire comes the shame that she shouldn't need affection and the fear that she might be rejected if she opens herself to being vulnerable to that need. The fact that the need has arisen, regardless of whether it is judged negatively by the significant other or not, can trigger feelings of having a bad or shameful part of herself exposed. She will most likely feel that she is being judged by the other in some way—catered to for being weak or indulged out of pity. She will find it hard to trust the other not to judge her because she is judging herself and will be tempted to project it outwards as a defense mechanism.

Other parts of ourselves, such as our feelings or our natural drives of sexuality and hunger, can also be bound by shame and repressed out of consciousness. Most people can remember an incident from childhood when they were told to "put some clothes on," or a situation where they were innocently displaying or exploring their bodies and they were unexpectedly reprimanded. They found themselves suddenly exposed and criticized for having shown a part of themselves that they did not know was wrong to show—a recipe for shame! Depending on a number of factors (the intensity of the parent's reaction, the sensitivity of the child, etc.) this can cause the child to have feelings of shame about her body and her sexuality that she could very likely carry into adulthood. "Sexuality is the core of human selfhood. Our sex is not something we have or do, it is who we are... Our sexual energy (libido) is our own unique incarnation of the life force itself... To have our sex drive shamed is to be shamed to the core" (Bradshaw, 1985, p.54).

Caregivers who constantly correct their children without the balance of positive mirroring can also distort a child's developing sense of self. Such negativity and perfectionistic standards can keep a child from being able to progress through Erikson's "autonomy versus shame" stage of development (Capps, 1993, p.28), since shame and self-doubt can stunt their ability to learn new skills:

> Whether in regard to exercising new functions, exploring the environment, acquiring language, or gaining control over bodily functions, shame can become a barrier to gaining mastery... If a significant other continually corrects a child's speech, he may become acutely self-conscious about talking and retreat from verbal interaction... Over-correction will induce self-consciousness and disrupt the learning of any skill. (Kaufman, 1985, p.59)

Kaufman (1996) notes that there needs to be "adequate and appropriately graded doses of shame that do not overwhelm the child but, instead, [sic] are effectively neutralized and counteracted" (p.147). If parents go beyond correcting the behavior of the child and say things like, "You should be ashamed of yourself," the child's sense of self is susceptible to further shameful wounding (Kaufman, 1985, p.18). McClintock (2000) states that people develop distorted views of self and destructive adaptive behaviors if such shaming language is experienced regularly. "If most of the feedback we get from our families of origin is that not only is our behavior bad, but it springs out of a core self that is rotten or defective, then we begin to cluster negative feelings around a base of shame" (McClintock, 2000, p.22).

Another form of inadequate mirroring occurs when the mother herself is shame-based. When this is the case often the mother has her own narcissistic needs that have gone unmet and she will not have the inner resources to be able to mirror her child in a "good-enough" fashion. Many mothers with this type of neediness will seek narcissistic gratification from their children, which prevents the child from being able to develop an authentic self (Bradshaw, 1988, p.44). In order to survive this situation the child will become complacent and develop a false self that can be used by the mother for her needs at the expense of the development of the child's true self. This results in the child building a false set of relationships and, over time, feeling isolated, unreal, and unable to be in genuine relationships or feel genuine herself (St. Claire, 2000, p.68). This false self is protecting the authentic self, which never had its needs met and was never seen or mirrored for who it was. There is an authentic self buried somewhere deep within, but it is likely fragile, insecure, and somewhat undeveloped since it was never seen and encouraged into being. "As the false self is formed, the authentic self goes into hiding. Years later the layers of defense and pretense are so intense that one loses all awareness of who one really is" (Bradshaw, 1988, p.14).

The starting point of our discussion about the development of a shame based identity was Kohut's (1978) self-psychology theory which states that, in order to develop a healthy sense of self, one needs to be mirrored and to merge with an ideal. Now that we have explored some of the results of inadequate mirroring, we turn our attention to the need for a child to merge with an idealized selfobject.

Idealizing needs are the needs "to experience oneself as being part of an admired and respected selfobject; needing the opportunity to be accepted by and merge into a stable, calm, non-anxious, powerful, wise, protective, selfobject that possesses the qualities the subject lacks" (Wolf, 1988, p.55). In other words, a child knows that it isn't equipped to survive in the world by itself, but "merging" with a selfobject (caregiver) who is equipped in these ways gives the child a sense of stability, safety, and strength. This is why a small boy faced by a bully might fearlessly claim: "You can't hurt me because my dad is bigger than you and he'll beat you up." Because the boy sees himself merged with the power and perceived "omnipotence" of his father, he sees himself as safe. However, if the selfobject is not experienced as possessing the qualities needed for a stabilizing merger (for example, if the parent is unpredictable, unavailable, or inattentive) then it is possible that the merger will not occur and the infant remains isolated and lives falsely (St. Claire, 2000, p.68). Austin (1991) highlights another aspect of developing a false self. "Unable to trust and depend on his/her feelings for orientation, the narcissistically injured person is forced to look to others for a sense of identity" (p.302). Not being able to trust her own feelings makes the already narcissistically injured individual vulnerable to further wounding since the opinions of others, both positive and negative, take on too much significance.

The other possibility for an infant with an unhealthy selfobject is that the infant employs the defense mechanism of "internalizing what is bad or frustrating in her environment." Fairbairn, of the British object relations school in the mid-1900s, examined the defense mechanism of splitting used by children who were in a selfobject relationship with an abusive caregiver. Since the child is dependent on her selfobject, regardless of how unreliable or even hostile the selfobject is, she chooses rather to "become bad than have bad objects in the environment, and so the child becomes 'bad' by defensively taking on the badness that appears to reside in the objects" (St. Claire, 2000, p.18). The child cannot control the badness of the object but needs to try to do so in order to have any sense of security:

> The child seeks to make the objects in his [sic] environment good, purging them of their badness by taking them on and making them part of his own psychological structure. The price of outer security is having troubling bad objects within, in other words, the world is good but now the child is "bad." (p.18)

For an object to have emotional importance for the ego, a piece of the ego must be attached to it. Therefore, the child splits off part of his/her ego and attaches it to the bad object, and then must repress both the split off part of the ego and the bad object.

The split off part of the ego then splits again into the libidinal ego and the anti-libidinal ego. The libidinal ego contains the normal needs of the child that are not being met but are "excited" by the possibility of being met by the selfobject. The child hopes that if s/he just tries harder, or is more perfect in some way, the selfobject will finally give her/him what s/he needs and thus stays attached to the selfobject. The "anti-libidinal ego" is the part of the ego that identifies with the rejecting/inadequate part of the object, taking a hostile stance against the libidinal ego and the normal needs of the child. (St. Claire, 2000, p.54). The anti-libidinal ego is also referred to as the "internal saboteur," because it attacks the child and her/his needs from within. "Fairbairn considered objects to be not merely internal figures or mental representations but agencies capable of psychological activity... the ego becomes a dynamic structure—that is, a psychic structure actively doing something to someone or something" (St. Claire, 2000, p.50).

This positioning of a dynamic structure, created through the internalization of a "bad" selfobject and resulting in an attack by one part of the self on another part of the self, is one explanation of how a person internalizes shame—that state of being where the self rejects the self. One often hears people talk of their "internal critic" or the *voices* of critical parents that surface from time to time and try to convince them that they are incompetent, unlovable, or in some way not good enough to do or be what they are attempting to do and be. The *voices* might have originally been the actual voices of perfectionistic, critical, or abusive parents but they have since been internalized as one of their own voices, the internal saboteur. The internal saboteur identified with the parent initially as a defense mechanism. If the person wants to get free of its attacks, the voice of the internal saboteur needs to be quieted because the need to defend has passed, and the voice is hindering rather than helping in the present situation. It is time to let other *voices* of acceptance, self-respect, and confidence, speak.

The internalization of shame happens in much the same way. A person internalizes a selfobject, and as we saw in the case of an abusive or critical parent, the internalization of the selfobject includes the shaming attitudes and behaviors the selfobject carries. When we internalize something we literally take it inside, through a process that begins with identification and ends with us incorporating the internalized object or attitude into our own identities.

Kaufman (1985) explains the role that identification and internalization play in shaping one's identity:

> Identity emerges haltingly out of the process of identification. Internalization is the important link by which identification leads to identity. Internalization involves three distinct aspects. We internalize specific affect-beliefs or attitudes about ourselves which come to lie at the very core of the self and thereby help to mold our emerging sense of identity. We also internalize the very ways in which we are treated by significant others and we learn to treat ourselves accordingly. This forms the beginning basis for our relationship with ourselves, another important dimension of identity… And we internalize *identifications* in the form of images—we take them inside us and make them our own. These identification images remain internal in the form of specific guiding images. Through internalization, the conscious experience of the self inside is shaped and a relationship with that self develops. This is identity. (p.37)

Children have a deep need to identify, to be deeply like the valued parent, and it is this need that enables the parent to transmit their ways of being, thinking, and feeling quite easily, often without intention, to the child (Kaufman, 1985, p.51). The first step of identification is for the child to observe, to see what s/he is taking on from the parent. Kaufman (1985) describes the visual process of mutual looking between parent and child that is part of the observing needed for identification:

> It is as though through the eyes we can see into one another, perhaps even experientially enter the other's skin and so come to know him or her from the inside… rarely do we sustain that meeting for longer than a moment, for the sheer intensity of the experience of mutual looking most often becomes too much to bear. (p.51)

Shame can interfere with this process of identification if the parent's own shame keeps her/him from being able to allow the child to see her/him this intently, or if the parent shames the child by being invasive through looking too long. Past a certain point of connection the looking feels to the child like exposure, and can interfere with the child's opposing need to separate.

If the models we identify with are shame-based themselves, and/or if they show attitudes towards us that are often inattentive and shaming of our feelings, needs, and basic drives, then we internalize shameful attitudes about ourselves. If shame is experienced as more than a passing feeling in isolated incidents, it can be internalized and felt indefinitely, thus shaping our emerging identity. "Our identity is that vital sense of who we are as individuals, embracing our worth, our adequacy, and our very dignity as human beings. All these can be obliterated through protracted shame, leaving us feeling naked, defeated as a person and intolerably alone," (Kaufman, 1985, p.7) as well as "flawed and defective as a human being"

(Bradshaw, 1985, p.41). Once our sense of identity is infected with shame, an inter-personal shame-inducing event is no longer required. Rather, the self can now autonomously activate and experience shame in isolation, when it is conscious of its limitations and failures, or of not achieving a prescribed goal (Kaufman, 1985, p.66).

Small children show feelings of shame by turning their faces away, averting their eyes, or blushing, just as adults do. Although it is momentarily painful for them, they do not yet have the cognitive or verbal skills to translate those shame experiences into words and create meanings about themselves. However, once a person is old enough to symbolize inner experience and use language they can:

> ... interpret shame experiences as signifying essential meanings about the self... Isolated shame experiences become magnified and fused via imagery and language. Scenes of shame become interconnected, and thereby magnified. "I feel shame" becomes transformed, given new meaning: "I am shameful, deficient in some vital way as a human being." Shame has become internalized... bound up with our emerging identity... It is no longer one affect among many, but instead comes to lie at the core of the self. (Kaufman, 1985, p.65)

Whitehead & Whitehead (1995, p.95-95) illustrate this point by telling the story of two young boys who are beaten up by older bullies while walking home from school. One boy comes from a family that has created a positive "holding environment" where he knows he can trust his parents to hear and comfort him. He returns home crying and tattered and tells his parents honestly what happened. They listen, comfort him, assure him that it was wrong for the older bullies to take advantage of him, and help him think of ways to keep himself safe while walking home (i.e. taking a different route, walking with others). The other boy does not come from a supportive "holding environment" and has heard his dad talk disdainfully about "sissies." He views being beaten up as his fault for not being strong enough or smart enough to get away or successfully fight back. He expects that he will be ridiculed and criticized by his father if he admits what happened, so he hides the evidence. He internalizes the experience as another "image" of how much of a sissy he must be and goes about devising ways to act tougher and bury his shame. In this way the second boy is linking past experience with present experience and building a shame-based view of himself as weak and less than a man.

We live in an ambiguous social state. We want to be seen, acknowledged, and respected, yet only when we feel adequate to be seen (Whitehead & Whitehead, 1995, p.94). Ayers describes our situation: "A central theme around shame, then, is about seeing and being seen when one wishes to hide, or of not being seen in the way one wants to be seen, or in a way that is congruent with what one is trying to show" (Ayers, 2003, p.18). A child craves and needs to be seen and mirrored to develop a sense of self, yet the warped reflection caregivers mirror back builds shame into the child's sense of identity.

Psycho-Spiritual Roots of Shame

Shame was put upon you.
It is not yours.
Your soul need not
Be limited by shame.

(Marion Woodman, 1998, p. 286)

Creating God in the Image of Our Early Selfobjects

Shame is a vast topic. I have limited my discussion to an examination of the psychological roots of shame as part of identity development from a self-psychology/object relations perspective. As Pattison (2002) says, "There is no one way of approaching or understanding shame, no one 'reality' that underlies all experiences of shame... There is no 'master narrative' that satisfactorily accounts for all, or most aspects of the phenomenon" (p.181). I chose not to review other psychological, social, theological, historical, and political perspectives on shame. However, given that one of the goals of this study is to explore how freeing the voice relates to pastoral counseling, I now turn our discussion of shame to a psycho-spiritual perspective.

The disciplines of self-psychology and object relations have much to say about the spiritual roots of shame and the corresponding image of the sacred one develops in support of a shame-based identity. As seen in our earlier discussion, mirroring, initially through the mother's eyes, and the internalization of a selfobject (the child's primary caregiver), is the material a child uses to develop his/her early identity. When the child isn't mirrored adequately, or the mother's attunement to the child is insufficient, or there is abuse, or the needs and drives of the child are unmet, ignored, or rejected, shame results. Initially shame is experienced as rejection or disapproval of some part of the self or the entire self by the selfobject. However, shame can become internalized as part of the child's view of his/herself quite quickly and can be re-experienced internally without further external rejection.

Anna-Maria Rizzuto (1979), in *The Birth of the Living God: A Psychoanalytic Story,* uses Kohut's concepts of mirroring transference and the selfobject bond to explain the early creation of the God-representation out of the experience of the mother. A child's representation of God "is the apex of the process of consolidating object representations into a coherent inner object world; it is compounded out of the bits and pieces of object representations the child has at her disposal... [Her] God is created from representational materials whose sources are the representations of primary objects" (p.178). The word *religion* comes from the Latin *religio*, which has a number of meanings, but the one important to this discussion is "to bind together" (Jones, 1991, p.43). Just as the child develops a cohesive sense of self through making use of a selfobject representation, often God, to mirror and focus the self's integrative processes, so religion psychologically serves to consolidate the bits and pieces of a person's inner representational world and bind experiences together (p.43). Rizzuto (1979) writes "the sense of self is in fact in dialectical interaction with a God representation that has become essential to the maintenance of the sense of being oneself" (p.50).

Masterson (1985) characterizes the individual's object relation as being more than just the internalized object. "It is the affective tone of the child's experiences—'his [sic] own inner feelings or states'—that form the core of the sense of self. It is these core affective states that are replayed in the transference and in all other relationships including the bond with the sacred" (Masterson, 1985, p.24). Therefore, when a pastoral counselor hears clients saying, "I think God gave up on me a long time ago," or, "When I feel like I need God the most, He disappears," they are providing a window into the affect states they experienced in their first selfobject relationship and the meaning they constructed from those feelings about self and about God.

James Jones (1991), in *Contemporary Psychoanalysis and Religion,* explores "the ways in which a person's relationship with what he construes as sacred serves as the transferential ground of the self" (p.65). He focuses not on doctrinal beliefs but on "how religion as a relationship resonates to those internalized relationships that constitute the sense of self— or… how a relationship to the sacred enacts and reenacts the transferential patterns present throughout a person's life" (p.65). As we saw in our discussion of shame, once shame has been internalized, something as innocuous as a glance from an authority figure (such as a voice teacher) may invoke an experience of shame, even if the glance wasn't intended critically. The glance was merely a trigger that put the person in touch with the shame that already existed within. However, shame is experienced as being caused by the judging authority. One can see that if this is the affect state a person carries into significant relationships, shame will inevitably be part of their experience of a relationship with the sacred.

It is interesting that the mirroring function of the mother who provides the material for the child's first self- image echoes the Biblical account of "God creating man [sic] in his own image, in the image of God created He him" (Genesis 1:27, King James Version).

Freud offered a different perspective:

> Freud found satisfaction in reversing the process and demonstrating through his lifework that it is man who creates God in his own image. Nevertheless, Freud remained in the area of reflection of images between man and God, thus confirming the paramount importance of the intertwining of faces by mother and child and God and man. (Rizzuto, 1979, p.186)

There is some truth in Freud's idea that "we make God in our own image," in that the image we construct of God reflects something of how we see ourselves. For example, a pastoral counseling client might say, "God is just like my father, angry and judgmental." By this, they are saying something about what they believe about the nature of God and about how they experience themselves in relation to that God—ashamed and rejected. Their feelings of shame and rejection have taken up residence as part of their self-image. In order to maintain that self-image, they must believe in an image of God that supports those feelings, an image that is like the angry, judgmental father with whom they experienced those feelings initially:

> The representation of God is given all the psychic potentials of a living person who is nonetheless experienced only in the privacy of conscious and unconscious processes. Other so-called actions of God in the realities of our lives (his responses to our prayers, his punishments, his indications of what we should do) rest upon our interpretation of events and realities to accord with our state of harmony, conflict, or ambivalence with the God we have. (Rizzuto, 1979, p.87)

This explains why clients who feel "God disappears" when they need God the most, are interpreting that "action" of God through their lens of abandonment experienced in early selfobject relationships. It will probably emerge in therapy that they have also learned to abandon themselves emotionally at difficult times. How could they experience God any differently? This self-abandonment often takes the form of a people-pleasing "false" self (Winnicott, 1971), created to protect the authentic self from rejection (Jones, 1991, p.89).

People who have created such negative, shaming images and relationships with the sacred face a number of challenges. Rizzuto (1979) says, "Once formed, that complex representation cannot be made to disappear; it can only be repressed, transformed, or used" (p.90). Those who repress the image often decide they do not believe in God because the God they experience hurts too much to be a God they want to have anything to do with. Rizzuto (1979) interviewed a number of people who said they were atheists, asking them what their image of God was. At first they replied that there was no God so they had no image to describe. When asked, "If there was a God, what would God be like?" they had a very clear image—usually of an angry, punishing, rejecting, or abusive God. It wasn't that they had no image of God. It was that the image they had wasn't one they wanted to be related to, which was part of why they had decided God could not exist.

People who "transform" their images of God do so as changes in their self-constructs occur. Rizzuto (1979) suggests "the God representation is reworked, added to, and transformed as the individual goes through life and brings new experiences to his or her inner representational world... One's image of God fits or can be reworked to fit one's needs at any given developmental stage" (Jones, 1991, p.46). Kohut suggests that change takes place because "new and more gracious interpersonal experiences are internalized as new psychological structures" (Jones' 1991, p.107). These "gracious interpersonal experiences" provide the material to make more positive relationships with humans and, in turn, "reverberate through a person's relationship to the sacred" (p.107).

Jones (1991) explains, "Every developmental stage is also a crisis of belief since it demands that the God image be reworked to fit a new conception of self... Internally the life of faith is an ongoing series of major and minor transformations and adjustments in the central image of God" (p.202). Often people don't manage to "up-date" their image of God along with the growth of their inner representational world. This could be due to their inability to let go of their defenses and adjust their representation of themselves, so their God needs to remain the same to support that self-image. It could also be that they decided to repress or jettison God altogether because the old representation was holding them back from personal growth and it was easier to just detach from God. It is also possible that they didn't know how to transform their image of God, or didn't know it was possible due to the overwhelming evidence in Western Christian orthodoxy that God actually is an angry, judgmental, fault-finding, shame-inducing, punishing, perfectionist who could never be pleased.

Images of God in Conservative Christian Teaching

> *You have taught me to worship a god who is like you, who shares your thinking exactly, who is going to slap me one if I don't straighten out fast. I am very uneasy every Sunday, which is cloudy and deathly still, and filled with silent accusing whispers.* (Garrison Keillor, 1985 cited in Pattison, p.229)

Stephen Moore (1996) expresses his view of predominant images of God taught by the Christian church saying, "The God of the majority orthodox tradition, with whose images I was confronted as a child, is a shame-generating monster." Moore describes the Biblical God as "a projection of male narcissism… the supreme embodiment of hegemonic hyper masculinity, and as such the object of universal adoration" (Moore cited in Pattison, 2000, p. 241).

How does one see God as a "shame-generating monster" when Christianity supposedly teaches love, forgiveness and grace? Jones (1991) begins to answer this question by using the example of abused children who held onto images of wrathful gods into their adolescence and adulthood because it supported their sense that there was something incurably wrong with them. "Often people who are abused feel guilty, partly because they imagine they played some role in the abuse and partly because they turn the blame and anger on themselves" (Jones, 1991, p.104). As we saw earlier in Fairbairn's theory, a child who has a "bad" (abusive) selfobject will "take upon himself the burden of badness that appears to reside in his [sic] objects, and in becoming bad himself makes the others in his world good" (p.104). Since the child can only control himself and not the object, s/he takes the badness into her/himself so s/he "feels safer in a world governed by good forces, even if the subject must feel bad about himself" (Jones 1991, p.105). As Fairbairn puts it, "It is better to be a sinner in a world ruled by God than to live in a world ruled by the Devil" (Fairbairn, 1943, p.66, cited in Jones p. 105).

People with internalized bad selfobjects need a wrathful condemning God to allow them to re-enact a relationship in which they are judged and found guilty, in keeping with their view of themselves. Many churches preach that humans are guilty sinners in need of forgiveness, and the emphasis is on the sinfulness, the guilt, and the "worm" theology of deserving nothing but condemnation from God. Yet, paradoxically, we are supposed to be able to shed all that badness and receive forgiveness and pardon through repentance. This teaching reinforces the already negative internalized image of self which holds the person stuck in a relationship with a judging God. What the person needs are experiences of grace and acceptance to help create new images of themselves and God. Ironically, this grace and acceptance are also promised by Christian teaching, but are hard to believe or access when sin and guilt are so over-emphasized.

A Theology of Shame Instead of Sin and Guilt

Lewis Smedes (1993), in *Shame and Grace,* gives the following account of his experiences of sin, guilt, and grace within the Christian church:

> When I heard at church that I was a sinner through and through, I only felt my old shame for all the natural goings on inside my body... hearing the message that Jesus died for my sins and I could be saved by grace... was the most perplexing part of my church experience... grace felt heavy for me. ... By the time the good word got to me, I was sunk so deep in my shame that I could feel no lightness in grace. Another thing that made grace seem heavy was the church's pre-occupation with guilt. Grace flowed from Jesus as pardon for the sins I was guilty of committing. But guilt was not my problem... What I needed more than pardon was a sense that God accepted me, owned me, held me, affirmed me, and would never let go of me even if he was not too much impressed with what he [*sic*] had on his hands... I found it hard to feel grateful for a gift when I was constantly reminded of how unworthy I was to get it. (p.80)

Smedes (1993) is not alone in his thought that "guilt was not my problem" and that shame was his more significant struggle. Pattison (2000) writes:

> Western Christian tradition has spoken chiefly in terms of sin and guilt, and has seen salvation principally as forgiveness of sins ... in trying to understand the nature of human alienation from neighbour and the divine... For most theologians, shame has not been a significant phenomenon as part of human experience or as a feature of the relationship between humans and God. (p.190)

Donald Capps (1993), in *The Depleted Self,* explains that there is a new narcissistic self in today's individualistic society that does not relate to the traditional language of sin and guilt:

> Something has changed, perhaps radically, in the way that we today experience a sense of wrongness—in our inner selves, wrongness in our relations with other persons, and wrongness in our relations with God. In our times we are much more likely to experience this "wrongfulness" according to shame, rather than guilt, dynamics. Thus to speak meaningfully and relevantly about sin, we have to relate sin to the experience of shame—not only, not even primarily, to the experience of guilt. Obviously, this will involve a reformulation of our theology of sin. (p.3)

Theologian Wolfhart Pannenberg (1972) was writing before Capps (1993) and before the use of narcissistic language became common, however, he identified the dilemma in virtually the same terms:

> In modern times a Christianity which takes its bearing from the problem of guilt has increasingly come up against lack of understanding and mistrust among people who

do not feel themselves to be sinners and who consequently believe that they do not need the message of forgiveness either. (Pannenberg, 1972, p.163)

Evangelists, who realized their former strategies of "convicting people of their sin and guilt in order to lead them to repentance" weren't working, also felt the need for this theological shift (Pembroke, 1998, p.15). Pembroke also realized that people were "experiencing a sense of 'wrongness' in terms of shame rather than guilt," and the new strategy would have to make use of concepts such as "exposure, acceptance, and fulfillment" for the gospel to make sense to the narcissistically wounded. "Just as forgiveness is what brings release for the guilty person, acceptance can repair the narcissistic injury in the shame-afflicted person" (Morrison, 1986, p.354, cited in Pembroke, 1998, p.15).

Capps (1992) formulated a theology of shame with theologically based therapeutic insights for the pastoral counselor. He drew on Biblical stories and images, such as Jesus accepting rather than humiliating the woman who anointed his feet with perfume, to illustrate an accepting God. This could be a healing image for some people but, depending on a number of factors that Pattison (2000) describes, it could be a negative image for others. "Images don't have fixed meanings, they can change across cultures and eras, and between people, so it's difficult to definitively label the functionality or dysfunctionality of an image" (p.232). Images reflect a social order view and theological images are no exception, emerging from a socio-political and historical milieu. If a society is shame-based then the ideas and images will reflect shame, often reflecting more about the human beings who constructed them and their world view than about the "true" nature of God (p.233). Liberation theologians have shown that "dominant images, ideas and texts are often created and sustained by dominant social groups and help to sustain the power of these groups and their views" (Pattison, 2000, p.233). Pattison points out that all such images are infused with a wide variety of meanings in the way they are used and, unfortunately, Christianity often doesn't dissipate a person's sense of shame but can actually engender, exacerbate, exploit, and ignore shame (p.231).

A Monarchical Image of God

Pattison (2000) outlines several commonly held theological ideas and images of God that promote shame. He begins with the dominant image of God in the Judaeo-Christian tradition in biblical and post-biblical development. He entitles this the "monarchical" model of God in which God is "King," and psychologically powerful and dangerous. This model of God gives humans strong emotions of awe, gratitude, and trust—the type of God that a weak, dependent child creates as an ideal selfobject to protect, direct, and accept her or him. Such a God also inspires fear and humiliation because this type of God can only be God if we are nothing (Pattison, 2000, p.235). The monarchical God is distant from the world, controlling through a mixture of domination and benevolence. "Most people have been exposed to this God through images and concepts of the monarchical tradition as contained in the scriptures, creeds, liturgies, and prayers of historic churches… This image of God and rise of human shame happened at virtually the same time in Judaeo-Christian mythology" (Pattison, 2000, p.235- 236). Shame makes its first appearance in the third chapter of Genesis when Adam and Eve disobey God and then feel exposed in the eyes of God, the creator. It is important to note that the "sin" here was disobeying God's command not to eat from the tree of good and evil and was not a sexual sin. One of the results of the knowledge they obtained from eating from the tree was that they realized they were naked and became self-conscious, but that was not the sin. This is important because some particularly conservative and inaccurate Bible teaching uses this passage as fuel to heap more prohibitions and shame on human sexuality.

Other biblical passages that are poorly interpreted and used to support further physical and sexual shame are found in the writings of Paul. Consider Galatians 5:16-19:

> But I say, walk by the Spirit, and you will not carry out the desire of the flesh. For the flesh sets its desire against the Spirit; and the Spirit against the flesh; for these are in opposition to one another, so that you may not do the things that you please. (Ryrie Study Bible)

It is difficult to imagine a reading of this passage that wouldn't induce some sort of idealization of the spirit and rejection of the body. "For much of history, Christianity has emphasized a strong separation of body and spirit leaving some to consider the body bad and the spirit good" (McClintock, 2001, p.42). This historical bias towards the separation of body and spirit is found in the translations of the Bible we read today, making it difficult for people to read it any other way:

> Much of the sexual ethic of western Christendom was tainted by the Gnostic-Manichean dualism that regarded matter as degraded, nature as the creation of demonic god, women as inferiors, and sex as lust to be repressed or expressed only within marriage. (Keen cited in McClintock, 2001, p.43)

Gnostic-Manichean dualism particularly distorted the interpretations of St. Paul by projecting a physical/spiritual split onto his writing, condemning anything of the flesh and exalting the disembodied spirit.

Sexual shame is a vast topic in and of itself, and could be examined from a number of angles that are beyond the scope of this study. One could look at feminist theory of oppression of minority groups, specifically women, and at how women's bodies have been the dumping grounds for much of society's shame, aggression, and angst. Or sexual shame could be examined through the societal, political, and cultural factors influencing views of sexuality in the present day and their historical roots. The prevalence of sexual violence is another point of entry into the discussion of sexual shame that would be relevant but is beyond the scope of this study.

Many Old Testament passages highlight God's deliberate shaming of humans. In Psalm 104:29, creation perishes as a result of God "hiding His face" and in Psalm 44:9ff, God covers His people with shame and scorn because they displease Him. In Psalm 2:4, God laughs scornfully at his enemies and shames them. Some people conclude from the Old

Testament that God is "a kind of all-too-human oriental despot who overtly exploits shame in the interests of bolstering his own power and control" (Pattison, 2000, p.236).

Many ideas and images of God do not directly mention shame, but still contribute to the development of shame in the human psyche and exacerbate feelings of unloveableness, humiliation, inferiority, and defilement. Pattison (2000) lists these commonly believed ideas, and shows how they can contribute to shame.

1. *God is wholly different from his people.* This creates dis-identification between God and humans. How can God mirror us adequately or be attuned to our needs if He is so different from us?

2. *God does not have a body.* The body is seen as the seat of shame as it is concerned with earthly matters, sexual reproduction, ingestion, digestion, and excretion. The majority Christian ideal, following in the steps of Platonic philosophy, sees God as disembodied... The ideal of disembodied spirit which has often informed Christian theology and spirituality fails to accurately mirror the reality of the human condition and may lead to its implicit disparagement and shaming.

3. *God is pure and holy.* God is not defiled by bodily functions that cause shame to humans, and can't look at or tolerate that which is shamed or defiled, so we are alienated from ourselves because we are not pure and holy.

4. *God requires people to be holy and obedient to God's will.* This could be interpreted that God doesn't mirror human needs and desires, and thus requires us to change, conform to His will, and not become our true selves. We must learn to mirror God instead of Him mirroring us, which echoes Winnicott's theory of a poorly mirrored child developing an outwardly conforming "false self" to please the parent.

5. *God is perfect.* According to some inaccurate readings of Matthew 5:48, we are also commanded to "be ye perfect as your heavenly Father is perfect." This is an impossibility for humans; it sets them up to fail and feel shame because they do not measure up and never will, no matter how hard they try.

6. *God is rational and does not have feelings or desires.* As humans we are all too aware of our feelings and desires, which are often based in the body. We know the disparity between us and the 'ideal, self-controlled, passionless God,' and feel we should subdue and deny our passions and overcome our bodies or suffer the shame of being bad and inferior.

7. *God is omnipotent.* The notion of an active, omnipotent God may play into human shame by emphasizing elements of passivity and lack of autonomy. "We have no power of our own to help ourselves," as the collect from the Anglican Book of Common Prayer for the Second Sunday in Lent reads. This makes people feel their actions and will have no significance.

8. *God is unbiddable and often absent.* God's ways are not our ways even though God supposedly works for our best as a loving parent. Much of the time we puzzle over what appears to be God's absence, which seems to reinforce our sense of badness, impotence, unwantedness, and fundamental flawedness.

9. *God is omnipresent.* This can feel persecutory and tormenting if one sees God as a disapproving deity, looking down with disapproving eyes of shame. Scripture verses such as, "Whither shall I go from your presence," (Psalm 139:7-8) can make one feel they can't keep any secrets, and are under perpetual surveillance.

10. *God does not need anything from humans.* It would follow, then, that humans do not deserve anything from God. Much Christian theological tradition emphasizes the asymmetrical relationship between God and creation, which compounds our sense of impotence and worthlessness. The price of developing a sense of absolute gratitude to and dependence upon God may be the acquisition of a diminished view of the power and value of the self. This may foster shame.

11. *God punishes wickedness and sin.* This can foster fatalism and passivity, as well as reinforcing the belief in ontological badness in the shamed believer.

(List summarized from Pattison, 2000, p.236-241)

The idealized God Pattison (2000) described would attract shamed, narcissistically wounded people since they would hope that a powerful, rational, disembodied God could meet their need to be made significant. However, "the God imaged in the orthodox tradition is unlikely to meet the real needs of shamed people and they might just have their powerless, unworthy, bad feelings reinforced" (Pattison, 2000, p.234).

Pattison (2000) draws a parallel between the characteristics of the monarchical God and the beliefs implicit in many dysfunctional homes that produce narcissistically wounded children. Alice Miller (1987), in *For Your Own Good,* describes these beliefs as follows:

1) A feeling of duty produces love.
2) Hatred can be done away with by forbidding it.
3) Parents deserve respect simply because they are parents.
4) Children are undeserving of respect simply because they are children.
5) Obedience makes a child strong.
6) A high degree of self-esteem is harmful.
7) A low degree of self-esteem makes a person altruistic.
8) Tenderness (doting) is harmful.
9) Responding to a child's need is wrong.
10) Severity and coldness are a good preparation for life.
11) A pretence of gratitude is better than honest ingratitude.
12) The way you behave is more important than the way you really are.
13) Neither parents nor God would survive being offended.
14) The body is something dirty and disgusting.
15) Strong feelings are harmful.
16) Parents are creatures free of drives and guilt.
17) Parents are always right.

(Summarized from Miller, 1987, p.59-60)

One can see a great deal of similarity between these values and those that built the monarchical image of God outlined by Pattison (2000) earlier in our discussion. Not only are there parallels, but many parents actually use God as a means of social control. This further blurs the distinction between God and parent for the child who is in the process of constructing an image of God. Meissner (1984) writes:

> The child's earliest imaginings about God are cast almost exclusively in the image of the parents… The confusion between parental and divine images is at first almost total (p.139)… There may be direct continuity between the parental image and the God image, so that they can be used more or less equivalently or as substitutes in the face of defensive pressures. Or they may be directly opposed, so that they become antagonistic, usually reflecting underlying processes of defensive splitting. (p.141)

A child faced by a monarchical parent as described by Miller (1987) will develop a "defensive self-representation" to protect himself. According to Masterson (1985) he can either be "a helpless child who is loved and rewarded for not asserting himself" or an "inadequate, evil, bad self who impels the mother to withdraw" (p.32). Either of these choices is not an expression of the true self, but is a defensive posture:

> In either case, the child fears that genuine self-expression will be punished with abandonment, and these two stances are designed to ward off that possibility or the memory of its past occurrences. Just as the parents emotionally, if not physically, abandoned the child, so the child learns to abandon his real self. (Masterson, 1985, p.15)

Interestingly enough, it is not only a dysfunctional family that encourages these defensive postures. One can find many examples of religious language pulling believers towards being either be a helpless, dependent, weak, needy child, or an evil, rebellious, willful creature who is always under the threat of divine punishment (Jones, 1991).

Conservative Teaching of Self-Denial Disrupts a Healthy Self-Image

Orthodox Christianity, which encourages a monarchical image of God, has no place for a strong, healthy self. "Self is seen by many conservative Christians as worldly-minded, as if the self is untouched by grace and unredeemed by the resurrection. Self is at odds with God; enjoyment itself is suspect. Individual autonomy in the form of personal appetite and a drive for achievement is seen as dangerous" (Thompson, 1996, p.149). Some denominations view the self as "a threat to the believer's salvation (as well as to the structure of their particular church organization)" (p.148). These denominations base their beliefs on selected parts of the Bible that emphasize the Old Testament hellfire and damnation themes, control being without rather than within, and "an obvious parent-child theme illustrated in the God-person relationship" (p.148). They argue that Christ urged his followers to be "meek and lowly" (Matthew 11:29, King James Version) and to renounce all earthly signs of power and acclaim. Christ urged a believer to "give up everything" (Luke 14:33), to "deny himself" (Mark 8:34), and to "lose oneself to find it" (Mark 8:34). Paul's writings also urge "humble self-negation as a term for spirituality," as seen in 2 Corinthians 12:10 (Thompson, 1996, p.148-149). Even New Testament stories that could be used to portray love and acceptance, such as "the prodigal son," emphasize the sinfulness of humanity. Thinking of this as "The Parable of The Forgiving Father" would focus attention on the love and acceptance of the Father, rather than the failure of the son.

Churches that engender these self-rejecting ideas often disregard theologians and are guilty of reading into scripture whatever suits their purposes (Thompson, 2000, p.148). Unfortunately, "Christianity, like other social institutions, engenders and promotes shame, often to enhance order and control. Shame can be used as a very effective means of manipulating people into obedience and compliance in the interest of the powerful who identify their interest with the will of God" (Pattison, 2000, p.229). There is a "basic misunderstanding of Scripture that equates passive self-denial with spirituality" (Rottschafer, 1992, p.151). The typical believer is taught to "interpret any form of self-love as synonymous with being sinful" (p.151). John Stott, a well-known evangelical Anglican theologian wrote an article for *Christianity Today* (1984) in which he tried to clarify the view of the self that was under debate:

> Christ calls us to self-denial… like Peter denied Christ, it's the same verb. He disowned him, repudiated him, turned his back on him. So we must do to ourselves… actually denying and disowning ourselves, renouncing our supposed right to go our own way. We are to deny our sinful fallen self: our irrationality; our moral perversity; our loss of sexual distinctiveness; our fascination with the ugly … our selfishness … our proud autonomy. (John Stott, 1984, cited in Aden, Benner, Ellens, 1992)

Shame Caused by Avoiding Pride

We have been looking at examples of conservative Christian teaching that encourage a weak, helpless self to be totally dependent on a monarchical Godobject. Rottschafer (1992) explores the "evil" self—the other possible view of self that can exist in relationship to the all-powerful, perfect, judging God. "Self, to many religious conservatives, is equated with a self-centeredness that includes rebellious questioning of authority, an indulgent preoccupation with self, and a spirit of worldliness that differs from traditional Biblical teaching" (p.146). In this way of thinking, the development of self is seen as a threat, not a normal part of healthy, human development. Self-reliance is condemned as being at risk of openly defying God and setting the self above dependence on God and the established order of church authority. Self-confidence is seen as cocky, and in danger of leading to the sin of pride (p.146).

There are numerous prohibitions against pride in the Christian tradition. It is seen as the first and most deadly of all sins (Pattison, 2000, p.248). Pride may be defined as "exaggerating our worth and power, and feeling superior to others" (Schimmel, 1997 cited in Pattison, 2000, p.248). Pride is "closely associated with arrogance, contempt for others and over-reaching proper personal and human limits" (p.248). Augustinian and medieval theology believed pride fundamentally corrupted the will and nature of humanity and ascribed the fall of Adam, and consequently humanity, to pride (p.248). Pride carries the connotations of direct rebellion and disobedience against God and failure to recognize one's proper place as a dependent human (p.248). Humility is taught as the counterbalance to pride, turning the world's values upside down by suggesting that the humble and meek are significant to God, as illustrated throughout Christ's Sermon on the Mount (Matt. 5-7) in which He explicates the meaning of "the meek shall inherit the earth." Jesus was an example of a humble servant, both in His teachings and in the example of His life. Paul's letter to the Philippians describes Christ's humility:

> Who, being in the form of God, thought it not robbery to be equal with God, but made himself of no reputation. And took upon him the form of a servant and was made in the likeness of man [sic]. And being found in appearance as a man he humbled himself and became obedient unto death, even death on a cross. (Philippians 2:6-8, King James Version)

There is little wrong with speaking against pride and advocating humility. "However, this is a classic case where theological ideas may produce secondary effects and interpretations in relation to shame that may not have been intended by their authors and perpetrators" (Pattison, 2000, p.249). Pride is so pervasively feared and rigidly judged that, even when expressed as self-confidence, self-esteem, and the enjoyment or excitement invested in the self or in successful accomplishments, pride is automatically assumed. However, these qualities are a type of pride that is necessary for a healthy sense of self-worth and accomplishment, rather than the assumed "egotism, inordinate self-esteem, and contempt for others" that they are often harshly labeled (p.249). This appropriate pride "is close to the sense of joy. It is far removed from the desire to destroy or domineer over others. It actually allows the self to experience itself silently and builds up a sense of expansiveness, efficacy, entitlement and necessary self-esteem" (p.250).

The type of pride that displays itself in conceit, arrogance, or superiority is an exaggerated pride, based on "a global over-valuation of the self as a whole rather than upon specific attributes or acts" (p.250). It is, in fact, another expression of narcissistic wounding that turns to grandiosity in attempts to compensate. The implications of this are that what has been condemned theologically as pride is, in fact, a symptom of shame; instead of receiving the understanding and help needed to come to a more accurate sense of self, the person will be further shamed by others.

Pride does have its dangers. But uncritical, un-nuanced notions of humility can be just as destructive. "The exhortation to be humble can be taken as an instruction to abandon all sense of autonomy or agency. It may amplify shame-induced passivity and depression as well as increasing self-obsession" (Pattison, 2000, p.250). There is a difference between true humility, where self-consciousness is absent, and false humility, which makes us so aware of ourselves that it paralyzes us from being able to act without myriad self-accusations and apologies. "Humility based on humiliation and shame rather than love and acceptance produces hatred, self-righteousness and rigidity, not change and reconciliation" (p.252).

Great things have been accomplished and selfless lives lived based on traditional Christian attitudes that condemn pride and exalt humility. However, the interpretation and application of these ideas to obedient parishioners and malleable children has often fostered an attitude of passivity and the fear that any form of self-assertion is a sin. This makes them helpless to defend themselves from further injury, and shaming and silences their voices (Rottschafer, 1992, p.252). Parents who avoid praising their children for their strengths and accomplishments, thinking they are protecting them from becoming proud, are neglecting the child's mirroring needs. This increases the child's sense of shame. The outcome might look more acceptable to the parents, since they will have succeeded in squelching the external display of pride. However, they will have passed on the legacy of shame and contributed to the narcissistic wounding of their child's sense of self.

As we saw in our earlier discussion of the psychological roots of shame, failing to meet external expectations or the internal expectations of an ideal self can cause shame. The word "perfect" in the Matthew 5:48 passage, "Be ye perfect as your heavenly father is perfect," has often been inaccurately translated to endorse unreachable ideals of perfection rather than the more accurate translation of "wholeness" or "single-minded devotion to God" (The New Interpreter's Bible, VIII, 1996, p.196). Berecz & Helm (1998) discuss the shame engendered by this inaccurate teaching:

> Christians may inadvertently cause excessive shame by cultivating unrealistic, unreachable ideals. The "Xerox" syndrome"—an attempt to "copy" the life of Jesus— sets too high an ideal for humankind and causes devout Christians unnecessary shame... Seeking to become "like God" was the original sin, and remains the sin of secular humanism today. Ironically, in more subtle forms it remains the goal of those Christians who strive to be "like Jesus," often leading to depression, shame, or grandiosity. A more appropriate goal is to become more fully human—like Adam and Eve—as God's children. This remains an achievable shame-free goal. (p.5)

Christianity possibly "produced more problems than it healed" (p.6) through preaching such high expectations of the ideal self that failure was inevitable, resulting in shame. The disparity between the ideal self and the real self was further widened through this teaching of perfection, producing yet more shame. Shame seldom fosters growth of the true self, only an increased attempt at building a false self. "The irony is that by attempting to produce better, kinder, purer people, the Christian church has produced more shameful people" (Berecz & Helm 1998, p.6).

The creation of such a "pure" false self is, in essence, "an effort to lose the self." Many have seen the self as "the culprit, the source of sin," so the elimination and "disowning of the self and all its attendant needs, wants, urges, schemes, lusts, selfishness, ambitions and pleasures" becomes the goal. However, it is impossible to lose our human characteristics, and the attempt has "led to the popular curse for so many religious people: guilt and depression" (Rottschafer, 1992, p.149).

I grew up being influenced by similar Christian teaching that I took very seriously. I worked sincerely towards perfection, purity, and denial of self to the point that I struggled with guilt and depression. Combined with a few other factors in my life, these turned into shame and self-loathing. This was particularly strong with regard to my physical and sexual self as evidenced in my journal entries in the introductory chapter. As a result of shaming these integral parts of myself, I struggled for years with my own layers of guilt and depression. Christian platitudes doled out as "encouragement"—such as "just have faith" or "read your Bible and pray more"—added another layer of shame and failure. I felt it was my fault that I was depressed, and I had to work still harder to pull myself up before God would accept me. Being told to "trust in his unconditional love" was no comfort because I couldn't feel that love. Allowing myself to get in touch with the primary mirroring need generated more shame that I "should not have needs"—an old defense mechanism I had used to cut myself off from my needs. I was in what felt like a self-perpetuating cycle of need and shame, and the "pastoral" advice and Christian encouragement I received only made it spin faster.

One of the core questions I held as I approached the study of pastoral counseling was based on this personal experience of shame and depression. I wanted to know if there was hope of truly experiencing God's love and acceptance in my feelings, and at the same time, coming to feel a measure of self-worth and acceptance. I couldn't accept myself until God accepted me, thus proving my worthiness. Yet I couldn't believe in God's acceptance until I could believe I was worth accepting—another spinning cycle that I couldn't break out of on my own.

We saw earlier that the primary mirroring experience provides materials for the development of the self and the image of God. According to Rizzuto (1979) the first image is permanent and can only be "transformed, repressed, or used." As an adult I was stuck using my original internalized Godobject from my earliest mirroring experience. Meissner (1984), in *Psychoanalysis and Religious Experience,* says:

> To the extent that the child's early experience with the mother has tipped the balance in the direction of more positive and gratifying experiences, a basic sense of trust is laid down that provides a foundation for the later development of a sense of trusting faith in the relationship to God. Where early infantile experience is discolored with insecurity, uncertainty, or anxiety, the foundation is laid for a basic mistrust that can contaminate and distort the later experience of God. (p.140)

My adult experience of God, and thus of myself, was that of being "contaminated" by my infantile experience. That experience was reinforced by years of being involved in conservative Christian communities, which:

> ... despite the "good news" of the gospel, were part of the long history of the church's tendency to deal harshly with people, much like angry, controlling parents [who] ... control the self with themes of guilt and punishment... dealing with God's children

not as though they are the redeemed but the condemned, not under grace but under the curse. (Rottschafer, 1992, p.146-147)

Now I see that I gravitated to these communities because they provided a selfobject that reinforced my weak, dependent self. Fortunately, I realized through "new more gracious interpersonal experiences" (Jones, 1991) with people, and with nature and art, that I could begin transforming my image of God and of myself and move towards the freedom of an authentic self.

One would hope that the pastoral counselor could be the source of "more gracious interpersonal relationships." Unfortunately, certain aspects of pastoral counseling can be the source of more shame rather than healing grace.

Pastoral Counseling: A Context for Further Shame?

Thompson (1996) and Scheff & Retzinger (1991) explore various aspects of pastoral counseling that can increase shame for both clients and therapists, beginning with the asymmetrical structure of therapy. "Clients are saddled with a 'double-burden;' they have humiliating secrets, and they are expected to disclose them to a stranger" (Scheff & Retzinger, 1991, p.135). Pastoral counselors don't join in the same intimate level of disclosure but "take the role of expert or authority while their clients assume the position of needy, dependent supplicants" (p.315). The pastoral counselor presents herself as "differentiated, with complete rational control of all emotions, entirely immune to self-doubt and shame, capable of boundless empathy and compassion, and able to accept whatever feelings and fantasies the clients bring to session." The client enters therapy "depleted by depression, torn by relational conflict and misery, and caught up in a storm of feelings they cannot identify, understand, or handle. They seek or sometimes plead for help, an appeal which is implicitly at least an admission of failure" (p.315). This sounds surprisingly like the relationship between the monarchical God and the depleted, sinful self seen earlier, and also echoes the dynamics of a child/parent relationship. The relationship being structured in this way could bring out transferential patterns of interaction and feelings of shame. Clients might also be tempted to compare themselves to the supposedly "together" and powerful therapist and feel shame that they are not as "together," thus believing the societal assumption that they must have a serious personal flaw if they are in therapy (Thompson, 1996, p.315).

Pastoral counselors "interpret" their clients, which tends to "objectify and humiliate clients while protecting therapists from similar experiences" (Thompson, 1996, p.315). When a pastoral counselor interprets transference, clients experience this as especially "devious" and feel it as an "indirect rejection on the part of the therapist" (p.315). Interpretations often expose clients' weaknesses, deficiencies, and failures and can even cause them to feel shame about their shame (p.315). Pastoral counselors will sometimes fail empathically, which could awaken the client's feelings of not being seen or understood and tap into the old shameful wound from their early inadequate mirroring experiences. If a client fails to improve in therapy they could feel it as another defeat, thinking they "can't even do therapy right."

The client is not the only one susceptible to shame in the pastoral counselor's office. Counselors are also vulnerable to the shame of their clients, and if they try to enter too deeply into the clients' emotional worlds without establishing some of their own protective emotional boundaries they can personally take on some of their clients' shame (Thompson, 1996, p.316). A client can also activate a counselor's shame by the questions he or she asks, or when the client's issues trigger the counselor's own unresolved conflicts and limitations, resulting in counter-transference (p.315-316).

Clients who feel ashamed in or by the presence of the counselor observing, probing, and interpreting their shameful experiences, could become angry and try to humiliate and belittle their counselor as a form of retaliation or defense. This retaliation may be conscious and direct, or unconscious and more indirect in some forms of resistance, but it can still be very hurtful and shaming to the counselor. If a client fails to improve, it can be felt as a challenge to the counselor's competence. A counselor may hold herself responsible for the client's failure and feel shame that "whatever I give isn't enough, or good enough" (Thompson, 1996, p.316).

Thompson (1996) suggests some guidelines for pastoral counselors who deal with shame in the therapeutic context. A pastoral counselor must first address her/his own shame issues. Counselors must know how shame affects them, what triggers their shame, how they try to defend against it, and how they inflict it on others. Being aware of and able to articulate one's own process of healing shame will be helpful in recognizing and validating a client's shame and knowing how to help the client move through it. Pastoral counselors who have unresolved shame might be tempted to focus on the client's failures, misery, and hopelessness. It is more helpful to mirror progress and work on balancing this viewpoint with authentic hope. At the same time, the counselor must come to terms with the cold hard fact that her ability to help is limited and, as Kaufman (1995) suggests, "accept feeling limited without feeling lesser for the limitation" (p.230).

Educating clients about how shame develops, and the protective role it could be serving in their lives, might help them recognize, accept, monitor, and perhaps even move towards healing their shame. The counselor needs to encourage the client to explore her shame, structure therapy to gently uncover rather than protect her from it, and accept the client's anger over having it exposed. Being compassionate, empathetic, and admitting and apologizing when a counselor hurts a client is an important part of creating a safe therapeutic bond which can act as a holding environment (Winnicott, 1971) where she can safely explore her shame. Within this safety, the counselor will occasionally need to risk "timely, respectful, non-intrusive self-disclosures about her own shame" (Thompson, 1996, p.30). Self-disclosure always increases the counselor's vulnerability. Although this is uncomfortable for some and not accepted by all as appropriate in the context of therapy, it could be used to lessen the power dynamic between therapist and client, which could reduce the client's shame.

Re-Imaging God as a Gracious, Transformational Selfobject

The new theology that Smedes (1993), Capps (1993), Pembroke (1998) and Pannenberg (1972) call for will recognize shame as a more relevant construct than sin and guilt, and will acknowledge grace and acceptance as the Christ-like response:

> The real gospel is, 'While we were still sinners, Christ died for us' (Romans 5:8)... There is no hint of performance to gain acceptance... there is an acceptance of our fallen human state and a realization that salvation comes from without—from above. There is no psychological bootstrapping to improve the self, no constant striving to become more perfect. (Berecz & Helm, 1998, p.8)

These authors and many others attempt to re-infuse some of the Biblical images of God with new, gracious meanings. They stress stories from Jesus' life that show him accepting sinners, the outcast, and the weak. Henri Nouwen (1992), in his book *The Return of the Prodigal Son,* has created a series of meditations on the Rembrandt painting of The Prodigal Son. He incorporates art, his personal journey, and the Biblical story to transform this image into one that focuses on the love and grace this parable was originally intended to hold. Unfortunately, some images will never be redeemed for some people. Associations of shame and control have become inseparable from Biblical stories even though the stories themselves are not shame-inducing when interpreted differently. We can also find gracious experiences and images of a God in other places—art, music, relationships, and nature. Anything beautiful carries grace if we open ourselves to it as part of God's gift of creation, reflecting God's love.

Christopher Bollas (1987) believes that part of what makes our first selfobject experience so powerful is that it is a transformational experience that collects up the emotions, urges, and fragments of the infant's being and organizes them into a cohesive sense of self (p.14). We learn to do this for ourselves as we mature, but the desire to have a selfobject that brings clarity, growth, and integration to our beings remains a strong desire throughout our lives and can be filled with a variety of selfobjects:

> We were not created in isolation and so the need for growth and change drives for a transforming object-relation that will sponsor that change... The ecstasy of romance, aesthetics, and religion become the potentially positive carriers of this necessary aspect of human experience (p.123)... The aesthetic space allows for a creative enactment of the search for this transformational object relation... In the quest for a deep subjective experience of an object, the artist both remembers for us and provides us with occasions for the experience of ego memories of transformation. (Bollas, 1987, p.29)

It is quite possible that the aesthetic, religious, or romantic experience is transformational in and of itself. However, it can also be a way of imaging or experiencing the ultimate transformational object—the sacred. In this way all beauty and love experienced is a glimpse of the greater love extended to us by God.

As we now turn our attention to music therapy literature as it relates to the use of voice, we will see how vocalizing with another person, an aesthetic experience whether in the context of a voice lesson or a music therapy session, can carry a transformational element, and can echo an early selfobject experience.

Music Therapy

During the early months of my study I was puzzled over how to include literature pertaining to music therapy. I assumed it should have relevance to the topic, yet the literature I was finding focused on the use of instrumental music. Music therapists who use voice, whom I know personally and have observed, sang and played to their clients as a form of non-verbal communication with them. The clients themselves didn't sing except in choirs or groups such as seen in the work of Susan Summers (1999). The literature on the use of choir work in music therapy focused on the social benefits of contributing to (and being included in) a group and sharing the musical experience. I knew a musical experience could bypass a person's defenses, and touch emotions that talking therapy couldn't. As an instrumentalist I had many such musical experiences, but I knew that what I experienced in voice lessons was something quite different. Musical experiences often brought my emotions to the surface and provided a release for them, sometimes affecting my playing temporarily, but I had not encountered these feelings of shame and exposure that totally blocked my vocal progress.

About half way through my study I was able to contact music therapy professor and voice teacher Susan Summers (personal interview, Jan. 24, 2004) at Capilano College in Vancouver to ask her about the therapeutic use of voice. She turned the lights on for me. She explained her work, as cited earlier in this literature review, and also directed me to the work of Diane Austin (1991, 1993, 1998, 2001). Austin began as a voice teacher, but was so interested in and puzzled by the number of students who would break down in tears during their lessons that she began studying music therapy and psychology to figure out how to deal with the emotions flooding her studio. She is now a professor of music therapy at New York University and specializes in the use of voice in her own music therapy practice. Austin (2001) uses a blend of self-psychology/object relations and Jungian analysis, combined with vocal improvisation in the context of music therapy to help find the "lost" selves within her clients.

Austin (2001) agrees with Winnicott (1971) and Miller (1981) that the authentic self can be "lost" behind a false self that develops to help a child survive, "sacrificing [the self] at birth to an empty parent... having it shattered into fragments from unspeakable terrors like abuse, neglect, and emotional and/or physical abandonment" (p.22). We have examined how parts of ourselves can be hidden away and bound silent and numb by shame if they were not welcomed, seen, mirrored, or valued. We looked at Fairbairn's theory that a child raised in an abusive or inattentive environment will split off parts of the self to survive. However, this leaves the child with an inner battle between the internal saboteur, usually associated with the advanced mental processes, and the libidinal ego, or the "feeling" part that is regressed (Austin, 2001, p.23). This makes it hard for the child to accept the shamed or cut off parts of self, and to genuinely connect in relationship. Austin (2001) describes people who develop such a split in terms of the effects it has on their voices:

> Children who are raised in an atmosphere of fear, hostility, violence or neglect, and children whose parents are alcoholic, emotionally disturbed, or absent (physically or emotionally), have been silenced... Needs and feelings remain unmet and the voice becomes inaudible, tight and tense, breathy and undefined, or simply untrue; perhaps lovely to listen to but not connected to the core of the person. In essence, traumatized individuals often survive by forfeiting their own voice. (p.23)

Re-inhabiting the Body through the Breath

For a person who has been split off from self and silenced, "the process of recovering one's true voice involves re-inhabiting the body" (Austin, 2001, p.23). This is because the connection between body, mind, and spirit was severed by dissociative defenses to protect the psyche during the trauma. Therefore, to bring parts of the self back together again, those connections have to be re-established. This can be very painful and resistance is common in clients attempting re-integration of themselves because they must "remember and experience the sensations and feelings that were overwhelming as a child, intolerable because no one was present to help the child contain, make sense of, and digest the intense affects" (Austin, 2001, p.23). However, part of re-claiming one's voice is "owning one's authority and ending a cycle of victimization" (Austin, 2001, p. 24).

Music therapy is particularly suited to helping clients re-integrate split off parts of self and access their authentic selves, because it bypasses cognitive defenses and taps directly into physically based emotions, giving the client a language to express experiences for which they may have no words (Austin, 1991, p.294-295). Singing is a restorative form of music therapy because it facilitates deep breathing, which "slows the heart rate and calms the nervous system, stilling the mind and body." The resulting relaxation helps those who are in a state of panic or anxiety or who are hyperventilating or breathing in short, shallow bursts (Austin, 2001, p. 24). Relaxation is helpful, but deep breathing has a much more significant psychological effect on our feelings. Austin (2001) observes her clients holding their breath when approaching an emotionally charged issue, controlling their feelings by restricting the intake and release of their breath. When she asks them to exhale fully "they often come in contact with a feeling they have been suppressing. Likewise, the inability to take in nurturing or other kinds of experiences and information is mirrored in restricted inhalation" (Austin, 2001, p.24). Austin is convinced, as am I after experiencing unexpected emotions through breathing related to singing, that "the way we breathe influences how we feel, and what we feel has a direct effect on how we breathe" (p. 24).

Rodenburg (1992) compares deep breath work related to the voice with "a diver going below the ocean... suddenly sensitive to the enormous pressure" (p.87). She has dealt with over seventy-five individuals who, when they released the breath from the lower abdominal area where they had been holding it, spoke of sexual abuse from earlier times in their lives. In most cases Rodenburg (1992) was the first person they had ever told about the incident and, at the time of the violation, the guilt they felt made it impossible for them to make any sound. "As they found themselves breathing without barriers to contain them, deep pain, deep experiences were suddenly released" (p.89). Before this experience of release their habitual unconscious response was to think, "If I don't breathe down there, if I hold it tight and wrap myself around the wound, I won't be reminded of the horror, the suffering, the guilt" (p.89). Rodenburg (1992) concluded "we can block and seal the memory of vile sexual penetration under the breath. We can hold and freeze it in the muscles of the groin... the breath can also thaw it, and bring it to the surface" (p.89). We hold other emotions, such as grief and rage in the "lump in our throat," tightness in the jaw, braced shoulders, and quivering lips (Rodenburg, 1992, p.91). These too can be released through deep breath work.

Singing not only accesses our emotions through the physical release that comes from deep breathing, but "it is a neuromuscular activity, and muscular patterns are closely linked to psychological patterns and emotional responses" (Newham, 1998, p.445). Since our body is our instrument, as seen in our earlier discussion, the vibrations we produce are felt internally and can "nurture the body and massage our insides. Internally resonating vibrations break up and release blockages of energy allowing a natural flow of vitality and a state of equilibrium to return to the body" (Austin, 2001, p.24). Clients who have frozen, numbed areas of the body that are holding the traumatic experience can find release through singing because it can help them discharge the residue of unresolved energy trapped in the nervous system through trauma, and give them a means to access and express intense feelings (Austin, 2001, p.24).

Vocal Holding Techniques

Austin's (1998) belief that singing is "a way to access one's deepest self... intimately connecting us to our breath, bodies, and our emotional lives," and that the voice "is like a bridge that we can connect the mind to the body and heal splits between thinking and feeling"(p.316), is foundational to her work as a music therapist. She has combined her vocal work with an object relations approach and developed an improvisational vocal therapy that she calls "Vocal Holding Techniques." Improvisational music is particularly useful in music therapy because "it offers an holistic form of assessment that is relational, noninvasive, and nonverbal, and that allows the identity of the patient to be revealed" (Aldridge, 1989, p.96).

Vocal Holding Techniques are based on Winnicott's (1971) concept of a "holding environment" created by the mother to provide a safe environment for her infant to be mirrored, merged with and, in time, moved through the separation-individuation process. Austin (2001) describes Vocal Holding Techniques as a method of vocal improvisation that:

... involves the intentional use of two chords played on an instrument [piano or guitar] in combination with the therapist's voice in order to create a consistent and stable musical environment that facilitates improvised singing within the client-therapist relationship. This method provides a reliable, safe structure... a secure musical and psychological container that will enable the client to relinquish some of the mind's control, sink down into his/her body and allow the spontaneous self to emerge. The simplicity of the music and the hypnotic repetition of the two chords, combined with the rocking rhythmic motion and the singing of single syllables (sounds, not words initially) can produce a trance-like altered state and easy access to the world of the unconscious.... For the client who is afraid or unused to improvising; it supports a connection to self and other and promotes a therapeutic regression in which unconscious feelings, sensations, memories, and associations can be accessed, processed, and integrated. (p.24)

Within this "musical container" the client can relate to parts of self that have been split off and integrate these parts back into themselves. They can repair developmental arrests, heal narcissistic wounding, allow feelings and images to emerge, and "explore new ways of being in the freedom of musical play and creative self-expression" (Austin, 2001, p.24).

The initial vocal holding phase begins with therapist and client singing in unison over the undulating chords of the piano. This helps clients who didn't have a "good-enough" experience of merging with an emotionally present, calm, and consistent mother to experience a symbiosis-like state with the therapist. The next phase is harmonizing, which can foster an experience of being separate yet related to and accepted. Mirroring occurs when the client sings a melodic line and the therapist responds by singing the melodic line back (Austin, 1998, p.317-318). Mirroring is particularly useful when a client is finding her own voice and needs support, and when parts of the personality that are new—or that had been cut off—are emerging and need to be heard and accepted (Austin, 2001, p.23). Mirroring happens not only on the level of therapist mirroring back to the client what she sees and hears, but the music itself is capable of mirroring the client's inner states and giving her a means to express them (Austin, 1991, p.305).

Vocal Holding Techniques are ideally suited for repairing a client's capacity for relationship, since they mirror the process of the primary source of connection between mother and child that, at an early age, was significantly shaped by vocalization. Infants begin recognizing their mother's voice already in the womb and it has been suggested that the mother's voice is just as important as the mother's milk in relational bonding. Pre-verbal wounds to the self, particularly difficult to access through "talking therapy," are more easily evoked and repaired through wordless singing in relationship to another person (Austin, 2001, p.25).

Resistance

For the same reasons that singing can be a powerfully healing experience, it can also be a powerfully threatening experience. Even if one wants to sing, fear of judgment or feeling vulnerable and exposed can produce extreme anxiety and hold one back. For clients who have learned to survive abuse by living in silence and denying emotional truth, finding their voices requires great courage. Clients who fear what will come out of their mouths sometimes find screaming and sobbing taking over their attempts to sing (Austin, 1998, p.316). Clients often know, or at least suspect, that music will get by their defensive barriers more successfully than words. The highly verbal client, who feels in control while talking, can find vocal improvisation very threatening because of the loosening of control necessary to improvise. For those who have rigid personality structures, or have a strong "false self," or believe their authentic feelings or certain parts of themselves are not acceptable, singing can be very threatening, since it elicits spontaneity which feels like having less control over what one shows outwardly (Austin, 1993, p.425).

Sometimes resistance is shown in music therapy by clients who "are merged with the instrument... one's whole sense of self-worth is riding on the performance... this becomes even more intense when the body is the instrument as in voice... because it is not once removed, but intimately connected to one's breath, body, and feelings and sensations within" (Austin, 1993, p.425). Bunch (1993) says that it is difficult but a student must learn "the difficult art of separating him/herself as an individual from the voice as an instrument so that objective learning rather than subjective inhibitions will take place" (p.18).

Transferential Issues

We have examined some of the reasons people might resist singing, both in therapy and voice lessons, but within the therapeutic context there is always the possibility of resistance to the therapeutic process because of what the relationship with the therapist evokes. Music therapy involves the musical experience *and* a relationship with a therapist, because both are important to the process of intervention and change (Bruscia, 1989, p.33). Austin (1993) describes how a patient might initially be attracted to music because it offers freedom to express repressed emotions and then develops into a means of gratifying the need for having the emotion seen and mirrored. It can be intensely intimate for the client to share feelings and the need to be mirrored with the therapist. Resistance occurs when fear of feeling intimacy with another person arises:

> The sharing of this personal gratification in front of another can induce feelings of shame, embarrassment, and guilt about experiencing pleasure, having and gratifying needs, and ambivalence over intimacy (fears of merging, engulfment, or abandonment). It is important to remember that these conflicts occur unconsciously and, therefore, the music is resisted due to its facilitative quality for expressing unconscious thoughts and feelings. (Austin, 1993, p.425)

Another cause of resistance can be associations from the mothering experience in infancy that is reproduced by the self-soothing quality of singing. This, in turn, can regress the client. "Relating to the therapist in this regressed way becomes threatening and produces ambivalence regarding whether to reveal infantile wishes and needs through music" (Austin, 1993, p.425).

When a therapist is using the Vocal Holding Technique of singing in unison with the client to create the feeling of "oneness," a client might show her fear of merging by avoiding singing in unison to resist the positive transference. The next stage, singing in harmony, allows for some separateness while still being accepted, but it might still be too intimate for some clients. It is also possible that the therapist will allow her counter-transference to affect the therapeutic relationship and avoid certain techniques such as singing in unison because she fears merger and loss of self (Austin, 1998, p.317).

A client who is just beginning to find her own voice often finds the Vocal Holding Technique of musical mirroring very gratifying since she felt "invisible" as a child and was most likely used to mirror her narcissistically wounded parents (Miller, 1981). The transference likely to occur for this client will be the temptation to fill the same role again of mirroring her caretaker. This will be acted out with the therapist when the client repeats the therapist's melodies and sounds, rather than getting in touch with her own. A narcissistically injured therapist might not see this and "may have counter-transferential feelings of wanting the client to take care of her in the music" (Austin, 1998, p.317-318).

A therapist can often hear a client's resistance musically. A client who sings with a lack of affect, or displays a musical affect that is in complete contradiction to her personal affect, is most likely resisting being emotionally present. A client who races the tempo, or slows it down so drastically that she controls every sound, or stops playing or singing prematurely, is also resisting emotionally (Austin, 1993, p.425).

Any therapeutic relationship holds the possibility of transference and counter-transference. "The intimacy of creating music together is especially challenging… because of the medial quality of the music." The unconscious contents for client and therapist are easily accessed through music; client and therapist can affect each other on a deep level that goes beyond words. Two people involved in singing and/or playing music together cannot be separated so neatly. "It is important to tell with complete assurance who owns which psychic contents in the transference/counter-transference process." This is very difficult to do when it is not possible to be sure who is in a reactive state to whom, or to what (Stein, 1992, p.69 as cited in Austin, 1998, p. 332).

This is true for music therapist and client singing together, and for voice teacher and student. Music has the same medial qualities, whoever is making it in whatever context, and breath work can unlock deep issues in the voice studio just as in the therapist's office. The only difference is that voice teachers may be less well equipped to deal with the psychological and emotional issues that emerge in their studios. They may mistake psychological resistance for lack of motivation, unwillingness to work, or indifference towards the teacher, so they push harder and exacerbate the problem. They are not necessarily equipped for the tears, the stories of abuse that pour out, or the extreme shame that keeps a student bound who wants to conquer her struggles but ends up fighting against herself. The voice teacher often carries her/his own unmet needs and unresolved struggles, which could emerge in the musical relationship with the student. If the teacher lacks the self-awareness and personal boundaries to keep his/her needs out of the relationship with the student, s/he could project them on the student and end up complicating the relationship and using the student for his/her own needs.

Without becoming therapists, voice teachers—like body-workers and massage therapists—should educate themselves concerning the possible side effects that come through breath work. They need to learn to listen for the self being revealed in the music and support that self appropriately. This might, in some cases, require professional therapy for the student. The teacher might also benefit from therapy to enable them to keep counter-transference issues in check.

Transition to Chapter Four

This interdisciplinary literature review has been an introduction to the relevant concepts pertaining to the link between voice and identity, breath, body, and emotions as experienced in singing. It has also covered the development of identity and shame from the self-psychology and object relations perspectives, the theological roots of shame in conservative religious teaching, and the link between early selfobject experiences and the personal God-images we create.

I began the literature review in the obvious place, reviewing sources on vocal pedagogy, therapeutic voice and body work, and literature related to performance anxiety for musicians. After this preliminary review I collected data by observing voice master classes, interviewing Annika and five master class students, and having my own voice lesson. From there I examined my data, particularly my personal experience of attempting to free the voice, and realized I needed to research literature on shame, identity development, and psycho-spiritual sources of shame, all of which I did from a self-psychology and object relations perspective. Finally I found relevant music therapy literature as I was able to meet personally with a music therapist, and confirmed the link between breath, body and emotions that is key to the process of freeing one's voice and self.

With the groundwork laid for understanding some of the forces that constrict a voice, as well as the way in which breath can release it, we now turn to the data of the study. We begin with an outline of the life experiences that affected Annika's vocal journey, then look at my experience of a voice lesson with Annika and Maureen, then examine some selected themes from the experiences of five master class students, and finally examine the theme of breathing in detail.

CHAPTER FOUR

COMING HOME TO MYSELF

Annika

Coming Home

"Coming home to myself" was Annika's description of her journey towards vocal freedom. This metaphor, which runs throughout Annika's vocal journey and is a strong theme in her teaching, is an image rich with meaning and deserves some exploration before we enter Annika's story.

We have many expressions in the English language that help us understand the meaning of "home." We "come home" after a hard day's work or an exhausting journey, put on a comfy sweatshirt, and flop into our favorite chair. We relax. We remove constraints and formal appearances and return to a more natural, comfortable state. We wake up weary with a cold and decide to "stay home" where we can take care of ourselves and nurture our bodies. Children and teens on their first time "away from home" struggle with a peculiar loneliness and lack of stability called "homesickness." They want to "go home," back to the people who accept and know them, back to where things are familiar, predictable, and safe. Their "home town" will always hold associations of their origins, their roots, the place they are from.

While away on a trip we set up a "home base" in a hotel, or a campsite, or in the back of the car—a temporary home where we collect ourselves, re-charge our energy, and store our belongings. If plans go awry during a long day of sightseeing and we are unexpectedly separated from our traveling partners, we are relieved to meet up with them again at "home base." We carry pictures of "the folks back home" in our imaginations, if not in our wallets, reminding us that "home is where the heart is" even if our bodies can't be there. When we feel "at home" with someone we let down our guard, and let our true selves show, knowing we are accepted. When we feel "at home" with ourselves we are at peace.

How do we go away from ourselves? We do so through disconnecting from parts of ourselves that are rejected or unnoticed by others and by cutting off from the aspects of ourselves that cause us shame and pain. We do so by creating a false self or a façade behind which we hide to keep safe. We do so by sacrificing the integrity of our selves in efforts to achieve unrealistic societal expectations of beauty, intelligence, productivity, and strength. Some of us are taught from early childhood that our self is not to be nurtured, respected, or indulged so we will not become "selfish." We are cautioned against expressing our feelings or allowing ourselves to feel them in our bodies so that we will stay pure. Some of us are socialized towards expressions of gender that might not feel true to us, but we try to fit the norm while inwardly feeling confused and losing another part of ourselves. These are only a few of the ways that many of us leave the home of ourselves, sometimes living estranged from our true selves for our entire lives until something tragic, or intimate, or difficult calls us home to find the lost parts we need in order to survive and be satisfied.

Annika could only have experienced a sense of "coming home" to herself if she first felt as though she had been away. As we journey "home to herself" with Annika we will see some of the influences in her life which drove her away from herself, and how her passion to sing, and its ability to re-connect her to her body, was her road home to herself.

Beginning the Journey

In Annika's words, she has been "singing since the beginning of time." She traced her vocal development as a vital thread of expression, influence, and energy beginning at age six when her parents put her and her older sister into a German children's choir. Annika's parents immigrated to Canada from Germany as young adults, and sought to pass on their German heritage to their two daughters. Their choir director, a retired opera singer also from Germany, quickly noticed their younger daughter's interest and ability and suggested Annika take private lessons. Even at that young age, Annika remembers singing as the one activity in which she could "be herself," a trait that wasn't encouraged in other areas of family life where obedience and doing what was "right" were emphasized. At age seven Annika was introduced to Mozart's opera, *The Magic Flute*, and remembers being captivated and excited by the dream that she might one day be on stage singing an operatic role.

Annika took voice lessons throughout her childhood and adolescence, and at the age of 16 she began working with a well known Canadian voice teacher who has produced a number of fine singers. This teacher "became a great buddy" of Annika's, but she had the well-deserved reputation of being ruthlessly blunt. "It's all very pretty, dear, but it's so boring," was one of her frequently used comments. Saying "You don't have enough fire in you to roast a wiener! You sing from [the neck] on up," was another way she challenged Annika to dig deeper into her body, her voice, and her self, to really communicate through singing. As Annika reflects on her voice at that time she says, "My voice wasn't free because I actually wasn't using my body. I was singing with my head, but not physically involved." She could feel the passion of the music and, "I was desperate to communicate it through singing but my body was closed."

Annika attributes this state of being cut off from her body to her strict religious upbringing. She said that the family philosophy was, "Deny the physical. The body is to be hidden, not something to be honoured as part of who you are. Nothing was acknowledged that exists from the neck on down. [The physical] was not discussed in any way... You just don't go there." The cultural and religious backgrounds of her parents were intertwined so they "shaped the way they saw the world and gave them their set of morals." Annika was expected to hold the same worldviews without questioning, just like her parents and her grandparents and the generations before that. This worldview disconnected her from, and condemned, the physical. "The big thing is the whole notion of sin. So much of it is evil, and all this is huge suppression of the physical. What's happening to the body upon getting messages of saying 'you are bad, you are wrong'… the whole body contracts and basically is denied, completely denied." This moral stance was not that unusual for a religious family in the 1960s and it shaped Annika's intellectual view of her body, her felt sense of it, and her ability to access it for singing. It was a time, she recalls, of "living in my head without being integrated into my body."

Vocal Affects of Being Disconnected from Her Body

Annika showed me how not being "integrated in her body" affected her voice by playing tape recordings made during her early twenties of her singing, and pointing out various vocal qualities. Even before she began her commentary I could hear that her voice at 20 was much thinner, with less colour and depth than the voice she sings with today in her early forties. Some of the change is due to the natural maturing of the voice, a process that takes until the mid-thirties for the average woman. However, she ascribed a great deal of what she heard in her voice from that era as the consequence of being cut off from her body and her breath. As we listened to a tape recording of her graduating recital from the conservatory in her home town when she was 20, she described having a "desperation to express the incredible passion that was trapped inside of me," but having no way to express it because, "my breath was caught and my body wasn't there to help me get it out." Her commentary while we listened to the recording continues:

> You can hear how the higher notes of my vocal range are disconnected from my breath and body. I could only sing these high notes by using my head voice—that is a smaller, thinner sound not supported by my breath and disconnected from my body. This is quite a contrast to the quality of my lower notes which had more depth and colour in their sound. Also, take note of how I am singing behind the beat. This is a result of my breath being locked and my sound not riding on my air stream. My body therefore is locked and held, trying to control and hang on instead of allowing it to let go and ride the beat. As I was unable to move my breath, I compensated by trying to convey the emotional content. But trying to do this with my body in a locked position only made matters worse in terms of slowing down the tempo. If my sound is not on my breath and in my body, all the emoting in the world will not communicate, as the sound will not be free to express the emotion.

Annika made similar comments about her disconnection from her body and struggle with the breath not working as we listened to a tape of her singing the Countess from Mozart's *The Marriage of Figaro*, recorded at age 23 during her time in university:

> I can feel myself getting excited and trying to prepare myself for the climax of this aria. My body wouldn't go with me… I did not have that connection to the low breath, or the energy in the body, to understand the concept of dropping into the body to help support the high notes. And it was really awful… I'd feel very caught in my body… it was like I couldn't quite express myself the way I really wanted to… Occasionally I did have glimpses—when it did work—and I could feel that my sound

was fulfilled. But more often than not I would be really struggling against myself in trying to get the depth into the notes and the freedom into the notes. You can hear how very audible my inhalations are here as I approach the climax. The loud inhalation already tells me that my body is very tense—that I have constricted the muscles in my throat because the breath that I took was very high in my chest. This tense inhalation has caused my jaw to tense as well, affecting the sound even further. By the time I reached the climax of the aria with the high notes, I didn't have a chance of reaching those notes with a beautiful free sound. At that moment my body was so locked, tense, and un-energized.

Repertoire demands

Annika's work with the Canadian teacher who challenged her to sing more than "pretty," and to go deeper into herself and her body, was the beginning of her journey home. However, a number of other factors challenged her to re-connect with her body and sing from a deeper place in herself. The repertoire she felt particularly inspired by, and which demanded more from her, forced her to find a way to get into her body so she would to be able to sing it. On the same recording as her graduating recital from her early twenties were some Rachmaninoff dramatic songs about which she felt very passionate and which were more demanding vocally and dramatically than her usual repertoire at that time. She commented as we listened:

> I had a vision of what I wanted from these Rachmaninoff dramatic songs, but I just completely disconnected the sound of my upper range from my body because I had no other way of doing it. But I knew what I wanted was an open glorious sound that did what it was supposed to do. The feeling of it being caught inside myself was so horrible.

When she left her home town and began university at age 20 she was challenged by a new context and by new ears responding to her voice. One particular coach at the university heard more colour and depth in Annika's voice than she was using, so he cast her in heavier operatic roles. Until that time she had always sung "ina" roles (characters such as Zerlina, Adina, Rosina, Despina)—light, cheery roles that kept her in a high tessitura vocally. She achieved this by singing in her head voice (a sound that was not connected to her body/low breath). Not only were they light roles vocally, but the characters were not deep psychologically or emotionally so she was able to remain in her head, somewhat detached from the characters. Annika reflects on an experience in university when a role she was given challenged her to find a way into her body to make the sound and characterization it required:

> I was 23… it was my last year in university and that was really the time when I was exploring heavier repertoire and doing things like the Countess [in Mozart's Marriage of Figaro] instead of Suzanna, who I would have done before. One can hear that the colour that role demands was absolutely right [for me] and yet I didn't have the… connection to my body.

A review in a city paper described a live performance of her singing the Countess:

Annika is a soprano who, despite her youth, has already begun to attract attention. Her voice is exceptionally beautiful, strong and securely pitched... the tone was somewhat covered at times... there is still room for emotional subtlety and range, and for clearer enunciation, even in recitatives. Her potential is great.

The review confirms that when Annika analyzes her voice from that era she is doing it with the finely tuned, self-critical ears of a professional who has discovered depths beyond what she was able to do in her early years. She was, indeed, a promising singer in her early years and was recognized publicly for it. However, the "room for emotional subtlety and range" was some of what she was struggling to find a way to express but which was locked in her disconnected body. Her relationship with her body was also a challenge when it came to the acting component of playing an operatic role. She spoke of feeling "awkward, embarrassed, and so naïve and green" when it came to moving her body on stage, particularly in a seductive or coquettish role. As she has become more connected to her body and more physically comfortable on stage she has come to say that the reason she loves opera is because "it gives me permission to take on a character that's so incredibly defined... I'm allowed to be wide open within that context, and express all those emotions the character would feel. It is a huge release, emotionally and vocally." When Annika began singing Wagner, "I knew I was where I belonged. Finally it was like my emotional makeup and my vocal makeup came together."

During university, Annika's lack of connection to her body was a struggle not only in her singing, but was also noted by others socially. Another singer she studied with at university met her several years later and made the comment, "You're really nice! It was hard to tell at university. You just didn't engage." Annika was puzzled by that comment at the time, but she now understands:

I was living so much in my own inner world—disengaged from my own body, and disengaged really from communicating with people—and all of that did have to do with a lot of my religious beliefs because, of course, I would never partake in certain things... I was setting myself apart and I was living in my own world instead of engaging in myself and in my body. In my very "Christian" way of thinking, I was very judgmental towards others at that time in my life. I am sure they must have perceived it at some level.

Annika found the shift that was trying to happen, the shift of moving into her body, a really huge transition."

Sexual Awakenings and Spiritual Struggles

When Annika was working with the renowned Canadian voice teacher, still in her home town, she sang in an opera workshop where she met a male singer with whom she became romantically involved. She refers to this as the "awakening of sexual energy," another way in which she became aware of and open to feelings in her body. She was still in a relationship with this male singer after her last year of university when she returned to her home town to sing the role of the Countess in a summer production of *The Marriage of Figaro*. Maureen, the soprano who had come over from Europe to sing the role of Suzanna, became close friends with Annika. They developed a "soul connection" which led Maureen to make sexual overtures towards her. Initially this was horrifying to Annika. She felt betrayed by even the suggestion of a sexual liaison with the woman she thought of as her closest friend. Annika described her mind set about homosexuality at the time:

> I was still very much in my deeply Christian way of thinking that was very black-and-white, very right and wrong. It was during that summer that a friend of mine, a guy, was going through his own emotional issues about whether he was gay or not. I was so upset and horrified that he would even consider such a relationship, I gave him the good Christian talk about how evil it was and how terrible it was and how he really should not respond to those feelings.

The "black-and-white thinking" of her Christian upbringing was disapproving or heterosexual activities outside of marriage and all homosexual activities. Her parents had given her a strict warning to stay away from boys. So, as she explained, "I was a virgin when I met Maureen—it was very clear to me that sex before marriage was not a possibility." But there was a strong pull between the two of them which Annika admitted to Maureen, saying, "If you were a guy we would be going out." This was the only way she knew how to think about the attraction she felt, since she was, in her words, "naïve, and so very green." Annika reflected on her feelings at that confusing time of her relationship with Maureen:

> It was all so intense and emotional. I was very confused by these conflicting feelings stirring inside me. On one hand I felt angry and betrayed by Maureen, and on the other hand I was experiencing a profound love for her with an intensity I didn't know existed. I knew I wanted to be with her, yet I couldn't comprehend how that could be. How could it be that I was feeling this way? How did the sexual part of it fit in?

At the end of the opera production that summer Maureen returned to Europe and suggested that Annika might want to come to Europe and continue her studies there, with Maureen's teacher. Annika's first reaction was mistrust of Maureen's motivation, but after a series of intense phone calls, letters, and a heart-wrenching parting in an airport, Annika decided to fly to Europe, to audition and set up her course of study for the following year. She arrived in Europe a few weeks after Maureen did, with the agreement being that she would stay in the basement of the house where Maureen lived, but in a separate, "safe" room in the basement. In Maureen's words, "As fate would have it," it worked out that there wasn't a separate room free for Annika and the two of them ended up staying in the same room and having a sexual relationship.

The morning after their first night together Annika got up saying, "I have sinned against God. I have done the most evil thing. You must help me to never let this happen again." But her resolve didn't hold. "That was a whole week of sex and very little sleep... singing auditions for various teachers in this euphoric haze, not really knowing if I was of this earth or not. But when I went back to Canada... I didn't talk to a soul about what had happened for

6 months. I'd sinned like mad for ten days, but if I confessed to God and asked for forgiveness then surely I could just forget that chapter in my life had ever happened." But it wasn't gone. The relationship with Maureen continued through phone calls and letters in which Annika would ask, "Can't we just be friends? The sexual part really doesn't have to come into it. I can't deal with it. I just can't see my way through it." And Maureen would reply, "How can you separate it?"

The turmoil and secrecy continued until Maureen's next visit to Canada when they were discovered together by the woman with whom Annika shared an apartment. At that moment Annika felt:

> My world had utterly collapsed because it was the first person who knew. And not only was she "any person." but she was the minister's daughter who represented the repressive Christian approach I was struggling against. I actually collapsed on the floor and came so close to throwing up because I was so utterly devastated and I felt my whole world had shattered… my world was just completely split, broken.

Maureen had to leave Annika in her distress that day to get to a vocal coaching. When she got there she couldn't sing because of her own emotional turmoil, and ended up telling her voice teacher the whole story. Annika and Maureen were coaching with the same teacher at the time, and when Annika heard that Maureen had told this woman about their relationship she felt horrified. "Up until that point I had this feeling that as long as no one knew about our relationship I could feel safe, and that somehow I would still be in control. It was very frightening to me to know that this was out in the open now. Looking back, it was, of course, a very important step in my journey to freedom."
Annika had her lesson with the same teacher a day later:

> It all sort of just poured out and [the teacher] was just amazing. She was the first person who I spoke to… If she hadn't been there for me I really don't know how I would have survived, because she really knew where I had come from, knew me so well through my singing. The voice reflects the soul and, of course, she knew what was inside.... If I hadn't been able to talk to her about it I think I would have been really stuck. I'm not sure how I would have been able to resolve that without her incredible love and support.

In a later section on the significance of the teacher/student relationship and its effects on the process of freeing the voice, I will explore this point further. However, I think it important to note here that when Annika felt her world breaking apart, and needed to confide and be understood on this very personal and intense issue, she turned to her voice teacher. She knew she was deeply understood by this teacher, had permission to be herself, and that her true self would be known through her voice. To her, that was a great comfort.

Annika says that coming to grips with her sexuality in her relationship with Maureen was a very slow process:

For years I was thinking—I can't deal with this. It's not that I didn't love her, but I felt like I was just going to be torn apart by this... It's not because I didn't enjoy every aspect of my relationship with her. In fact, I was transported by it. And the love-making was a part of my spiritual relationship with her. The dilemma was that I really truly did think that homosexuality was a very evil thing—that I would go to hell. It was how I understood Christianity to be, the whole thing of what is right and wrong in the world...it's black-and-white...You were either a born-again Christian and you were this way, or you weren't and you would go to hell.

That was Annika's firmly held moral stance, all she had ever considered to be a possibility, and yet her experience was screaming something different:

It was so profoundly shocking when I found myself with these feelings for Maureen. I just couldn't make sense of them. I was feeling this passion for her so powerfully. I felt I had touched on some deep truth, experiencing love in a way unknown to me until that point. Everything that I had been told—that [a homosexual relationship] wasn't love, that it was bad—how could that be when I was experiencing what I was experiencing on such a profound level? It was a connection on a very deep level that really transcended the here and now—a spiritual connection.

After listening to Annika describe her dilemma I tried to summarize what I thought I was hearing. Her deep spiritual connection with Maureen was pulling her one way, but pulling in the opposite direction was the black-and-white, "deep" spiritual teaching that condemned her experience. She had never questioned these teachings before, but her spiritual connection to Maureen seemed much deeper and more real. When I shared this summary with Annika to make sure I understood she replied:

Yes! I think you've just hit the nail on the head. It did have to do with my relationship with what I understood God to be, which was the most important thing in my life. In a sense my spiritual life is still as important to me as it ever was, but has shifted enormously in terms of its structure. I grew up with a very narrow concept of what it was to be a Christian. It took me some time to open up and expand to the concept of what I thought my Christianity was... The whole issue of sin I just don't buy into anymore. I don't believe that we are born into sin. I think that there is [something] of God in all of us. With this concept of being born into sin, there is so much negativity and fear. So much of my own negativity towards myself stems from this very basic thing. If I am not able to love and accept myself, there seems little chance of really being able to love and accept others.

Having my own feelings of shame from my Christian upbringing, my ears were attuned to the language of shame that I heard in Annika as she referred to feeling guilty, and believing there was "something bad" about her. I asked her if shame was also part of her experience. At first she was puzzled as to the difference between guilt and shame, so I explained that shame was having the sense that *you* were bad, whereas guilt was about having *done* something bad. She then explained, "Maybe I've got the two of them together; I do mean guilt as also being shame." As seen in the literature review, shame is a way that we cut off a part of ourselves. Within the metaphor of "coming home to the self," this is the equivalent of throwing part of ourselves out the door to shiver in the back yard. Very early in life Annika had been taught to cut off from her sexuality, in order to be pure in her Christianity. Now that her sexuality was knocking at the door, asking to "come home" and be reintegrated into her self, she was in turmoil.

Maureen blamed the church for Annika's long lasting struggles with accepting her whole self.

> Maureen: There were just these underlying things that came up for so long, these blasted feelings of badness, disappointment, judgment, that just sent me around the back twist because there was all this imposed stuff that has nothing to do with Christ's message.
>
> Annika: I still sometimes get glimpses and shadows of just "being" bad.
>
> M: I find it just unfathomable, to see someone eating themselves up like that. You know, it makes no sense and it makes me angry.

Annika and Maureen were expressing some of what I expressed in the literature review on the psycho-spiritual roots of shame. Conservative Christian teaching had given Annika a pervasive and lasting sense of "badness" in general, and specifically with regard to her sexuality. She was bad on two accounts—first, because she was a sexual being, and second, because she was expressing it in homosexuality. Maureen made the point that "this imposed stuff has nothing to do with Christ's message." In a later interview, they expanded on this, articulating the belief that Christ's message should be about "love and acceptance."

This feeling of "being bad" followed Annika into her into professional singing career, making it difficult for her to take criticism or suggestions from others in rehearsal. Annika thrives on the thrill of performance and on releasing spontaneous creativity, but rehearsing is difficult for her because of this sense of badness. She remembers back to her piano lessons at six years of age. Already, then, she "shut down and barely responded" when she was corrected. The same was still true in university 15 years later. Maureen described her behavior:

> If she didn't like what somebody was asking her to do or it didn't agree with her she simply got very stony... Sometimes it was her judgment, but sometimes it was just her backing off into herself in insecurity. She used to remove herself, withdraw any emotional involvement.

I asked Annika what she was feeling just before she felt the need to withdraw. She had to think for a bit, and finally said it was "probably some frustration and anger." Maureen said that it appeared to her to be "nastiness turned in on yourself... your self-hatred. You seemed to be punishing yourself." This resonated with Annika's experience.

> Annika: It does seem to be a reflection of the dark, very punishing thing, and it's this feeling somehow that I'm not good inside.

Maureen: That fucking Christian guilt and justifiable punishment shit that still comes up… The last time I was making some suggestions about your singing you reacted in an "old" way. Your response was that you were feeling so horrible and that you thought you were horrible. When I give my comments about your singing you decided to use it as fuel for hating yourself.

As seen in the discussion about shame in the literature review, the criticism of another person seems to be what activates feelings of shame. However, shame already exists in its victim as self-rejection that has suddenly been seen by the eyes of another person. In this case the eyes belonged to Maureen, who spoke out of love and good intentions. Annika thought again about her reactions to being corrected or given suggestions for improvement in rehearsal:

> I would say that insecurity and fear really set up a reaction like that. There is still a fear issue that I need to work through—it just comes over me. Certainly a large contributing factor to that fear in earlier years was wondering if my parents would find out about my relationship to Maureen.

Annika went on to describe another aspect of her "spiritual expansion" having to do with years of arguing with Maureen about Christianity being the only religion that held the truth. Gradually she came to the realization that this was also far too narrow, that there are certain truths in all religions, as well as negative aspects, but that what it really came down to was "one's connection to the divine."

What I heard Annika saying was that she expanded her relationship with the divine beyond "keeping the rules to please God." Rather, it became an experiential relationship that opened her to intimate connection with the divine and with others. She now brought her whole self into relationship, including her sexuality, and because she was bringing more of her authentic self rather than her false, people-pleasing self, she was able to let herself be seen, to feel genuine and loved, and to let herself be her authentic self. After several years of turmoil, she finally accepted herself and her homosexual relationship with Maureen when she realized "how wrong it was to push it away… seeing that shift, realizing that it was basically just there and that I wasn't gaining anything by denying."

Although Annika had to work through a lot of turmoil as a result of entering into a sexual relationship with Maureen, the relationship also carried a lot of positive effects, including another level of coming home to her body. Maureen noticed vocal changes in Annika as a result of their sexual relationship, describing them as "tangible release and space" and "an opening up of the body for those resonances to happen." These resulted in a new depth in her sound. Annika reflected on this process of change in her body, her emotions, her beliefs, and her voice:

> As I was slowly able to get into my body more, breathe deeper… many of those things did relate to letting go of my own emotional holding patterns and what was happening in my own life… in my first relationship with a boyfriend I started feeling more things in my body, and then when I met Maureen it was a completely deeper

level of getting into my body, so then I really understood... the sexual experience was complete, so therefore I felt the release, I felt the understanding of that energy and of being grounded and anchored in my body. And so that was a release of all that emotional stuff—thinking that it was so wrong and so bad... Can you ever really get that low in your breath if you've never had a sexual experience? Maureen and I couldn't really answer that question.

We saw in the literature review of the use of voice in music therapy, that breathing deeply brings one in touch with one's body, and thus with one's emotions. In a later section we will look further at the mechanics of breathing as taught by Annika and Maureen in the master class—how proper breathing releases the voice to sing more freely and, in turn, releases the emotions. I think it important to note here that Annika's "emotional stuff" was a significant block in her ability to "get low enough in her body" to sing well. The emotional and physical release that came from the sexual experience, and the changing views, which allowed her to enter the sexual experience without feeling it was "wrong and bad," contributed to her ability to move towards vocal freedom. Annika's answer to the question, "Can you ever really get that low in your breath if you've never had a sexual experience?" is "No." Perhaps, for other people, who have a different relationship to their sexuality, the question might be answered differently, but in Annika's experience she needed to open herself sexually and release the negative beliefs, guilt, and shame, to go a level deeper of her voice.

I asked Annika how she saw a person's sense of identity, including sexual identity, affecting vocal freedom. She responded, "The two are so closely entwined. Our voices, like our bodies, can only reflect what's going on inside. If what we're holding is a lot of negative emotions, then what comes out in our sound reflects it."

Annika said she knew some people who found singing very straightforward and not fraught with this type of emotional turmoil. She believes that, for those people, singing was not the place they were challenged to grow in life, and they came to singing with a basic sense of self-acceptance, of being at peace with themselves. She said how nice it would be for all singers if they could set up their breath, posture, and throat openness technically correctly and be assured that a high C would pop out. However, from her teaching experience Annika believes:

> The root of all technical problems is not technical; it's a process of finding the voice. I think it's the singers who struggle with issues of self acceptance that struggle also in terms of finding their vocal freedom. All those emotional things come out so clearly in their voice. A basic belief in self needs to be there, in order to create a certain sound.

I asked Annika if accepting her sexuality was part of "coming home to herself" and she answered, "Yes, because I think part of accepting the sexual part of myself was really getting to know who I was. It's really not the fact that I was straight or gay. It was like finding out about the sexual part of my being, whichever way it was."

Was it "coming home" to herself sexually? It was in the sense that she had to get to know herself sexually, and her relationship with Maureen was the context in which she did that. But was it a coming home to a part of herself that, because of her religious teaching and conditioning, she had denied and later gave herself permission to express? It was, in the sense that she had been cut off from her body and sexuality and was now getting in touch with them and allowing herself to feel and be sexual. However, unlike many people who struggle with homosexual feelings from childhood and feel released when they finally give themselves permission to express those feelings, the thought of a lesbian relationship had never entered Annika's mind before she met Maureen. She explained her experience this way:

> I don't know [whether] if I didn't have Maureen... I'd be with another woman. I might be with another man—that's quite possible—and the same is true for Maureen, because she had many more relationships with men than she ever did with women before she met me. I would say it had more to do with connection with my "soul mate" than it had to [do with] coming out in terms of being gay.

Fear and Physical Illness

Within a year of the time Annika and Maureen became involved, Annika moved to Europe to begin her vocal career. Although they were not living together for the first few years, Annika and Maureen continued their relationship. It was during this time that Annika was in a state of turmoil about the sexual part of her relationship with Maureen. This resulted in Annika often pushing Maureen away, asking if they could "just be friends." But at the same time she felt the sexual attraction, the "beautiful connection" and "transcendence" of being intimate with Maureen.

A few people in Canada had discovered the nature of Annika's relationship with Maureen, and that had forced her to own it in a limited way. However, Annika had not told her parents, sister, or anyone else. She lived in perpetual fear of her parents' reaction if they were to find out, as seen in the following excerpt from an interview with Annika and Maureen:

> Annika: The fear levels were just enormous... wondering whether Mom and Dad would find out about our relationship, or what would happen or how they would respond or if Dad would... actually become violent knowing this information... just the fear of them knowing was just so huge.

> Maureen: It ruled our lives in many ways.

> A: I was really driven by this incredible fear... it's shifted now, but up until very recently even being with Mom, this fear would just well up inside me. Just the sound of her voice—the tone of her voice—would instantly bring up that fear. It's just a reaction that's so immediate... so strong.

I find it fascinating that, separate from our discussion about her singing voice, Annika spontaneously identified that her mother's voice stirred up fear, and that her own voice changed to reflect that fear. Whenever Annika was talking to her mother on the phone, Maureen knew, because:

> My voice would go very high... very out of my body. It was like I tried to remove myself... the fear was so great and gripped at such a low level... it grips in my gut and it's so squeezed there that the only way is up... iron bars down either side of my stomach just gripped... I still get twinges if I've had a conversation that's been particularly upsetting, if an unexpected telephone call from Mom has caught me off guard.

Even with Annika's parents in Canada being separated by an ocean from Annika and Maureen in Europe, the fear that their relationship would be discovered ruled many of their decisions. They set up their schedules to be sure they were in the right place at the right time to receive phone calls from Annika's parents. Even though Annika wanted to stay with Maureen for her first Christmas away from home, she feared it might look suspicious to her parents. Instead, she went to Germany to stay with German relatives, which pleased her parents. However, the emotional strain of holding so much fear and secrecy manifested itself in physical illness, as seen in the following excerpt from an e-mail communication from Annika to me on March 12, 2003:

> Of course the whole breathing issue is the thing that very often releases things if we are indeed breathing low and deep in our bodies. Guess what happened to me when I moved over here to Europe? I literally could not breathe. I spent a week in hospital with acute bronchitis and asthma, and subsequently spent years trying to sort out my bronchitis/asthma/allergy problems. And they were so directly a result of my emotional turmoil at the time—trying to come to terms with my relationship with Maureen, all the terrible fear and guilt, and all that stuff with my parents... feeling that intensity from my parents and, in a very different way of course, from Maureen, ended up with me not being able to get my breath. Isn't it just so incredible how our bodies don't lie!

Annika's breathing problems continued for months after this visit to Germany. She returned to her home and to voice lessons, but illness was really hampering her progress. "I started my lessons again, but I was weak. I was really struggling." As seen in another excerpt from Annika's e-mail of March 3, 2003, it was her voice teacher who addressed the real issue holding up her singing:

> One of the most incredible things said to me at the time was by my singing teacher here in London who, having heard about my time in hospital and asthma and stuff said, in her thick accent, "Darlink, vhat is da matter? You don't haff asthma. Tell me, is it a man?" Terrified that I would have to talk about my personal life and relationship with Maureen, I quickly responded, "No!" "Ah," she said, "then it is a woman!" She then said, "It is really very simple—if you feel the relationship with Maureen is what you want then you must do it, but not feel bad about it and drive

yourself with the guilt and bad feelings that are making you ill." Really, [it was] one of the most helpful bits of advice.

In an interview with Annika she commented that, "In her instinctual knowledge my voice teacher just knew. It was incredible that she just said, 'You're not really sick.'" This is another example of how the relationship between voice student and teacher can have an incredible impact on the progress of the student. The following is an excerpt of an interview with Annika about what effect it had on her that she had this particular teacher and this particular conversation with her.

Joan: How did that affect your studying with her?

Annika: It was just such a relief, a huge relief. It was sort of like another person knowing, and at that point not many people knew. But there weren't a lot of people. Did it affect our working together? I mean not hugely. It was incredible that she went there, because she wasn't one to... talk about emotional things. But just the recognition that she instinctively knew was enough. It changed a lot for me psychologically, because I felt she understood where I was coming from, which enabled me to relax more. So that affected my singing.

J: If you look at it the other way, if you hadn't told her and you project forward, what would that have looked like?

A: I suppose I may not have continued, I don't know. It is a good question... I think it would have been different. There's a good chance. It's hard to project. Very possibly I could have just gotten more and more uptight in my body, trying to do what I did in Germany and just making it okay... trying very hard to appear that it was okay when it wasn't.

Body Work: The Alexander Technique, Craniosacral Therapy, Osteopathy

One of the ways Annika sought to re-inhabit her body was through doing various kinds of body work. She explains this part of her journey home to self:

My early phase of life I spent so much time moving out of my body. I'm sure I was in it as a child, but then I moved out of it because we are told not to do this and that and to behave in a certain way, and so basically the body closes up. Then there comes a certain point that you try to inhabit it again, but it's not such an easy process and it involves trusting the body to know its own wisdom and understand how it is to do its thing the right way.

I would say that so much of how I found my way into my own body really did not have to do with singing, it had to do with all the body work I had done—Alexander, and my incredible osteopath—I guess those were really two huge people for me... I could get so far [with the singing] and then something was in the way and I had to look at issues of holding patterns, and sometimes they are physical and you need help. What's so wonderful about Alexander is that they can really train you. The osteopath can make an adjustment to ease... pain, but somebody like an Alexander teacher can actually make you re-think how you use your body.

As we saw in the literature review, the Alexander Technique is "a subtle method for changing habits and attitudes, which releases the body and mind, enhances body awareness and functioning, and gives the body new freedom, coordination, and energy" (Leibowitz & Connington, 1990, p.xv). Annika began learning the Alexander Technique as a teenager before she started university and has continued practicing it throughout her vocal career. I heard many aspects of Alexander philosophy coming through her teaching and beliefs about the unity of body, mind, and spirit, and principles of control and release.

Along with her practice of the Alexander Technique Annika has worked extensively with an osteopath and a craniosacral specialist to free her body of tensions that were blocking her vocal freedom. She explained her experience of craniosacral therapy:

> Annika: I think one of the most powerful treatments I had was with a craniosacral person. I had gone to see him and Maureen found me in a heap on the floor by the time she got back. I remember being leaned up against the wall. It was absolutely extraordinary. He had made some adjustment on my neck and… what it did was release something… all of the sudden it released… these whooshes of, not blood, but it felt like waves, just opening up. He basically opened up my cranial rhythms and all of a sudden everything started shifting… That was just so weird, these whooshes of these rhythms that I had never felt before… absolutely amazing and scary at the same time because it was such a new sensation to me. Having released that in my head, I would say that it was a process of working with another osteopath who basically started releasing things all the way down my spine. I can remember an incredible session on something at the very bottom of my spine—these fluids started going up and down my spine. Also this whole area of my lower back… it was just so amazing.

> Joan: Did you feel your singing changing with that?

> A: Yeah, I did. That coincided with the start of working professionally. Yeah, I would say that it was reflected in my singing, that it was the beginning of finding more the depth of my voice. It was an ongoing process. I think I saw her in and out for about eight years. But she was also so intuitive and she was so incredible. When mom and dad were about to come over and visit, and they didn't know yet [about her relationship with Maureen], we had sort of agreed that what we would do was rearrange the house to make it look like we each had a bedroom. I was in a session with the osteopath, who sort of had her hands on me and was doing her stuff, and as I was telling her what was coming up, and she basically said, "If you go through with it you will pay for it in your body, your body will react. If you feel you really need to do that I'll be here to see you through on the other side but you'll pay very heavily. You have a choice. You actually do have a choice. You don't have to go through with it." And I left . And I thought, "I do have a choice, and do I want to put my body through that? No, I don't think I do." After living years of secrecy and deception that was it, that thing from the osteopath was the moment that I thought, "I can't deny it any more, I'm denying myself and the most important thing in my life and my body can't take it any more."

Osteopathy and craniosacral therapy are based on the same foundational principle of the Alexander Technique—that body, mind and spirit are an inseparable unit and that, if you affect one part, you affect the whole. This was clearly illustrated in Annika's experience described above, where the osteopath encouraged Annika to take care of her body by taking care of her emotional life. A craniosacral therapist is:

> ... the ultimate biofeedback machine. Connected to the patient's nervous and muscular systems through touch, responding to signals so faint that the patient is unaware of himself as the source, amplifying those signals to bring them into the conscious awareness of the patient, the therapist makes manifest the self-healing organism. (Manheim & Lavett, 1989, p.4).

Annika mentioned several times how intuitive her body workers were, whether they were craniosacral therapists, osteopaths, Alexander Technique teachers, or voice teachers. I include the best of voice teachers in the category of body workers since they sense their students holistically, paying attention to the body, mind, and spirit and realizing that the voice reflects the state of all these components. Voice teachers also work with breathing and posture, key issues in the therapies we have examined, and at times will use gentle physical touch to guide a student into a different posture or help them sense their breathing. Moreover, just as Annika's osteopath spoke words of insight to her about the physical fallout she would experience if she continued hiding her relationship with Maureen from her parents, so it was her voice teachers who intuitively spoke up about how her relational turmoil was affecting her singing and her physical health.

Rejection and Depression

Annika ended the secrecy of her lesbian relationship with Maureen when they had known each other for ten years and had been living together for eight years. She wrote a letter to her parents telling them about the true nature of their relationship. As she had feared, they were far from accepting. Annika's reaction to their rejection was so strong that she "literally could not stomach the force of it." Not being able to "stomach" the rejection gave her years of irritable bowel syndrome, Candida infection, and respiratory problems, as well as plunging her into a depression that lasted for years and negatively impacted her career. In the following interview excerpt, the two women discuss the far reaching effects of Annika's parents' rejection:

> Maureen: Annika's career was starting to take shape... but after this thing with her parents, her work really did fall off... There were various reasons for that, but basically her energy for the work vanished and she was just depressed. There were a couple of years where she would just say things like, "I don't know why I'm here, I don't know what I'm meant to do, I really don't know why I should be alive." It wasn't that she was weeping depressed all the time, though there were several months of that initially, but it was just this sort of deadness that came over her as a result of no longer having this parental approval really, and feeling so undermined. It was very alarming to see and to witness. There was nothing to do but wait. It was not a time for her career to be moving forward. She simply didn't have any confidence.
>
> Annika: Those were difficult times for me.

Joan: Was this when you had Candida and all those stomach problems?

A: Yes, it was at a time that I had some wonderful work. A time in my career where doors had been opening and I had some rather high profile concerts, but they were at time where I was physically very weak. It was such a struggle just trying to get through rehearsals and performances.

M: At a time when you didn't have the resources to do it.

A: So the work fell off and conductors stopped using me.

M: And every occasion was a challenge, whether it was social or professional. You had to sort of "gird your loins" and force yourself out. It was bleak, and it lasted several years.

A: It was pretty alarming how long it went on for.

J: And the singing wasn't good then?

A: Singing takes a lot of energy and I just didn't have it to put out there. The illness and the physical weakness were reflected in my singing. Auditions were a great struggle for me. I remember one audition that I did for an agent. The rejection hit me very hard. It was also the moment that I understood how raw any rejection left me, after my experience with my parents.

M: So you got to the point where you stopped doing auditions for anybody, just because you couldn't face more rejection.

A: I could not cope. I really just could not cope with the rejection. It really was devastating.

M: So a phone call, even… there was potential for rejection in all kinds of situations. You just couldn't deal with it.

A: To some degree it is still difficult, and I still struggle with these issues.

This specific rejection and her upbringing in a church that stressed "guilt, punishment, and sinfulness" (Maureen's description), left Annika with a permanent self-view that "I'm not good inside." To this day she struggles with "shadows of just being bad," which Maureen sees as the impetus for a lot of her self-punishment and not liking herself—a very difficult stance to sing from with confidence and freedom. She continues to heal, but there are still "shadows" at times.

Annika tried to maintain contact with her parents, but for a year the only response to her friendly Christmas letters and birthday wishes were occasional letters of condemnation laced with scripture passages that "proved" her sinfulness. After a year they had a meeting at Annika's request. It was excruciatingly painful for Annika as she faced the rejection in person. This added to her stomach problems and brought on the years of depression mentioned earlier. Eventually a bit of thawing occurred, and they resumed some very superficial communication at a more bearable level.

Father's Death

Annika's father died unexpectedly of a heart attack several years later. Annika flew home immediately, and she and her sister worked together to support their mother through this difficult time and to help with funeral arrangements. Annika's sister had known about Annika's relationship with Maureen longer than her parents had. Although she initially had some similar reactions of judgment, she had come to accept it and had resolved her issues with her sister years earlier. I asked Annika to reflect on how the death of her father affected her:

> Annika: It was a deep and profound experience, an experience that shifted something inside me… a heightened time emotionally. A bit like living in a different reality, a bit like glimpsing things on another sphere of existence. I feel his presence now more than I did when he was alive. Through his death he's been released from so much intensity and struggle in his own life that he had no way of working through. I can almost feel that release for him.

> Joan: And does it bring any release as far as the rejection thing you were working through? Or was that already done for you?

> A: That was sort of done for me… Interestingly with Dad I never really felt that he rejected me… He certainly disapproved of what I was doing, but I never felt the rejection of me as a person. I would say that he never withdrew his love in the way that I felt that Mom did. So I never had those issues so much with Dad. My relationship with Dad in a way was much more straightforward.

> J: Did you notice your father's death doing anything to you vocally or emotionally?

> A: I would say yes. Emotionally there was a lot of release going on at that point too, for me. Dad's death was really a very profound experience for me that added another layer of depth to my own spiritual path. because I had some very, very profound moments.

Just a few months after losing her father, Annika performed the role of Abbigaille in Verdi's *Nabucco* in her home town. She was a brilliant success, as seen in the following newspaper review from the local newspaper:

> Annika does a very credible job… blessed with perfect pitch she is able to absolutely nail the octave-spanning highs and lows… In Annika's most convincing and emotionally powerful scene she wonders aloud in a beautifully sung scene alternating elegiac lyricism with dramatic melodies. Her singing has a rounded, velvety quality that's very attractive. Some might prefer a voice with a greater dynamic edge for this role, which is so melodramatically over the top. Nonetheless, no one can deny Annika is a gifted singer capable of navigating one of opera's most arduous journeys.

Another reviewer of the performance wrote, "Annika lets her acrobatic voice soar in song… she more than holds her own on stage. She steals the show with an incredible vocal range and athletic delivery that takes her from high to low C."

98

Following an interview with Annika, another reviewer wrote:

> Annika was reported as saying that she believed she was entering a mature phase of her career. She's becoming increasingly interested in singing operas requiring considerable heft—Wagner for example. Although she looks younger, Annika turned 40 a few weeks ago. "It actually feels quite good to have arrived at 40 and feel that people won't say, 'Oh, you're much too young to sing this role,' she said. "I feel like I've arrived."

I was able to attend this performance and thoroughly enjoyed it. It is a very demanding role that spans an incredible range—from high C to middle C in the matter of a few beats and she effortlessly flew from the top to the bottom of her range with great accuracy and a consistent full sound. It was the best I have ever heard her sing and her acting was energetic and commanding. Another layer of physical, emotional and spiritual release was reflected in the clarity, power and energy of her voice that evening.

Release of Dreams, Settling Into Home

In the last few years Annika has continued performing internationally and has begun teaching voice. Knowing how significant being a teacher has been to my own understanding of flute, I was curious to find out how teaching has affected Annika's voice and views on voice. I asked Maureen to be part of the discussion about teaching since she co-taught the master-classes and because she has had the unique position of observing vocal changes in Annika up close for the past 20 years. Following is an excerpt of our discussion.

> Joan: Maureen, how have you noticed Annika's voice change since she started teaching?
>
> Maureen: I would say that over the last few years she's found her sound and her core and her colour to an extent that she has never had so consistently before. That may well be because of having to analyze it. I can't say, I'm not quite inside of Annika's head. I can't say how much it coincides with teaching and how much it coincides with her coming into her power in herself and of her voice. Her voice has narrowed and gotten deeper, and the top is much more in place. I mean she's always had really good, really high notes, but the sort of middle high from e or f up to b or b flat was a bit of a funny zone where the sound would spread and not work consistently. But then if she had a very high note it would always be fine, she always knew how to get there.

The two women discussed how they thought the recent settling of Annika's voice came to be:

> Maureen: It's taken until the last couple of years for that to come into place. But a lot of it, I think, has also coincided—funnily enough—with an acceptance on Annika's part that she may or may not be having a career as she dreamt of it. So I don't know how much has to do with letting go of self imposed expectations and judgments, how much has to do with teaching, how much has to do with a physical coming home... I don't know what all... but she has certainly moved into a time of coming into her own power.

Annika: It also coincided with my having come out of my years of working through the rejection of my parents and working through my ill health. It's been about four years now that I actually feel in great shape physically, so it's corresponded with that and it's corresponded with that emotional freedom that has given me the vocal freedom.

Annika's "coming into her own power" vocally and personally was about her feeling physically well and strong, and in a better place with her family emotionally, and with her self-acceptance of her life as it is. As Maureen says, "What was going on inside was reflected in her voice." Now that she was settling into herself emotionally and physically it was reflected in the consistency and deepening of her sound as well as a "coming into line" of the middle-high register, which had been so scary and disconnected from her body in earlier years. Both Annika and Maureen linked Annika's ability to come to grips with her career expectations with the power and freedom released in her voice and life at this point:

Annika: I spent a lot of time [in the past] feeling horribly guilty for not doing a lot more auditions and feeling that I should be driving myself. I had a fixed vision as of where I wanted my career to go. My dream was that I would have a very busy career singing in all the big opera houses around the world. I would say that I have now let go of the expectation, which is not quite the same as letting go of my dreams. When a great job comes my way, I now see it as a gift to be enjoyed rather than something that my whole life depends on.

Maureen: No, it's a very clear moment and it's very different. It's as much a release [as] an admission of defeat... It's important to stress that you realize that it doesn't' fit any more to hang onto these things, it isn't where your life is. Okay, so neither of us is ever going to sing at the Met—does that really affect our validity? No it doesn't, so let's just let it go.

A: Yes, this thing of pleasing other people... I'm finally letting go of it and finding the freedom of knowing that I am really doing it for me, not anyone else! Some people would think that you weren't valid until you sang with a certain conductor, or opera company, or in a certain venue. For me it's not about that myth, it's about letting go.

Annika was released to begin teaching as she let go of pleasing others and seeking her validity in external accomplishments. She and Maureen discussed how she came into teaching in the last few years:

Annika: I never sought to start teaching because I never ever thought that I'd enjoy it. I didn't know if I'd be any good at it, and I never thought I'd do it until I could sing perfectly myself!

Maureen: You had a very fixed idea that you would teach after you'd had a career. When you were miserable about not having work and sometimes miserable about the money you weren't earning, I would say, "How about some more teaching?" There was huge resistance because you felt that it would be admitting failure. You would say, "But I should rather be using my time and energy pursuing work—I should be learning things, I should be sending out resumes because that's what I want to be doing rather than teaching. You saw it so clearly as failure—you would get miserable and blue when I would propose it so it was just kind of serendipitous that some people started asking for teaching. There was no way I was going to work with some of those kids so it had to be Annika—no way out. You didn't even like it very much at first.

A: I think back to before I met Maureen—I was very much in a singer-y, ego singer-y place. I was immersed in that world and all the expectations of behaviour that went along being "a singer." I would never have considered teaching in those days because, in my own mind, it would have defined me as a "failed" singer.

Annika explained that she is still enthusiastic about performing when the opportunities arise, but she felt "releasing" the dreams and ambitions—and letting her career be what it was rather than trying to force it into something pre-conceived—had further released her voice.

Listening to Annika describe her journey home to herself was both inspiring and painful. I related personally to the beginnings of her journey, being cut off from her body, living in her head, and singing from the "neck up." Her passion to find a way to express her authentic self through repertoire that moved her fueled her determination to face her fears and re-inhabit her body. She was also propelled by passion for her soul friend, Maureen. In the context of that relationship she came home to her body sexually, and experienced some of her greatest joy and deepest spiritual connection. However, she also faced some of her darkest turmoil and fear in the context of this lesbian relationship with Maureen and the rejection and depression that resulted from the reactions of her family. As I listened to this part of her journey I couldn't contain my tears, partly for the pain she had endured, and partly for the love that she continued to show to her family despite their rejection. She worked through these issues to the point of being able to separate from their judgment of her and embrace her self, voice, and lifestyle decisions. As she released so much of the fear, loss of parental approval, guilt, and black-and-white thinking, she came home to a healthy place physically and emotionally, which settled her voice. She also released the need to please others (not just her parents) or to try and fulfill their expectations to prove herself, and is settling into the fullness of singing freely to please herself and encourage her students. Her voice is reflecting this centered, purposeful yet undemanding approach to herself, her body, and her life. She sounds free, flexible, and powerful in voice and spirit, and finds great satisfaction in helping her students move towards a similar place, celebrating their vocal and physical "homecomings" as they occur.

Now we turn from the story of Annika's life journey home to herself through pursuing vocal freedom, to the story of my first step in the process of freeing my voice in a one hour voice lesson with Annika and Maureen.

My Voice Lesson With Annika and Maureen
(Joan)

Without our body we cannot speak truthfully.
We may think we are speaking the truth,
But if we lie down
And somebody puts a hand
On our heart and belly,
We will cry.
There's truth in those tears.
(Marion Woodman, 1998, p.92)

> Maureen: Okay, why don't you lie down on your back on the floor, knees bent up so you can balance, and I'll put this book under your head so it's a little easier on your neck.

I was getting in position for my voice lesson with Annika and Maureen, with Maureen taking most of the teaching initiative. As I got into position on the floor Maureen leaned over me and placed her hand on my abdomen. I felt some anxiety flitter through my body—what did this feel like? Like lying on a doctor's examining table—not my favorite place to be. But I told myself, "Try to stay in the moment and just do what she tells you."

> Maureen: Breathe so you feel it extend through the whole column of your body, from your pelvic floor to your soft palate in the roof of your mouth. Now breathe out as a sigh—ahhhhh.

> Joan: Is it supposed to go anywhere in particular?

> M: Go anywhere? No, but I want you to feel it. Imagine that you have vocal chords there on your damphiene (lower abdomen where Maureen's hand was resting), and that's where the noise is coming from.

I sighed out another "ahhhhh," trying to imitate the sound Maureen made before me. I was not sure whether to focus my attention on the sound of my "ahhhhh" or on my breathing, but the pressure of her hand held my attention more strongly on my abdomen.

> Maureen: The whole throat is in neutral and there are just two little flaps in the throat that happen to catch in the wind and make a sound as you centre your breath.

Maureen continued to make sounds for me to imitate—sighing out an "ahhhhh," then turning the sigh into a more active, undulating sound, like a car engine revving, coaxing me to a lower pitch, a louder range in volume, all the while with her hand on my abdomen reminding me to centre the breath there.

> Maureen: Can you make the inhalation silent… a lower deeper sound… Nothing changes in the throat as you "ha ha ha." It stays the same. Say "no" to any muscle killer involved in the throat. Inhale the sound and make sure that the inhalation doesn't stop before the exhalation starts.

I made a couple of "ha ha ha" sounds that were slightly deeper and freer, thinking about making the sound as part of the inhalation rather than after the beginning of the exhalation.

> Maureen: Good! That was a good one. You were letting the resonance sort of happen. Now it goes "Ha Ha Ha" but no "H" just a puff of air from the abdomen.

> Joan: I actually feel it here (pointing to my throat).

> M: Yeah, but you're not doing anything there in your throat.

Maureen tried to re-focus me on my inhalation and the action in my abdomen. As I continued to "Ha Ha Ha" and do the car revving sound she was one minute pressing on my abdomen, the next tweaking the top of my head to encourage me to feel the breath from palate to pelvic floor. It took me a while to get used to all this physical contact and to keep up with what part of my body I was supposed to feel when. As soon as I was making sounds my attention automatically went to what I was hearing and I couldn't feel my body, but when she would touch me somewhere, my attention would go there and I would lose the focus on the sound. It was a balancing act of sounds and sensations that took some getting used to. I felt a improvement from the beginning to the end of the lesson in my ability to hold onto more than one physical sensation at a time, but it was somewhat disorienting at this stage.

> Maureen: You can have even less glottal attack with the chords, just "ah ah ah"—feel my stomach as I do it.

Maureen placed my hand low on her abdomen, drew a deep breath, and puffed out some "ah ah ah" sounds. I felt her stomach going in with each puff, and when she put my other hand on her throat I felt no activity there. Feeling her body in action was much more effective than just telling me how my body should be moving, but it introduced another level of physical contact that I had to adjust to—me touching her. Again, nothing insurmountable, but something for me to get used to that took my attention away from my task for a time. I tried again to breathe and make "ah ah ah" sounds. Maureen stopped me.

> Maureen: I want your abdomen to go the opposite direction.

Annika, who had been listening and watching, interjected at this point.

> Annika: Was it going up while she was exhaling?

> M: Yeah.

> Joan: My stomach was supposed to be going in while I did that? I don't know how to do that.

I experimented with my abdominal muscles for a minute—pulling in, pushing out, trying to remember how I breathed for flute playing. I felt a very weird muscle in my tail bone twitching which distracted me completely from my abdominal muscles. I didn't want to mention it though because it was "down there" in my body, where I didn't like to think I even existed.

Maureen put my hand on her stomach and throat again, and had me feel the difference between pushing out with her abdominals while making the "ha ha" sounds and tucking the abdominal muscles in. Annika commented that pushing out was a rigid way of breathing that causes more activity in the throat. I couldn't figure out which way to move what when. What she described as tucking in felt like pushing out to me and vice versa. Annika made the comment that many of the students in the master class had the same question: "Which way does it go?" This highlighted for me just how difficult it is to get another person to connect with a physical sensation in the way it is described by the teacher. Even if the student manages to make the same physical motion as the teacher, there is no guarantee they are sensing the same thing, or focusing on the same muscles, or that they would describe it in the same way.

After some discussion Maureen and I realized I was thinking about the action of a slightly higher part of my belly, which, in flute playing, is supposed to pop out. This helped me realize that part of my confusion came from my habitual way of breathing while playing the flute for many years. I told her I found it difficult to feel the breath properly lying on my back—that maybe if I stood I could feel it more as I did in flute playing. It was harder than I thought to become aware of what my muscles were doing when, focusing on an activity like breathing which is unconscious and habitual most of the time. It seemed nearly impossible to change it, particularly when her hand on my abdomen and the sound I was trying to make distracted me. I realized just how little awareness most of us have of our bodies most of the time, and how complex something as natural as breathing is.

After Maureen had taken the first 20 minutes to make her point about breathing, we switched from "ha ha" sounds to a swoop of connected ascending notes. She sang me an example and I tried to imitate her. Half way up the scale my voice wobbled and I instinctively choked it off. I laughed nervously and Maureen asked, "Feel a bit scary? Okay, start lower, more in the range of your speaking voice—you have good resonance in your speaking voice." So we worked on finding my low notes, and breathing in the full length of the "tube" or "column" that extended from palate to pelvis. I calmed down some and continued trying to imitate the examples Maureen sang for me. She tried to get me to move the exercise up to a higher pitch. I wasn't anticipating it would be much different than what I had been doing, so I took a breath and began imitating the higher pitch. Quite unexpectedly I found my voice choking off as I went higher. My eyes flooded with tears and my body tightened. I turned my face away, embarrassed. Maureen still had her hand on my abdomen but when she saw and felt my tightening, she leaned back from me. When I had the courage to turn my face back towards her I saw that Maureen had tears in her own eyes.

Maureen: Ah ha, I can feel...

Joan: You can feel me fearful.

104

M: I can feel the vulnerability… you're very brave.

We were quiet for a minute while I tried to get a grip on my tears.

Maureen: There's something there from your childhood.

I nodded and wiped my eyes. I was surprised that she knew that, but also comforted that she connected so immediately without me having to explain. Maureen gave me another minute to compose myself then started trying to normalize my experience.

Maureen: It's ridiculous what singers do! It's ridiculous to ever want to feel vulnerable, ridiculous to ever want to put ourselves in that position of exposing ourselves, you know, and you see these singers at the master class all week voluntarily exposing themselves in such a way

Joan: Yeah. But I think it's what being alive is.

M: It's true, so just stay home, as the pitch goes up, don't go up into the heart chakra—scary and vulnerable there—just let the pitch go up. But you stay home.

This was a remarkable experience for me. I had approached this vulnerable place before in previous voice lessons, but each time my voice started tightening and the tears welled up, I had withdrawn. I felt so ashamed that I would be seen in my vulnerable state—as if I was completely exposed, standing there naked with nothing to hold onto, or hide behind, or protect myself with. I was ashamed to be seen so completely and deeply, fearing I would be judged and rejected. Some of those feelings were threatening to overwhelm me again, but the tears in Maureen's eyes let me know that she wasn't judging; she saw me, and saw my vulnerability, and accepted them. Her intuitive understanding—that something deep within me was being touched—helped me resist shutting down my voice and myself, and trust her enough to stay with the process.

Hearing her tell me I could "stay home and not go to the scariest place" was also very significant to me. Part of my fear of judgment and rejection came from my own judgment and self- rejection. "Staying home" was not easy for me to do since I was used to abandoning myself at these vulnerable moments, rejecting myself for being weak, vulnerable, or broken. When I took my first voice lessons I was so entrenched in this self-rejecting attitude that I simply could not stay with myself. I wouldn't have even known what it meant to try. However, through my last few years of counseling studies, and through doing my own therapeutic work, I had come to realize how damaging my self-rejection was and I had been consciously trying to stay with myself. Her suggestion that I "stay home" was the reminder I needed to work against self-judgment in this vulnerable state, and try not to project my judgment onto Maureen. Her gentleness and visible emotional connection to my vulnerability were also examples to me of how I could be compassionate with myself as I faced something shameful and frightening.

Maureen had me stand up and led me back to breathing and vocalizing, this time asking me to be aware that the sound was being made by two tiny vocal folds flapping against each other in the wind. She held two fingers in front of my face as a focal point and asked me to keep my awareness totally on the "noise maker" while I inhaled and exhaled. I tried, with mixed results.

Maureen: Does that work at all for you—keeping your awareness [on the throat]?

Joan: I felt it less helpful than when it was on my abdomen because I'm already going to grab things in my throat.

M: I was thinking that you might be able to stay there, focusing on the vocal folds, rather than trying to escape… That's where the noise is made regardless of the pitch, so why go anywhere else?

I tried again, but there was another "escape" point in my voice where I lost contact between the voice and the breath, and there was a break in the sound. Maureen suggested it was probably a register change where a different part of the vocal chords engage. We continued working with an ascending swoop, changing focus back and forth from the abdomen to the vocal chords, and a few times I was able to connect to both at the same time and a more consistent sound would pop out.

Annika, who had been listening and offering the odd comment but not teaching as actively as Maureen, then introduced one more concept—that of raising the soft palate at the back of the roof of the mouth. I have heard this described a number of ways, most commonly as the cool feeling at the back of the throat when you take a deep sniff of a rose and the soft palate lifts in response. Annika cautioned me against using an extreme method such as the sniff or forcing myself to yawn. These methods would put me into a rigid set inside my mouth and produce a hard surface that wouldn't be good for resonating. Her way of helping me raise the palate was to stand behind me and gently pull up on both ears which manually raised the palate for me. As she pulled up on my ears I was to gradually bend my knees so I was going down into a half squatting position, and sing an ascending scale on an "ahhh". Bending my knees was to help me maintain an image in my mind of staying down as the pitch went up and help me access my abdominal muscles.

As Annika stood behind me pulling up on my ears, Maureen stood in front of me with one hand on my abdomen and sometimes a few fingers on my throat. I felt a little claustrophobic with that much physical contact, but focused mainly on the feeling of my throat opening at the back from the ear pulling. I maintained the lifted palate half way up the scale and then felt it pulling closed against my will. I tried to resist the closure, some times more successfully than others. Annika could also feel it through my ears, and described it as an internal struggle that I finally won in the end. It seemed to me that this was an example of "my body not lying"—part of me was really afraid of opening myself that vulnerably and it was looking for another "escape route," as Maureen called them, this time by lowering the palate.

Maureen reminded me again that I didn't have to go to the scariest place. I could stay home and focus on the deep muscles in my pelvis, opening and widening, allowing the sound to drop down into my body. I was actually more "at home" thinking about my soft palate being open than the nether regions, but I think her strategy was to keep me from fixating on the part of me that was in danger of tightening which, in this case, was my throat. She asked me to inhale a tube of colours, I chose blue and silver. These colours would fill a narrow column down to my pelvis as I inhaled, make a turn at the bottom and come back up my spine and out the top of my head as I exhaled. Maureen and Annika had both used this image of inhaling a tube of colours throughout the master classes and it seemed to help some students. I got caught up trying to analyze it briefly, knowing my breath couldn't actually move up my spine and wondering just what they meant. I use images a lot myself when teaching, but they are images that have presented themselves spontaneously to me through my experiences. I realized how tricky it is to use images in teaching because the student might focus on a different part of the image than you intended, or interpret the image in a different way, or not connect with the image at all. Yet if you ask a student what something feels like in her body, she will more often than not respond by giving you an image of it rather than a technical description. So it seems that images are part of most people's thinking and are useful in describing sound and sensations. It's just a question of finding images that can be mutually understood and carry the right focus.

> Maureen: If you have the courage this time when you're inhaling the colours and exhaling the ascending "ahhhhh" sound, just keep your eyes with me and I will help you. Usually your eyes go up straight to the ceiling and then they go around like mad— zig zag zig zag.
>
> Joan (laughing nervously): Come on, I'm looking for help!
>
> M: It seems like you're saying, "Get me out of here!" There's probably all kinds of past life adventures under that, that have to do with what you're trying to work through.

I tried a few more breaths and swoops, realizing how embarrassed I was to look Maureen straight in the eye. She continued to remind me to try and look at her, thinking it would help me focus the sound and stay home in myself. I tried several more times, going in and out of focus with the sound as well as finding it very difficult to look her in the eye for more than a second at a time.

> Annika: It's really interesting, I can feel it from your ears that your throat wants to close.
>
> Maureen: I feel it's when the fear comes in.
>
> Joan: It's funny, because I can feel something in me closing it against my conscious will—it feels like fear.

A: Well part of it is habit too, I mean those muscles aren't used to it, and it's strange to get both ends of your body together because they are opposites—it's hard to touch them both—the depth down low in your abdomen and the space up high in your head.

M: It's like patting your head and rubbing your stomach.

J: And to stare you straight in the eye at the same time!

Maureen told a joke to dissipate the tension, and when I tried again I was determined to look her in the eye. Over the next few tries I looked her in the eye more, and finally did one swoop where I stay connected to her eyes the whole time.

Maureen: You didn't seem scared!

Joan: Yeah, I didn't. It was better!

M: Such a relief.

J: You absorb it all don't you?

Annika: Maureen absorbs it all incredibly—she gets the sensations.

M: Yeah, I absorb all the fear you're throwing off—right at me!

J: Oh, I'm sorry.

M: That's alright. It's just how I'm made. But you weren't afraid that time, and it was very nice. It seemed that it helped you stay focused on my eyes.

That was an understatement! I felt that I had jumped a huge hurdle by staying focused on Maureen's eyes and letting myself be seen in them. I had the sense that she really had helped me up the scale—ascended it with me and not against me. This was another miracle of trust and acceptance for me, since it is so hard for me to believe that people are with me, supporting me and not judging and rejecting me. It took several tries, but once I had settled into her eyes I drew strength from them and felt much more calm. She could feel the absence of fear as well as hear it, and Annika could hear it and feel it in my ears as the struggle lessened of my throat wanting to close.

As I listened to the tape of this voice lesson, transcribed it, and re-read the transcript to analyze my experience, it struck me how little this lesson had to do with music and how much it had to do with my body. I had taken and taught many years of flute lessons, and been through breathing exercises in that context. Sometimes there was a small amount of physical intervention from the teacher, and instruction to pay attention to what it felt like to breathe, but the goal was to get on to the flute and the music. The focus was predominantly external—learning how to manipulate an instrument held outside of your body, in your hands and against your lips. In a voice lesson, so much time was spent feeling the breath and being aware of your body. If you worked through all that and actually sang, you weren't supposed to listen to yourself, but to focus on the sensations in your body. The focus was completely internal—something new and shaming for me who was very distant from my body.

As noted in the introductory chapter, I was raised in a context similar to Annika's where I was encouraged to cut off from my body and live from my head. I was unaccustomed to paying attention to what my body was feeling, and actually quite afraid of it. It was beginning to make sense to me why earlier voice lessons had been so hard for me. They challenged me to move into my body, which went against years of conditioning, body habits, and moral beliefs, and it scared the life out of me!

Introduction to Student Interviews

We now move to the data collected from five of the students present at the master classes. I had one-hour interviews with each of these students and began each interview with the question, "What does 'being in the process of freeing your voice' mean to you?" I have quoted their answers to this question at the beginning of their interview material. I asked the students a few questions about their vocal journey and they provided information about themselves and their vocal backgrounds which shed light on their experience of the master classes. I also asked some questions directly about their experience of the master classes, their private lessons with Annika, how the teacher-student relationship affected their vocal progress, and how they worked through vocal blocks. (See Appendix B for further details of questions asked.) These were informal, semi-structured interviews so I did not ask all questions to all students, but adapted the interview to the responses I received to what I had observed of the student in master classes and private lessons.

The following are summaries of the interviews with the students, combined with my observations of them in master classes. Pseudonyms are used for all students and identifying information has been changed to protect their identities.

Student Interviews

Lisa

Freeing the voice is "learning to sing with the total instrument as opposed to what we understand in the western world as singing from pop culture and speaking voice. It's always done in a small range—small volume. Learning how to use the entire instrument and to let it resonate—to be able to use it freely to interpret the vocal literature."

Lisa, a Canadian singer in her late thirties, started voice lessons at the age of 15 when she had a chance to sing in a high school musical. Beginning at age 16, she spent a few years studying with the same renowned Canadian voice teacher that Annika did and, in fact, looked up to Annika when they were both teenagers studying at the same conservatory. She learned some things from this teacher but, in her words, "She's a tiger! She's scary! She used to terrify me! I liked her being honest but she was sometimes just a bit too brutal for me… I was only 16. It's different when you're 25 and you've got a great big ego. I needed more love and support."

Lisa found that this teacher "used a lot of imagery that didn't work for me. She used to talk about balancing on tight-ropes and being at the top of a water spout… but she never gave me any kind of understanding of how you breathe. There's nothing wrong with knowing a little bit of anatomy." Her teacher used to tell her that she was "too scientific" in her approach, which might have been a true statement with regard to singing, but she was on her way to university to become a medical doctor where a scientific approach was an asset.

Lisa stopped singing for the entire time she was in medical school. When she was 26 she had a life threatening tumor removed from her chest and was very depressed afterwards. She thought at the time, "I'm only 26 years old and I might die, and I don't think I've ever done anything that I've ever wanted to… If I come out of this I'm going to change some things." During the depression that followed surgery she was looking for something to make her feel better and decided to start singing again. She was excited to start again. "It's like everything that I've been missing, the whole half of me that's been cut off and hasn't been used— singing is the way I can get to it. It's something special for me and takes me away. I don't have to think about all those other things that I do during the day. It's an escape. I go to a different place."

Lisa was glad to be singing again but she never felt that she had learned to breathe properly and she struggled to find a teacher who could explain it in a meaningful way. She knew there was a problem, because "I had only one dynamic level—I couldn't go really loud or soft. There were these singers who had that glorious sustained, beautiful ebb/flow, and they molded the phrase, and I couldn't do that. I thought, 'I'm not singing, I'm just kind of talking.'"

She finally found a teacher who gave what her scientific, medical mind needed—a technical explanation of how everything worked anatomically. "He was the first one I ever got real concrete advice from, and exercises designed to try and help me free up some things." (Refer to the section on breathing for further details of Lisa's experience of breathing at the master class.)

Master Class

The first time Lisa sang in master class she had a very serious look on her face. Her eyes were fixed open in what appeared to be fear and her mouth was drawn tight. She held herself stiffly, turning her whole body as a fused unit from the waist up, looking as if she was on the offensive, bracing herself for a fight. Her sound reflected this tightness with a covered quality that pulled her below the pitch in the upper register. Annika asked her what she was thinking. Did she really want to sing? It appeared that part of her did not and that part was affecting the part that did. Annika asked her to say the phrase "I want to live" several times, trying to get her to take hold of the meaning of the phrase for herself. Annika explained that our negative

110

thoughts send messages to our body which hamper our singing. The impression I had from watching and listening was that Lisa was working very hard and concerned about getting everything "right," which must have been Maureen's impression as well, because when they first began working with Lisa, Maureen said, "Now, let's have fun with it!" Lisa was singing a boisterous opera aria with a humorous text and lots of flashy coloratura passages. Maureen encouraged her to think about the text and the dance-like quality of the music—anything that would help her tap into its energy. Since Lisa was still having trouble letting go of her tight control, Annika asked the whole class to dance around the room while Lisa sang from the stage doing some limited sway-dancing of her own. This helped all of us feel what the music was really about, since we were then connecting it with our own bodies, but it was hard to tell how much Lisa's performance of the piece changed since we were so preoccupied with our dancing.

After Lisa left the stage and sat down in the seat in front of me she turned around and said, "If you're looking for someone with vocal blocks to interview for your study, I'm your person. Sometimes I'm just a brain on a stick!" I asked her during our interview what she meant by that and she replied, "I was just thinking about how I can get so stuck... You know, you can really let your head eat you up." She referred to how impressed she was with another singer who had shown signs of struggle at the beginning of her master class session but had made an obvious choice to push the negative emotions aside and just concentrate on getting the work done while on stage:

> I sometimes start to feel so small and I can't do it any more because I can't stand it. My blocks are always mental. I think, "I can't do that, I can't let go, I can't be that expressive person." It's this immediately negative thought. I'm a pretty detailed person and if you try to make me be some loose, creative singer like the other singer we heard yesterday... if I could ever achieve that space I think that would be inner peace. It would be like that beautiful expression that Annika always has, that love of life. That's one thing I would like to take from singing into the rest of my life, that sort of love and peace.

I commented to Lisa that maybe singing was her way of trying to get to the place of love and peace, and she responded:

> Yeah, maybe that's the avenue—I can't really see any other way of getting at it. You approach singing in the way you approach every other problem in life. I'm very diligent. Why else would I do this at this age, still trying to figure it out? I still want to learn and figure it out because I get this huge emotional benefit when I do. It's like flying; it's like this pure joy. When you get it right it's just fabulous. So it's those moments you have to feed off [of].

I asked Lisa how her singing life fit with her life as a medical doctor, and she said:

> I always feel like I'm two different people—the singer, and then Little Miss Anal Doctor, detailed control freak. When I'm at work I think about holding myself in good posture. I see all these people slouching and I think, "You're only 40 years old,

stand up straight! Look like you like yourself!" I'm always kind of marching around. I'm very busy. I always get a headache on my work days and have to take an Advil. I hold myself very stiff. People tell you terrible things about how sad their lives are, and you have to take it all in, and you try not to internalize it but some of it does get you. So I get very stiff and find it very difficult to relax enough to sing on those days. Although on occasion I have come home and sung during lunch hour and it was fabulous—I feel so happy, like I've had the most marvelous break. In my off time I'm quite a bit more free and relaxed... my singing self is part of my "off time" self.

A day after this conversation Lisa sang again in master class. From the moment she walked on the stage she appeared less rigid in her body. Her sound was brighter, her face less frozen, and she was able to take a lighter, faster tempo. Annika and Maureen immediately congratulated her on the change and were quite surprised that she could be so markedly different from one day to the next. The whole class responded with enthusiasm that she seemed to be much more alive, musically and physically. I asked her about the difference afterwards and she said that she realized through our interview the previous day that if music was her road to peace and love, then she needed to approach it that way and get back to reaping the benefits. It was very satisfying for me to hear this, and to have seen first hand how a person's mental state can so completely change their vocal expression.

Control

Lisa obviously realizes the stiffness and scientific self of her working life affect her ability to loosen up to sing. However she does not seem to be aware how much stiffness remains in her body all the time, holding her back from a truly free singing self. The fact that she consciously "marches around holding herself in good posture" at work, a posture she admits is very stiff, sheds some light on her rigid stance at the first master class since, as she said, "You approach singing the way you approach any other problem." This fits with her thoughts about control in voice:

> I don't like being asked to lose control. I find it counter-productive... it comes as a criticism that you're a person who's uptight all the time... Control is already an aspect of my personality—a big thing for me... My best singing doesn't come when someone says, "You have to let go." It comes from saying, "Think yourself into the song more." When Annika said, "You have to lose control to gain more control," it didn't bother me so much because it wasn't a command, she was speaking in more generalities and she said, "You have to allow it to sing, you have to feel it," and maybe that feels like losing control but it's really gaining more control over the sound.

Teacher/Student Relationship

Lisa said it was important for her to trust her teacher. For her, trust was based on whether they were giving her accurate information:

It's important to trust... or you go home and think, "I wonder if this is right? That's probably part of my habitual stop-and-start thing, I think, 'No, no, no, that can't be right. There must be something different you can do.'" It totally destroys my whole musical idea. I'd be on tenterhooks the whole time thinking, "There's got to be a better way."

When I asked what helps her trust her present teacher she replied, "She taught me to breathe, the basis for all singing... She gave me information but she was patient and used demonstration, immediate positive feedback, and constant reminders of how to breathe."

It was also important to Lisa that the teacher figured out how to work specifically with her, and not overwhelm her with too much information or criticism:

> In those master classes when they're all over people... you could kind of see the frustration building on their faces. You just can't take that amount of information. I can't take it when my present teacher starts yelling things. "Do this. Do that. You can't do that." I'm just paralyzed. I feel like I'm being attacked, I feel like I'm being pulled to pieces by a pack of wolves! I get furious—really upset. She's only done it once and she must see that I get upset. She certainly has figured out how I learn best now.

This would explain some of Lisa's reactions to her first teacher, "the tiger" described in the opening of Lisa's story, and also her need for correct, anatomical information and a clear explanation without much imagery to suit her scientific leanings. As we will see in the stories of the other students, this is not the case for everyone. In fact, many singers thrive on a very different approach. Lisa's final words of appreciation—that her teacher has figured out how she learns best—is a good goal for all teachers to strive towards. That is, it is important to take the student's strengths and ways of being into account as they explain, correct, encourage, and try to build rapport.

Carolyn

"Freeing the voice is something that you never stop learning as a singer. It means trying to get through the technical obstacles—it's an ongoing process—and getting through the emotional things."

Carolyn, a 25-year-old Canadian who had studied voice in Canadian universities, opera programs, and privately in England, was one of the most advanced singers in the master class. She sang with confidence, had an energetic stage presence, and was very engaging musically. Carolyn, like most of the singers I talked to, had thought deeply about what singing meant in her life and whether or not it was worth all the work and struggle. The question came up for her while in University when she had been involved in two car accidents:

> [The first accident had left her] very disturbed. I had post-traumatic stress syndrome and I was really screwed up. I continued going to school pretending I was fine, and

then, at the end of my second year I had a break down and really freaked out because I had been trying so long to ignore all these feelings of fear and vulnerability and anger. I had whiplash and jaw problems and I didn't feel like I was getting recognition from people—I had a huge problem psychologically but the university didn't acknowledge it because I didn't have a visible injury, like a cast on my arm.

It is really unfortunate that Carolyn's voice teacher was not more aware of how her accidents could have impacted her singing, and did not refer her for further help:

> It is very important that a voice teacher knows about any major injury or illness someone may have suffered, in order to provide the best kind of work... Good osteopaths, orthodontists and Alexander technique teachers are valuable allies for a good voice teacher. Voice work includes working with the whole physical apparatus. (Rodenburg, 1991, p.63)

After a summer break and psychotherapy Carolyn went back to University and found it "easier to be more open and vulnerable, emotionally and musically—both go together." She was just starting to get back on track musically and personally when she was involved in another car accident, this time injuring her hip. That weekend the opera production opened and she was determined to perform. "I soldiered on... the show must go on, people were relying on me... It was like a true division of body and voice or... not body and voice, but body and emotions... My voice was not as open as normal. It took more energy [to perform] and I felt pinched or something."

Should I Continue Singing?

Her teacher during university, who was "harsh" and "not very nurturing," also affected Carolyn's vocal journey. Working with her was very frustrating:

> I never felt like I was doing enough and I thought I was the worst singer. I felt like, "I can't sing, I'm terrible!" I was really quite annoyed with singing. I went and did a summer program in New Brunswick that really gave me a new burst of energy for singing because the way this teacher in New Brunswick was teaching was much more connected... it just felt better. It feels nice to have that connection and I really started to embrace singing again.

The physical and emotional issues that emerged from the car accidents, coupled with the lack of connection with her primary voice teacher in university, caused Carolyn to "re-visit why I enjoyed singing. I went through that whole process of, 'Am I going to sing again? Do I really want to do this? Is it worth the struggle?' I finally decided that yes, it was worth the struggle. But it took a long time."

Joan: What helped you make that decision?

Carolyn: Just the fact that I enjoy it so much. It's like an addiction almost... Of course, I still have thoughts of, "Am I going to be able to make it in this business?" I think everyone does.

J: What does it feel like for you to be singing?

C: It feels really good sometimes. Not all the time, but sometimes… it's freeing. It's a bizarre feeling to have the sound coming out of your own body… I don't really have a concept of what I sound like, even on a tape recorder since my voice is quite big so it doesn't really [show on a recording]…I just like the way it feels. Sometimes when I really hit a sweet spot, like when everything's free and working properly, it's like you are able to just let everything go and it feels just so good to have the energy flowing in the right direction.

Another thing that helped Carolyn come back to singing was working on her identity and emotional life separate from singing:

I found that after the car accident when I couldn't sing I was very lost and depressed because I thought, "I can't sing so I'm worthless." I felt terrible because I couldn't sing. Coming back to finding the joy in singing was finding other things that I can identify or create as an identity for myself, you know it's not just the singing. Singing is a very large part but it's not everything. I want to be able to go kayaking, not as a singer but as Carolyn, who happens to sing as a career. Everything was a mish-mash before. If singing wasn't going well and I was tight and had a lot of jaw tension… I think it was a result of my emotional life… [Now] I've really tried to regard singing as a job, and still always bring myself into it, but not bring my problems of that day... If I've had problems I try to put them into a little box and say, "I'll deal with you later."

Control, Letting Go, Vulnerability

I observed Carolyn in a lesson in which Annika asked her to lie on the floor for some breath work. Then she gave Carolyn the image of "sending the air in a column up her spine" as she was singing an ascending passage that went right to the top of her range. Carolyn took the image of "sending the air up the spine" and thought of it as singing into her back. This had very audible results of the top notes sounding more secure and free, and not getting thinner as had happened with the way she was singing before. Carolyn describes the experience:

Carolyn: It really worked well to think that the sound was going into my back. It was quite extreme, not just a little change. It felt weird—great weird! I wasn't doing almost anything to make the sound, it was like just vomiting it out—there were no blockages. Obviously there was effort because I was doing things in order to make that happen, but there was no effort to make the sound happen, there was effort to make the tension not happen. It was pretty exhilarating. I'm at the point that I really want to let go… I've been treading on this line for a long time—6 months maybe. I don't think I would get this feeling of loving singing so much if it didn't happen and having a sense of control over when it happens.

Joan: Has the scariness ever held you back?

C: It's like something is holding, I think it's really even a deeper level of a conscious awareness, "No, I don't want to go there"… I can't describe it because I don't think you're conscious of when your body, or your everything just says "not today"…Whenever I'm really tired, in both therapy and singing, I'm way more free, because you don't have enough energy to have your guard up…I've done a lot of voice programs and a lot of them have been about opening up and letting go and this letting go and letting it all hang out—it's hard for me because I can fake it very easily on stage. I'm performing for you but it's not really that intimate for me, and I can do that very easily because I can act as well. I'm ready to go to the next level and I'm ready to bare it all, and it's scary but I'm ready. I'm getting all the tools here to peel layers off.

J: How does it show in your voice?

C: I can't tell what I sound like but I think there's probably a bit more soul, if you can understand that metaphor in voice, like a little more depth—a little less showing and a little more doing.

J: What does it feel like vulnerability wise?

C: It's really scary, like I'm very fragile right now, but it's also really neat—I'm teetering and I'm vulnerable but I'm not going to go over the edge, and I'm not going to go, "I'm too scared to do this," and hold back either. So it's like this nice line that I can explore more.

J: What would you attribute to being ready now? What's been changing in your life?

C: I think the fact that I decided that I wanted to sing because I liked singing and not because my parents had told me I was a good singer or I had a teacher who said, "Oh you could do this for a job." That did happen to me when I was younger because I had this big instrument and it was exciting, and I went to university, but it became this job and I really didn't enjoy it. I had to re-discover it as I've already told you. Knowing that I want to do it has basically given me so much more freedom because now I can just say, "I'm doing this for me, I'm not doing it for anyone else and if it works it works but I'm going to try my damndest to make it work." Maybe I needed to get to that level of vulnerability to proceed further and I think that maybe necessity is what made me open up.

J: Necessity helped you open up—would you say that singing is also a way to open up?

C: Oh, definitely, I mean it's so therapeutic… When I was a teenager I used to bang on the piano when I was angry, but now singing is almost the same. It gives me a sense of calm, and it's very therapeutic because it is physical. You can't help but feel it through your entire body so it's not just your brain anymore, everything's going "Okay, I can calm down, I can deal with this situation." I think a lot of the things I'm doing vocally are creating the vulnerability, and the vulnerability is creating the medium for me to be able to do the things vocally…They are going hand in hand like a nice circle.

Teacher/Student Relationship

I asked Carolyn what she needed in a voice teacher:

Carolyn: I don't work well under someone who is hard on me all the time, although I do want it sometimes. I want someone to really lay down the law occasionally, but I also like the balance of nurturing and some indication that progress is being made… and a real person, someone that's real and isn't a caricature of an opera singer, I just find that so false.

Joan: How much do you want to talk to a teacher about personal problems?

C: It depends on the rapport— you don't want to feel like you're complaining. You know singers, every little thing can be a problem, but I think it's important to be able to talk to your teacher about important things—because you can't separate things.

During the week of master classes Carolyn re-visited a deep personal issue that challenged her emotionally. Part of working through it was talking to Maureen about it:

Carolyn: This week is my Mom's death anniversary…and I looked at Maureen and I realized that she is very much like my mom in her frank manner, and I'm very much like my mom too. Maureen and I get along very well, we have a rapport and just the freedom of, "I don't care what anyone thinks of me," sort of thing. It's because of this anniversary …I'm feeling quite emotional. I talked to Maureen about it and she was very nice about it and understanding… I didn't want to sing today… it was really, really helpful talking with her, we had an intense discussion—intimate, didn't have to skim over anything. We just sang a little bit, it was good. It helped my overall trust in Maureen, and nice to know I have support… It's helpful for a teacher to be understanding and acknowledge how you're feeling and what's going on because if you start getting into this pattern of pretending that you're ok then you're holding everything.

Joan: What role does trust play in your relationship with your teacher?

C: Trust is definitely a big issue—I think that was one of the problems I ran into with my primary teacher at University. I went when I was young and I was so excited to be accepted into this great school for music and with a really famous teacher… I implicitly trusted her, I trusted whatever she said as "the law" and I think I ran into some troubles there because I trusted too much almost… You have to understand that they are not the only person that has something to say…With my present teacher he really pushes but I can also say, "Stop, that doesn't feel good." Or I can say, "Yeah, I can do this." So you have to trust your teacher but you also have to trust your own instincts. You have to be able to say, "I'm not comfortable, that's not something I'm able to do."

J: What about the use of language –how a teacher explains things?

C: I like the use of metaphors, I'm a pretty visual person. But I'm also very aware of my body and my musculature and anatomy because of the car accident, so I think it's fine to have a balance of the two. Sometimes a teacher will have a catch phrase that makes you go, "Ok, I understand that concept now that someone else has been telling me in a different way." The metaphor of "up my spine" really worked for me in the lesson with Annika.

Sandra

Freeing the voice for Sandra means:

> ... being able to sing freely without tension, singing in a voice that is really yours and it's not manufactured. You are able to sing from a deep place comfortably, and if you're not you need to look at something—find what issues are blocking you—physical tension, old anger, past histories, or not wanting to show emotions.

Sandra did not begin singing as a teenager, as was the case with all the other master class students I interviewed. Instead, she was involved in acting and studied theatre and English as a university student. She developed a successful career as a writer and editor and it wasn't till her marriage was ending in her early thirties that she felt that "the arts were missing" from her life, so she joined a community choir. The choir director noticed the potential of her voice and suggested she take private lessons. Sandra has now been singing intermittently for ten years and although she says it is one of the hardest things she has ever done, and she often thinks of quitting, she keeps singing and opening new parts of herself through her musical endeavors.

Master Class

Sandra was particularly courageous in one master class, singing even though she was feeling emotional, suffering pain from a deep massage the previous day, and not in her best singing form. This class was a good example of the way Maureen and Annika drew the best out of their students without using some of the demanding and damaging techniques common to many music teachers. Sandra described her master class experience:

> Sandra: I can only say that I wasn't crying because I was nervous. I was emotional, but I wasn't nervous, I wasn't shaking or I didn't have any of those fluttery nervous feelings. Mostly, the emotion was coming from the massage pain. I trusted Annika and Maureen that they would know what they could do with me if I wasn't in an ideal state... although I actually *was* in an ideal state because you know, I had my little cry in the washroom... we could get something interesting out of this emotional state, and this particular piece too, which was a French art song, kind of a sad, a bittersweet memory that someone was having, set in autumn, so it's kind of a melancholy song.

> Joan: What was it about Maureen's approach that was helpful to you?

> S: She let me just sing within myself, which is something I wouldn't have thought of because I would have thought that would have been self-indulgent. But it was a really neat point she made that when I first sang through the song I kept trying to project outward to the audience, but it wasn't working for that song, or maybe for me that day. So that really helped, just giving me permission to be introspective in that piece, then having me sit [Maureen asked her to sit on the stairs at the front of the church, looking at the floor with her elbows resting on her knees and her head in her hands] so that I didn't feel like, "Oh my God, what do I do with my arms? I'm out here alone on a stage!" I just sat, and as she said, "Pretend it's just you and you're just sitting there

talking," and then she added herself, "Pretend you're talking to me," [at which point Maureen sat down beside her on the step]. So suddenly it was not, "Here I am, a singer, and I'm performing this song and communicating an important emotion." It was, "This is me and I'm just telling a story." She was sitting very close to me which was fine. It was very grounding for me and it also helped me imagine that I was telling it to someone so it changed the flavour of how I was singing it. So it was helpful that way, and I guess also being emotional—sitting down is more helpful because then the breath isn't all stuck up here in your chest, so just from a physical point of view it might have been helpful in that respect.

Posture

Sandra explained at a later point in the interview that part of what was contributing to her emotional state the day of this master class was related to her ongoing struggle with posture and extreme tightness in her back.

> Posture has been the bane of my experience! It's a constant struggle… and it's not just singing, I mean my whole life has been a postural nightmare. From the time I was 16 and I was standing like a piece of wheat in the wind people were saying, "Stand up straight!" I have a very traumatic history about people telling me to stand up straight, so when I first started singing I felt like people were criticizing me all the time. I just went right back to my teenage years when I felt inadequate, when I looked ugly because I wasn't standing up straight… Now I understand that posture is integral to singing and so necessary… they're not criticizing me personally, it's that I have to get this right to get the voice I want. That's why I was frustrated yesterday (in master class) because I know how it sounds when it's right, and how it feels, it feels great. But I'm not there, I'm only there some of the time—it's kind of in and out, so it was a kind of a beating myself up moment, thinking, "When the hell am I going to get this!" So posture for me is just really hard. You know I've done everything—Rolfing, Alexander technique, massage, acupuncture, craniosacral, chiropractic, the equivalent of osteopathy. I have done them all and I've started to realize, especially right now at this workshop, that it's not about being broken and needing to go get fixed all the time, but that I need to adopt a daily practice. I need to do yoga or something as part of what I do every day, not just an isolated habit applied to singing.

Teacher/Student Relationship

I asked Sandra how other teachers dealt with her in emotional situations and she recounted a situation with her present voice teacher:

> I'm not prone to talking a lot about my personal life in my lessons, but we are personable… so I'm starting to sing this sad Italian art song, and I was going through a separation from my husband at the time which was very painful… and I lost it. I absolutely burst out crying which really surprised her because I might have mentioned that I was going through some stuff, but I hadn't gone into detail. So I absolutely lost it, you know, in a way that one couldn't cover up. She was very comforting. She went, "Oh, are you okay?" And I said, "I'm okay, I'm just emotional." She got up from behind the piano and came and asked me if I would like a hug. And then she said, "Well you know, there's no point in singing if you feel so emotional." I agreed and I told her why I got so upset—she didn't ask me but I told her why. So we ended

the lesson, which was the perfect thing to do. It wasn't like we sat down and had a big therapy session, but it was a great gesture. That's what I would want from a voice teacher. Some people would want less and some people would want more.

Sandra also said that she valued supportiveness in a teacher:

Supportive in terms of a teacher is someone who recognizes that you will often have more than a mere technical struggle with something, and as a singer, inevitably aspects of your personal life will bleed into your singing life. I don't think that's a bad thing. As you can see from the master class that I did, sometimes you can get stuff out of that. So that's supportive—for a teacher to recognize that will happen and have an appropriate and professional way of dealing with it. But that does not have to extend to knowing every detail of what's going on in your personal life. It also means she recognizes when there's an issue that's so big that she might have to say, "You might want to consider talking to someone about that because it's beyond my scope as a teacher to deal with it." This could apply to physical stuff too, like my teacher commenting on my neck and my posture all the time and saying, "You really need to go to yoga or something because we're never going to get anywhere because you're stiff all the time." Supportive is also a teacher giving you signs along the way that you are improving, and helping you set goals. Another kind of support that I really like is when teachers attend your performances.

Singing Authentically—What Has Held Her Back?

Sandra's definition of freeing the voice included the concept of "singing from a deep emotional centre" which she later described as singing "authentically." She described to me some of what she had to work through to access her "authentic self" in singing:

Sandra: I have a bit of a complex with my singing… I want to sing but I don't want to sing because people might think I'm showing off… My mother thinks what I do is showing off. Now she never said that to me, but I have picked up that she thinks it's showing off and I wouldn't quite say it's disapproval but the tiniest bit of feeling that the arts are frivolous. I've come around to completely the opposite conclusion, that the arts are essential and music and culture are how humans express themselves—the most fundamental way of people communicating with people. But for a long time it affected me. Someone once said to me that if you love singing and people want to hear you, you should get up there and deliver—or you're hiding your power.

Joan: How do you think that affects what you actually do on stage—the freedom of your voice?

S: It definitely affects it because if you are not singing from a place that is authentic, then you're not singing properly… Being afraid that I might be showing off means I would not be pulling deeply from myself, I'd be covering who I really am… I'd be putting a barrier between the audience and me—I'd be creating a façade.

J: That's interesting that when you sang in master class yesterday, something about having been emotional and then just being allowed to be in yourself—there was an authenticity, I felt like there was some sort of relief in being allowed to be yourself.

S: Yes!

Why Do You Sing?

I asked all the participants why they sang, but I was particularly interested in Sandra's reasons for singing since she had come to it later in life and had made several comments throughout the week about how difficult she found some aspects of it. She answered:

> To create beauty and to tell the human story over and over again, even if I am the only one hearing it. That's a good question because most singers I've been around say, "Because I love singing," and I never say that, which really makes me question my motives. Why *do* I sing? It's such a challenge. It's so damn hard! This is a weird kind of reason to do something, but I've never tried so hard at something and felt so constantly challenged by it. I want to give it up and then I don't want to give it up. Obviously I get pleasure out of it because I never really drop it, but I certainly want to drop it all the time, and that might be because I'm not getting enough pleasure from it because I'm not singing properly. I'm not singing freely, and certainly when you do, when my teacher gets me to do it or Annika and Maureen have done it here, you suddenly go, "Oh, wow! It's so easy and it's not hard work!" So many times for me it's bloody hard work… I guess another thing that attracts me to it is that it's performance, it's communicating, and it's theatre. I'm quite an intellectual, too, so you get to learn languages—expressing yourself in a different language, and it's about poetry—some really beautiful poetry. I think that's why I haven't gone back to piano since I started singing because piano is just piano, whereas singing is the melody and the text and the languages, and I just love all those challenges.

Control

In the area of control, Sandra—like other students I interviewed—said high notes were an issue. She described an experience of relinquishing control in a lesson with her present teacher:

> She got me to sing a really high note that's super free… it's kind of scary because it's so free, it's a new sensation. My teacher told me that she's had students who've experienced that and actually ran out the door because they were so frightened by it… it was so alien to them, that really free feeling, and probably because they had a voice that they didn't know was there, or it didn't feel like them, but actually that is the voice that's them—that's part of it too.

Further discussion of Sandra's experience of trying to let go of holding her breath, which was one manifestation of her struggle with control, is found in the section on breathing. I asked Sandra about her ability to go deep into the breath, wondering if the same need to control that was causing her to hold her breath would affect her ability to get low into the breath:

I don't have any problems with letting the breath go deeper now. I might have three years ago because I had all this emotional stuff. I did that music healing [referring to some workshops she had attended] and we did toning and stuff. It was so ready to come up and be dealt with—that deep stuff just came up. Now, since I went through all that, I can dig down there, and I also can feel it down there because before, I wasn't ready to deal with those issues. I wouldn't go down there so I was kind of singing from the waist up, from the chest up.

Julie

"Freeing my voice is about using my body, space, and breath when I sing. I need to trust in the sensation, believe in myself, and try to experience different sensations."

"Two Voices" in Master Class

Julie is a 22-year-old black Canadian singer who had recently completed her Bachelor of Music in Voice Performance degree when she attended the master classes. The first day of class each of the singers performed one piece as a way of introducing themselves to the class and getting the initial nerves out of the way. There was no teaching done that day and the only comments made were a few words of praise and support. When I heard Julie sing I wrote in my field notes, "It sounds like she's singing with only half of her voice—she's pinching off the bottom of her resonance. There is an obvious break between her little head voice and her chest voice."

The next time Julie sang in class, Annika and Maureen commented on the break in her voice and did some breath related exercises to help her open up the top of her voice, but she made little headway. After class I asked Annika and Maureen what they thought was going on for Julie and Annika replied that she thought Julie was doing some serious holding. She knew this because of her sound but also because she was complaining of back pains, so they had suggested she see a chiropractor. Maureen wondered if Julie came from a similar background to Annika, that is, whether she was taught to cut off from her body, contributing to her vocal tension. Julie had told Maureen in a private lesson that she knew that she needed to work on her confidence, thinking that would fix the problem. Maureen didn't think that "applying confidence" over top of what she was doing was the answer. She needed to get in touch with her body and sing from a deeper place which would feel more stable and free, thus naturally increasing confidence.

Avoiding Ethnic Stereotypes

Later in the week there was an evening performance given by Louise Rose, a Canadian black gospel singer. After the performance I gave Julie a ride back to her hotel and we discussed the concert. Julie did not seem as excited about the performance as a lot of the other singers had been. She told me that she never wanted to be seen as a singer "like that." When I asked what she meant by "like that," she said she did not want to be stereotyped as a "black gospel singer" and she did not want people assuming she was part of the black church subculture. We didn't have time to talk much more before I dropped her off, but we agreed to have a formal interview the next afternoon. Here is an excerpt from that interview:

> Joan: Last night you said something about stereotypes, not wanting to have that "heavy" voice of black gospel singers. What do you associate with that kind of heavy voice that you don't want to have associated with you?

> Julie: I guess the gospel sound, the black choir sound. It's so funny, I want some of it and don't want other parts of it. I would like to be able to have the agility [black singers have] but I don't want it to be assumed that I am a part of the stereotypical black church subculture. I don't want people to think, "Oh, there's the black girl, this is how the black girl should sound." I would ask them, "Why didn't you expect me to sound that way?" and they would never say anything, but I knew that's what it was. One girl said to me, "You should sound more black!" And I said to her, "How do I do that? I don't know what that means."

A student in the master class then told her, "You're black so you need to sound like Louise Rose." She was offended because she saw herself as a completely different person with a different sound. She cited a number of successful black singers she did not want to sound like and whose repertoire, like the song *Summertime*, she had purposely avoided in the past. Julie continued describing her feelings when people were surprised by her voice.

> Julie: In a way I like when people listen to my voice and go, "Oh, I never expected that sound to come out of her." Now I'm starting to realize that maybe that wasn't my true voice and that's why people thought it sounded different than they expected. I liked feeling unique but at the same time it didn't work for me.

> Joan: It sounds like you were trying to make something happen that wasn't really your voice.

> Jul: Exactly, and I don't know if that is just me trying to emulate a sound that I like, or if that's how I truly thought my sound was, because I have had moments when I have sung from my body and the reaction I get from people was, "Yes, we want more of that!" But I couldn't tell the difference. Even when I started this week and Maureen said it sounded like there are two different voices, I didn't hear that.

I asked Julie how much emphasis was put on her cultural heritage in her family. She said her family had taught her to be her own individual. However, some of Julie's black friends worry that she has cut herself off from the black community. "While I feel that I am a member of the black community, I am not interested in being a part of the black gospel church subculture. I do not want to be a gospel singer and I don't want to be labeled as that. I've almost gone to the extreme." However, Julie's interest in her black roots and heritage was sparked when her mother gave her a book of Jamaican folk songs. I commented to Julie:

Joan: It sounds to me that this could be part of where the two voices come from. You are on a journey to figure out how to integrate the "blackness" that you embrace and still remain separate from the stereo-typical black gospel church subculture.

Julie: Right! Yes, because I listened to Leontyne Price [a black classical singer] and I hear a rich sound but I don't hear the stereotypical black gospel sound by any means. Whereas if I listen to Jessye Norman [another black classical singer] I can hear it—I mean she's done gospel stuff. I listen to Mahalia Jackson [also a black singer] I mean it's beautiful. Oh, my gosh, what a big sound!

Identity as a Black Woman

Julie's vocal challenge of integrating "two voices" appeared to have its roots in wanting to avoid black stereotypes and to have a distinct, unique identity. This attitude showed up not only in her voice, but in her body image. Julie commented on an experience she'd had just a few months before the master class:

Jul: I was kind of laughing because I was looking at pictures of myself and thinking," I'm a black woman!" I'm shaped like a black woman. Obviously I knew that I'm not shaped like Caucasian people, but it was just funny to look at a picture. In the last few years I've gained a lot of weight which sort of bothers me, but it sort of doesn't because weight is not an issue for me. It's funny to be in university and to watch these girls have their little salads, and I was eating—food is meant to be had, and that's a very black thing. So I was looking at that picture of myself and I thought, "Well you know, I am a big person, I'm a black person, that's who I am." I had to laugh at myself.

Joan: Was that new to you? Seeing a picture of yourself and realizing that?

Jul: Well, Yes. I see myself as a person first, I'm Julie first, woman next, black third. Like the fact that I'm black—I'm not that first, and a lot of people who I've met, their blackness is what makes them, and that's not me.

Julie had recently attended a concert of a black singer with one of her Caucasian friends who told her he could hear some of the same colours in her voice. He meant it as a compliment, wishing he could have some of that colour in his voice. When he explained this it was the first time Julie had realized, "I'm already unique, I have this unique sound already just due to the fact of where I live—in Canada, with predominantly white people. In fact, I'm unique anyway. Everyone has their own unique sound."

Control, Vulnerability, Letting Go

Julie sang in another master class and it came up again that she had two separate voices, with the upper register being very thin and small with a tight vibrato, and the lower register having much more resonance, colour and depth. Annika had worked with her in a lesson on feeling the connection to the breath and deeper resonance of her speaking voice and "laughing" voice, and reminded her in class to stay connected to that part of the voice while she was singing. Annika encouraged her to "not worry about making bad notes—go for the sensation." In class Maureen worked with her "inhaling the sound" and carrying more of the weight of her voice into the high notes. She made noticeable progress in this class and her high notes were starting to have some body to them and sounding less disconnected from the low register. Following is an excerpt of the interview I had with her after the master class:

Julie: I used to feel that I had no control—I still kind of do, but in a different way now. I felt like I had no control over what would come out, even though I was completely controlling the sound, so of course I was completely singing from my throat and not from my body. My previous teacher used to ask, "Which singer do we have today? You, or your younger sister?" I was always scared of what would be coming out. I didn't necessarily hear this two voice thing, but I'm starting to realize it now by sensation. The sensation today [in class] was more trusting, just letting it happen, just setting myself and my body up the right way, knowing and trusting that it would happen and not trying to make it happen, because making it happen, really was not working for me. I heard the difference today—it feels bigger, but as I told you after the Louise Rose concert, I didn't want to have that stereotypical big sound. When I took lessons with the previous teacher I almost felt like a bigger sound was being imposed on me, and I wasn't sure if that was my voice or not, I couldn't tell. I felt pushed into having that voice and so I think that vocally I forced a lot, I pushed a lot. But today in class the bigger voice felt completely different. It felt more inside. The breath felt lower and deeper. I just felt like I had more space. It was like an out of body experience. A friend of mine described the breath while singing like "a wind going through her." I never understood what she meant until feeling it today. I just feel so open. It's scary sometimes to be that open because you want to keep a part of yourself, at least I need to keep a part of myself. I just don't want to give it all away. I try to keep certain emotions inside. I don't want people to be able to read me.

J: What kind of emotions are you more tempted to keep inside?

Jul: I guess it's partially a fear of not being accepted. I am always worried, have I offended that person? I want everyone to like me. I sort of realized that if people don't like my voice, well this is my voice... It feels like, you know you have an onion or a nut, and you've taken all the shell off and then it's like the most vulnerable part. I don't want to share that, which is funny because I feel like I'm a very open person just in life, but put me up on stage and that's where my introverted self wants to come out. My friends have always commented, "We don't understand how you can be so confident in normal life and then put you up on stage—it's like a switch of a person." I've had this sensation before but there is something in me that won't trust it enough. I think that I'm starting to now see the benefits of actually working within my own body. I haven't come up with the reasons as to why this scares me, the sound or the sensation. I think it's more of the sensation that scares me more than anything else, and I think it's just the lack of control because last year Meribeth Bunch (2000, *Handbook of the Singing Voice* referred to in Breathing section of this chapter) had us do this thing where we had to write down the things that are going through our brain as we're singing, and my one thing which I took with me all this year was that I wanted to be perfect... I don't know what that meant, I don't know what perfection means to me, but it just made me realize that I won't be perfect, so I guess I'm just sort of letting that go. It was just like letting go and just trusting that I don't need to control the sound to get the sound that I'm looking for because controlling the sound doesn't help me.

J: How have you been able to move forward a bit through that fear? Where is it the easiest for you to push that fearful boundary?

Jul: It would be here in master class. Just having Annika there to remind me helped me go through. Annika is very loving, and nurturing and she has that very motherly quality, and she makes me want to try to figure myself out. I don't know if she can notice but there are times when it doesn't really work, it's because I've gotten nervous, and my first instinct when I get nervous is to cry—that's sort of my defense mechanism. I'm not a risk taker in that sense of you know, jumping into the pool or skiing, I don't do those kind of things, that's not me. I'm a very "feel it out" sort of person, so I guess that maybe in voice I've always done the same thing, been very scared of taking risks.

Part of Julie's fear of taking risks and not being able to achieve the "perfection" she looks for manifested itself in a fear of cracking.

I say to myself all the time, "Do what ever you need to do, to not crack," and what I want to do is just hold it so that I won't crack, so it feels very tight in here [her throat], so then once I start getting frustrated it's the first thing that goes... actually doing that will probably make me crack even more.

Identity and Need for Approval

Within the context of her voice studies, Julie realized that a lot of her self-worth was wrapped up in her singing and that her singing was affected by her lack of confidence:

Julie: I have this real complex of not feeling that I am as worthy as the other people who are here [in master class]. I always put myself vocally on the bottom. I feel like I'm the one person who sticks out. For a long time I always wanted to prove to people that I deserved to be there, and I think it was me trying to prove to myself that I deserved to be there. I'm still working on that—I mean, I tell myself, "You have your Bachelor of Music! You can sing." People tell you, "You can sing," but there's still that fear in me that I'm always on the bottom... with voice I always have wanted to hear from a teacher, "Yes, that's what you are supposed to do, there is nothing I can teach you, you've reached perfection." And you're never going to hear that because there is always something to work on. So then I started to get rid of that and that's when I started to realize that the voice doesn't make me as a person. I made the voice "be" me, as a person. So if I was a bad singer, as I considered myself a bad singer, it therefore made me a bad person. It's something I still struggle with a lot and I just started to realize that I am not my voice. I almost wonder if that's why there's such a break [in my voice]. It's almost like I'm trying to escape from the fact that the voice is still mine, but at the same time it doesn't make me the person.

There is a close relationship between one's sense of identity and one's voice as seen in the literature review and in Julie and Carolyn's experiences. Julie and Carolyn both realized, for different reasons, their need to work at being able to separate their personal identities from their vocal identities to achieve more vocal freedom.

Shauna

"Freeing my voice is a huge technical process that comes with hard work and practice to acquire the technique to perform music with ease and the ability to express myself and my personal feelings. It is learning to channel emotions and let go."

Shauna was a 22-year-old voice student from Scotland who had been singing since she joined the school choir at age 14. She decided at 15 that she wanted to study voice seriously and possessed the self-motivation to enroll herself in a boarding school that focused on the arts and gave her many musical opportunities. Around the same time she heard Annika in performance and talked to her briefly backstage afterwards. She was so impressed with Annika as a singer and a person that she began corresponding with her. Annika, who is very gracious in her encouragement of young singers, responded to Shauna's letters and she and Maureen opened their home to her for visits. Shauna's parents had moved to the United States while she was in boarding school, so her visits with Annika and Maureen took on even deeper significance since they were accessible for frequent visits and understood and supported her in her vocal pursuits. Shauna was also trying to come to grips with her homosexual identity, and found Annika and Maureen to be accepting role models who were more understanding of this struggle than were her parents. With all these points of personal connection, Shauna felt that Annika and Maureen were like "aunties," giving guidance and a "safe" place to go when her parents were so far away.

Teacher/Student Relationship

Shauna did not study voice with Annika and Maureen between summer master classes and, although this was her third year of class with Annika and Maureen, she did not consider herself one of their students. She was quite definite about her boundary in this regard, saying, "I would hate to become one of their students because I would lose their friendship then. They're very close to me on a personal level, but I like to keep the music out of it. If I go to their house it's not music and they have never taught me." This being said, Shauna was struggling during this master class feeling that she was "crossing into" the position of student. This was affecting her emotionally and, in turn, affecting her singing.

Master Class

When Shauna sang in master class she performed well but made a small slip, showed her displeasure visibly on her face, and continued singing. While Annika and Maureen were working with her, Shauna was noticeably frustrated and, at times, acted sullen and disinterested. Annika and Maureen appeared to be struggling to engage her fully and then shifted the focus of their comments to a discussion of general principles of performance that were loosely related to Shauna but addressed the master class as a whole. Shauna told me that this also frustrated her because she wanted to get on with singing and their generalized discussion was keeping her from receiving as much personal attention as some of the other singers during their allotted half hour on stage.

In my interview with Shauna I asked her what she was feeling and thinking during this master class. She told me:

> I'm just beginning to wonder this year if I can't work with Annika and Maureen because I feel like I'm crossing over. I'm dealing with that on the stage and it makes me angry. I feel like I'm letting them down in a bigger way than if I didn't really know them or didn't care. In the master class I wanted it spot-on perfect. I feel I have something to prove or show because I've had a year's gap (since I last sang for Annika and Maureen) and that's the only time they hear me. I started singing and thought, oh, this sounds like two years ago. I am very lucky to have Annika and Maureen, I've put them on a pedestal because to me they are also my idols and I want to be so careful with them, I kind of need them.

Shauna's raised expectations of wanting to impress Annika and Maureen, and her strong "self-criticism," made her "angry and frustrated" and tightened her upper body—shoulders, throat, and jaw, so that, "everything is held, even my voice, and it's on the verge of tears. Then it shakes, so there is a lack of control." When her body tightens, as part of her emotional reaction, she senses her voice as," cloudy, tight, trapped, and small." She feels her breath change "going higher and higher. I can't go deep. It's held." When she realizes where her breath is she gets angry with herself and jumps to judging herself, thinking, "I can't do this on stage. I know it's because I'm not doing something—I'm being lazy somewhere, or I'm incapable, maybe I'll never have what I want in my voice."

One sees how a small mistake on stage, when the expectations and need for approval are high, can lead not only to self-critical thinking but to tension in the body and breath, which further constricts the voice and compromises performance. Shauna said she is always waiting for someone to tell her, "Your voice is fine, it's an instrument that will sing." She says that if she doesn't have what it takes to be a singer, "I want to know now rather than letting me go on struggling, because singing is not easy and I'd stop now if I knew that I would never have the top notes." When teachers give her some of the reassurance she is looking for she says, "It helps, but I still doubt them. I'll think, 'That's right now, but I'll do it tomorrow and it will be gone,' or I'll think, 'I had to do all this work, maybe it won't happen on stage.'"

All the singers I interviewed agreed that it is difficult for a singer to have a true concept of what they sound like because they hear it from inside their own bodies where the sound is being generated. This is more disconcerting for some singers than for others. Shauna sees it as another reason to doubt herself: "I know that other people hear me differently. What I hear in my head is very thin and I don't want people to hear what I'm hearing because then it sounds like I shouldn't be singing!"

Trust

Trust has been an issue for Shauna in working with various voice teachers:

> I haven't trusted my teachers; that is why I've had so many. My teacher now, I would say I trust the most but even then there is something as soon as I feel anything that hurts, I'll tell her straight away—that's a part of me not trusting. She knows there is a bit of that, and then I don't trust myself either so there's a combination of the two.

Shauna says that the main thing she struggles to trust is that what they are instructing her to do won't cause her vocal damage. This is always a concern for singers since they have to trust their teacher to coach them towards a sound that they can't hear objectively. They also have to learn by sensation, but the way one person describes sensation does not necessarily correspond to how another person experiences sensation.

Control

When asked about approaching a vocal block, or something that was difficult for her, Shauna said that she struggled with high notes. She felt that when she attempted to sing high "there's nothing to hang onto."

> It's taking a risk, like when you let go and you're not quite at the other end of the swimming pool and you don't know whether you'll ever reach the edge. You could just go down and drown, but I could also swim. I might not swim there, I might struggle to get there, but I don't know for sure that I will. I'd like to be closer to the edge of the pool, or never to have been thrown in!

I have sought to present the main themes that emerged in each of the student interviews. Certain themes were similar across the interviews, in part because of the questions I asked (see Appendix B). I analyzed the themes partially as I presented them here and I will do further analysis of the material in Chapter Five.

Breathing is a prominent, consistent theme throughout—in Annika's journey home to her body, in my voice lesson, and in the student interviews. Breathing is central to singing and to re-connecting with one's body and emotions. Therefore I have chosen to highlight breathing in a section of its own, presenting data from interviews, observations, and my personal voice lesson experience, and integrating it with relevant vocal pedagogy literature.

Breathing

"Trust in your breath. It is the lifeline for the voice" (Arman, 1999, p.47).

Everything begins with the breath. "The mechanisms for sustaining life and sustaining voice are intricately bound up together. Our lungs give us the breath, which supports our life; they also supply the breath stream on which the voice rides" (Martin, 1996, p.261).

Whether singing or teaching others, Annika began every master class, private lesson, and pre-concert warm-up with the breath. Whatever technical issue she was addressing, she always brought it back to the breath, agreeing with Maureen who maintained, "If you get the breath right, there is the potential for everything else to free up." When Annika and I listened to recordings of her voice from her early twenties, her analysis led back to the breath. "I do believe that those problems [tongue tension, not being able to focus the sound more narrowly] were all a manifestation of not being able to breathe properly. Because my breath wasn't working for me, and it really wasn't low enough in my body, that was where it got stuck." Therefore, to free the voice we must focus first on freeing the breath. Annika believes we all instinctively know how to breathe if we can just trust our bodies:

> We must trust in the body's wisdom and get out of our own way... We are all born knowing how to breathe deeply into our bodies, and somewhere along the way we have lost our way.... I think that everybody knows and can re-connect to the breath. There are so many blocks, physical and emotional, that get in the way. It does seem very simple really, just trusting that your body will respond, that your vocal chords will respond, that your breath will go where it needs to. It's a process of getting out of the way.

Annika asserted, throughout the process of coming home to herself through freeing her voice, that getting low enough in her body with the breath was the key. In my voice lesson, and in the experience of the master class students I observed and interviewed, the releases and discoveries, vocal and emotional, were connected to deepening and freeing the breath. Moreover, as we saw in the review of music therapy literature, the breath plays a large part in "the re-inhabiting of the body" and in controlling our emotions (Austin, 2001, p.24). Therefore, it is essential that we examine breathing in our exploration of the experience of freeing the voice.

Breathing is also very controversial. "More than any other area, the field of voice and singing is fraught with differing perceptions of how the act of breathing occurs" (Bunch, 2000, p.11). Alexander, founder of the Alexander Technique, said:

> Surely no organ or system of the human body is at present completely understood anatomically or physiologically. It would be difficult however, to single out one vital organ concerning which more has been written, on which more lively differences of opinion are still expressed in print, and of which more remains to be learned, than the mammalian lung. (Alexander cited in Alcantara, 1997, p.90)

The differences of opinion are due to multiple factors. A few cited by Alcantara (1997) are: faulty sensory awareness (see the Alexander Technique in Chapter Four for further explanation), the tendency for people to breathe "badly" and assume it is natural when it might be habitual but quite unnatural, and the fact that it is very difficult to observe natural breathing accurately. In the account of my voice lesson and that of some of the master class students, I noted the limitations of language to adequately describe what one experiences while breathing. This is due to the variety of meanings that can be derived from a particular description, and often from an inaccurate use of terms (p.91).

Richard Miller (1977), a well respected vocal pedagogue and author on vocal technique, sees part of the controversy being the national differences in approach, as he explains in *English, French, German and Italian Techniques of Singing*. McCallion (1988) suggests one of the reasons for the proliferation of breathing techniques:

> is the fact that there are so many possible ways of performing the act. The equipment is so designed that variability of its use is part of our natural adaptability to changing circumstances. We change our breathing in response to emotion, and each emotion has its breathing pattern. (p.43)

The "many possible ways of performing the act" of breathing are described at great length by Miller (1977, 1986, 1993), Husler & Rodd-Marling (1976), Titze (1994), Vennard (1967), and Bunch (1993, 2000) to name a few of the well-known vocal pedagogues. One thing they all agree on is that one must understand some basic anatomy to understand breathing properly, so their descriptions are accompanied with anatomical diagrams displaying the lungs, muscle groups, and passageways that make up the breathing apparatus. Husler & Rodd-Marling (1976) say "the mechanics of breathing is a problem requiring on one hand the detailed knowledge of a classical anatomist and on the other hand the analytic understanding of an engineer"(p. 49). Bunch (2000), who has had a great deal of influence on Annika's views about breathing in the last few years, says, "to understand this action, first study the anatomical description of respiration. This will form a basis for objective observation, rather than dependency on hearsay and descriptions altered to fit the process of singing" (p.11). Annika agrees, saying:

> It is important to know what your instrument is. We can see very little of our instrument, unlike say, a brass or wind player who can easily take their instrument apart and examine exactly how it works. For this reason there are many misconceptions in the singing world, partly because many singers and teachers prefer to deal entirely in metaphors and sensations. They do it because they are ignorant of the anatomy, or they are afraid too much emphasis on physiology will inhibit the natural voice.

It is beyond the scope my research question to explore the numerous approaches to breathing and the debate between them. That would be a thesis in itself. However, since releasing the breath, resisting the temptation to hold the breath, and getting low in the body through the breath are foundational principles of Annika's teaching and her own experience of freeing the voice, I will examine breathing from her perspective.

Annika's philosophy of breathing has evolved over her lifetime of singing. It has recently been strongly influenced by her work with Dr. Meribeth Bunch, the noted vocal pedagogue and anatomist who has worked extensively with medical doctors and dentists and has dissected cadavers to understand the physiology of the breathing apparatus and the vocal folds. Annika and Maureen have developed their own techniques for explaining breathing and exercises to help students experience the breath. Annika described her philosophy of breathing in an interview and I saw her demonstrate it in master class and experienced it for myself in my voice lesson (see My Voice Lesson with Annika and Maureen for further details). Following is a blend of Annika's description, the descriptions of some of the master class students, my observations in class, and my personal experience of what it means to breathe in the context of singing. Annika began her description as follows:

> When you inhale what actually happens physically is that your lungs fill with air. As your lungs fill with air your diaphragm, that muscle that's attached all around from the front of the sternum around to the bottom ribs, going all the way to the back—the diaphragm gets displaced by the air which causes it to go down. It's like a balloon—the lungs get filled with air which pushes the diaphragm down and all the internal organs—everything gets displaced. If you're in a relaxed state your lower belly looks like a balloon because everything gets displaced down there. If you're allowing the breath to go down deep enough then you can breathe all the way down to your pelvic floor. So the inhalation—we encourage to go very, very low and we think of it as being in our lower belly, where our entrails are, 5 finger widths below our belt buckle. That is sort of where our engine is, where the breath drops down from. That is also the place where the energy comes from in Tai Chi.

Bunch's (2000) definition of breathing is essentially the same, except she is speaking in medical terms instead of the simplified metaphors of balloons that Annika uses for teaching:

> For an easily produced voice, the inspired air must silently pass through a spacious, free throat and wide open vocal folds, into a chest in which the upper part is stable, not rigid, and the back and lower portion is flexible and mobile to permit lateral and posterior expansion of the rib cage. At the same time, the abdominal muscles need enough stretch in them to allow the downward excursion of the diaphragm. During expiration there is a recoil of the elastic lungs and trachea, balanced and slowed by a combination of maintaining good posture and active contraction of the muscles of the abdomen. When the head, shoulders and hips are aligned, the breathing mechanism performs these actions with minimal energy and without muscular compensation or physical or vocal distortion. (p.13)

In order to get us to feel the breath deep in our bodies, Annika and Maureen had all of us participating in the master class stand with our backs flat against the wall with our knees half bent. Standing in this position releases the muscles of your lower abdomen to breathe freely without pressing. Then we moved away from the wall and squatted right down on our haunches, and were told to breathe deeply while looking at our crotch. In this position we could see that we were, in fact, breathing right down to our pelvic floors. We also lay on our backs on the floor and placed our hands on our lower abdomen to feel the breath at work down low. (See the account of my voice lesson for further description of breathing while lying on the floor). In a subsequent class we got down on the floor on all fours like a dog and, as we inhaled, gravity helped pull our abdomens towards the floor. During the exhalation, it was clearer that the abdomen wanted to contract to expel the air by pulling up away from the floor.

Annika and Maureen often used the phrase "inhale the sound," meaning that the singer was to inhale with the same openness, posture, and freedom she used when she was going to exhale. Annika stressed thinking of "a lovely column up your spine" which was to be maintained at all times. The column of air that was inhaled from the soft palate down to the pelvic floor, then sent back up the spine on the exhalation, was likened to those toy plastic tubes filled with liquid and coloured glitter that swirl when you shake them. Singers were encouraged to focus on this column or tube of colour when inhaling and exhaling and to fill it with colours that suited the energy and style of the music they were about to sing. Annika described the breathing column as follows:

> The column is our breathing column, where the sound is. It's an imaginary thing, and it remains the same width from the bottom to the top.... It's air, it's posture, it's also colour, because we can create colours in that column of sound where our air goes up and down.... It's like an artist having a palette and choosing colours depending on what song it is, and how you would like to hear your sound. For instance, if you're singing a Handel aria with lots of florid passages, it might be rather nice to fill your column with blue and silver strands because it will give image and colour. And, as singers, what we have is images to respond to... Colours are a very, very powerful thing. Colours have different vibrations and we respond to them, therefore it's not a surprise that the sound that is formed as we think about colour will also affect our thoughts.

Annika uses the concept of colours when working with her students and has good results. One of her young students used this concept in preparing for a music festival, and after her performance the adjudicator commented directly on how lovely her vocal colours were!

The language about maintaining this "lovely column" and "sending the breath up the spine" was also used to image the posture to be maintained during inhalation and exhalation:

> You always want to physically stay in position so that your column never gets scrunched up... As the balloon increases as you inhale, your rib cage is naturally going to go out, and as you exhale it will come in but you don't want it to collapse. What you want to do is work your lower abdomen muscles more to keep a steady flow of breath and send the breath up and not collapse the ribs in the process. It will go down a bit anyway, but you don't want this motion of an accordion—then the body shrinks.

There was one singer in master class who quite visibly collapsed her ribs like an accordion as she exhaled, and her chest caved in slightly and her shoulders moved forward. In order to help her sense what her body was doing, since she was completely unaware of this collapse, Annika stood behind her and placed her hands high on her ribs on either side. As the student sang in her usual way with ribs collapsing, Annika provided resistance against this motion by pulling up and back with her hands on the ribs. This intervention gave the student a physical understanding of what her body was habitually doing, and what it should be doing. (See the discussion of the Alexander Technique for further explanation of impaired body perception.)

In a subsequent master class with the same singer, who hadn't completely broken the "accordion" habit, I was asked to stand back to back with her as she sang (since I was the same height). She and I together monitored her tendency to collapse by concentrating on always having our whole backs touching, especially at the top of the ribs and the shoulders where she was tempted to pull away during an exhalation as she collapsed forward. It was suggested that she should sing with her back against a wall to self-monitor while practicing at home. It was a very interesting experience for me to stand against her and feel her body breathing in connection with her sound, since it vibrated in my body and not just in my ears, giving me the sensation that I was doing the singing. That might be the closest I ever come to feeling the exhilaration of a free singing voice, and it was glorious!

This idea of "refusing to collapse" reflects a view of breathing that agrees with that of the Alexander Technique, but which is at odds with the common view of controlled breathing or "breath support." Michael McCallion, (1988) author of *Voice Book*, who also follows the Alexander Technique principles, says:

> Support for the voice is strength with direction, and it comes about when the breathing muscles are working in a state of co-ordination with a good head/neck/ back relationship. To put it simply, it is the refusal to collapse, and the physical means whereby you make your breath last as long as you want, at the pressure you need to make whatever sound you want, whatever volume, pitch and resonance is called for. (p.41)

Seen in this light:

> Support is not something you do, but something the contrary of which you inhibit—a non-doing rather than a doing (p.94)... *Let* is the operative word. This applies to both the inhalation and the exhalation, which Alexander wrote should be, "a controlled movement which allows the air to escape, not a special effort to 'drive' it out." The most important thing about breathing then is not to do it, but to allow it to happen on its own. Ideally breath 'takes itself' rather than having to be taken. (Alcantara, 1997, p.97)

Annika speaks to this "letting out" of air and "non-doing" in the following description of the exhalation:

> As soon as you start letting the air out, the balloon is going to go down (deflating). Now this is the bit where there are pushing out techniques which Maureen and I feel very strongly against. Pushing out techniques cause a lot of tension because, if you don't go along with the flow of the natural way of breathing, you're causing tension rather than enhancing the normal flow of the breath. What you want to think is that the muscles, way down in your lower abdomen, are involved in the process of letting that air out as the balloon goes down.

"Breath support" is a term that Annika rarely uses because, in some schools of breathing, the phrase is linked to the "pushing out" techniques she is trying to avoid. However, "breath support" is the term used by many teachers to describe the exhalation as an active suspension system for the voice to ride on, without being a forced or rigid "pushing out" of the air. The struggle to find terminology and imagery that carry the same meaning for teacher and student is very difficult in the area of breathing. This was evidenced in my voice lesson when the exhalation was described to me as a "tucking in" or "pulling up" sensation in the abdomen but I experienced it as a pushing out. In master class there was similar confusion among the students when Annika and Maureen came around to each of the singers, placed their hands on their abdomens, and tried to help them feel the muscle action as they exhaled. Lisa, a master class student who had a clear grasp of anatomy from her career as a medical doctor, said:

> Although I think their description of breathing seems to be working, what they're saying and what I'm doing isn't quite the same. That's what I think the problem is, because their description of the muscle kind of coming up, sucking in, and pulling, creates a lot of tension. I don't truly think that's what they're doing—when Maureen put my hand on her stomach it wasn't going in, it was staying out in the same place and the muscle was going in, so it was suspended but moving and elastic –that's what my other teacher talked about—the elasticity of the muscle, the rebound, always ready to move when it's needed.

When I described this confusion to Annika, she explained:

> The pulling up I was just describing to you is that if your lower belly is relaxed and you're opened to your pelvic floor in your inhalation then as you exhale that area is going to contract and the motion of the breath moving inward and up the spine, in a column… that is the correct motion. What you really don't want is that as soon as you start exhaling you push out as if you were about to sit on the pot and have a really big poop. And that is pretty much how some people are taught, and also in those words. Another term that's used for that is "a bearing down." It is very important to stay very grounded and to stay low in your body, but if you're actually pushing out and causing that tension it will effect the instrument, as I was describing about the air pressure too, it will interfere with the air pressure. If you are lying in bed and you're very relaxed, just watch what happens… your tummy will fall when you exhale. Many people as they start to make the motion conscious, either because of what they've been taught, or sometimes because they're thinking very hard about the breath and thinking about what to do, they will actually go contradictory to the very basic natural motion, completely the opposite so that when they exhale they try to make their stomach bigger.

Richard Miller (1993) has adopted the Italian concept of the *appoggio* technique of breathing, which literally means "to lean upon," for his description of "breath support:"

> It is a special method of managing the breath for the tasks of singing, in which the gesture of inspiration resists the gesture of expiration… the upward movement of the diaphragm and the inward movement of the rib cage are retarded. (p.25)

In *appoggio* breath, "suspensory muscles in balanced tension… provide necessary resistance to economize the exhalation of the breath" (Reid, 1983, p.13).

McCallion (1988) provides a concise description of the process of exhalation in the context of singing, which is anatomically clear and avoids the "pushing" imagery:

> As you breathe out during vocalization, the abdominal muscles shorten and pull the ribs down. If the breath is not to be pushed out in a great whoosh, the rib muscles and the muscles which support the spine need to resist this downward pull, otherwise the whole rib-cage slumps towards the stomach, the spine bows and the out-breath is uncontrolled—collapse has occurred. The important thing to note here is what is happening to the spine, because if the spine is maintaining its lengthening tendency the rib-cage cannot collapse downwards. However, the ribs are left free to move. During the out-breath, the ribs, which are anchored to the spine at the back and to the breast bone in the front slightly rotate (or depress) while the lower ribs move in towards the centre of the body. This has the affect of making the chest noticeably narrower from side to side and slightly narrower from front to back. But the chest is not seen to slump in the slightest, the shoulders are completely uninvolved and stay open and still. How much the ribs move will now depend on the intrinsic strength of the rib muscles and the quality of sound you wish to make from moment to moment. (p.41)

According to Annika, the constant flow of air in the exhalation is what makes a free sound:

> You never want to interfere in the exhalation, because if you stop the air it's very hard to get in motion again without causing a lot of tension. There is some pressure from below the cords which is balanced from another pressure from above the cords and what you want is a perfectly consistent pressure to go through those cords to create a free sound.

This corresponds directly to the definition of a free voice given to me in a personal interview (June 25, 2003) with Professor Bruce Pullan, Head of the Voice Department at the University of British Columbia: "A free voice is the antagonism between breath pressure and resistance… achieving a coordinated balance between two opposing forces." It also agrees with Giovanni Battista Lamperti in his book *Vocal Wisdom*:

> Singing is accomplished by opposing motions and the measured balance between them. This causes the delusive appearance of rest and fixity—even of relaxation. The singing voice in reality is born of the clash of opposing principles, the tension of conflicting forces, brought to an equilibrium. (p.41 & 116).

We have discussed the inhalation and the exhalation, but perhaps one of the trickiest aspects of the breathing cycle is the point between the two. Annika explained:

> The inhalation to the exhalation is also a very important time because you don't want to stop the breath at any point and set the voice for the upcoming phrase. Breathing is one continuous motion that should never stop. [Between] the inhalation and the exhalation there is a turn about, but the whole thing is one fluid motion.

Throughout the master class Annika pointed this out to many singers, who would take a breath and then hold for a split second before they began singing. This moment of hesitation, which involves closing off the air stream by tensing muscles that should not be engaged, is common for young singers but must be eliminated because it introduces unnecessary tension. To demonstrate the continuous motion, voice teachers often have students move their arms in one long fluid line or a large unbroken circle while inhaling and exhaling. This gives them a physical picture of the continuous motion of the breath, even though there is a turn-around point from inhalation to exhalation where the air changes directions. Some use the image of a swing, saying that there is a point at the top of swinging up that the motion changes direction and you begin swinging back. At this point you don't consciously hold, or stop the swing. You just keep riding with it and the direction changes itself.

Joan Patenaude-Yarnell (2003) uses the adage, "Begin singing on the gesture of inhalation," meaning that the direction of the inhalation helps coordinate breath pressure and vocal fold tension. She also encourages singers to think that "the tone begins where the inhalation ends" (p.185).

Sandra, one of the master class students, explained her habit of holding her breath:

> I've struggled with holding my breath, which is basically—I keep trying to control the experience. I have that kind of attitude. "If I can really get control of this song, I can get it just the way I want." You can't really do that if you want to have a free voice. It's kind of a funny balance. Breath for me was, and still is, about holding it, and then trying to control it, and learning not to do that, and to breathe more deeply.

Sandra said that her ability to go deep into the breath was affected by emotional issues she had held in her body and breath for years. She resolved these emotional issues through a vocal healing workshop and was now able to dig deep into herself, her body, and her breath, which contributed to new vocal freedom:

> One of the most common faults in breathing is the following pattern; breathe in— hold—breathe out... The hold disconnects us from an organic and releasing breath position... This hold can also stop us from communicating a vital emotion, like showing rage at an inappropriate moment or the way we fight to hold back tears. (Rodenburg, 1992, p.146)

This connection between breath and emotions is very apparent in music therapy literature. Austin (1998) believes that singing is "a way to access one's deepest self... intimately connecting us to our breath, bodies, and our emotional lives," and that the voice is "like a bridge that we can connect the mind to the body and heal splits between thinking and feeling" (p.316). She also states, "The way we breathe influences how we feel, and what we feel has a direct effect on how we breathe" (Austin, 2001, p.24). Rodenburg (1992) cites examples of clients who had blocked and sealed the memories of sexual abuse by habitually holding and controlling their breath. When they "found themselves breathing without barriers to contain them, deep pain, deep experiences were suddenly released" (p.89).

Reid (1983) explains that the breathing and vocal problems of many singers occur for emotional reasons which result in a "failure to release expiratory tension:"

> A basic human characteristic is to erect defenses against anxiety by restricting respiration (hence the sigh of relief when danger, real or imagined, has passed). Consequently, natural inspiration, which is perfectly automatic when expiratory tension has been properly released, is impaired. (p.44)

> The entire body, and especially the respiratory system, responds to pleasure by expanding and responds to fear and anxiety by contracting. When expansive movement is encouraged during training, the anxious student will often respond to the feelings aroused by inhibiting the respiratory function. The specific nature of this physical inhibition is an inability to fully release expiratory tension (holding caused through fear of 'letting go'), with the result that both inhalation and exhalation become shallow. It is the "holding" through inhibition that lies at the root of many singers' vocal troubles. (p.49)

Reid (1983) attributes the physical inhibition to "an inability to fully release expiratory tension" or a "fear of letting go." The inhalation is affected by this tension, but it is in response to the tension of the exhalation. Therefore, the key to freeing the voice, and perhaps the starting point of the breath, should be thought of as the exhalation.

Everyday expressions, such as "I'm not holding my breath over the outcome of such and such" or "I let out a big sigh of relief," reflect the emotional tie to the exhalation that we instinctively feel. Rodenburg (1992) has encountered clients who, upon discovering buried emotions when encouraged to exhale freely, unexpectedly started screaming or sobbing. When we feel the need to hold back emotion—screaming, sobbing, rage, telling someone what we really think of them, or even letting ourselves know what we think of ourselves—we hold our breath. Rodenburg (1992) says that "It is a breathing habit very common to women who are neither listened to nor respected" (p.146). It's also true of anyone who is unsure of their own ideas and feelings, who hesitates or "edits" what they express. Cognitive self-editing translates into a physical manifestation of tension in the exhalation. Since the voice is activated by the movement of air through the vocal cords, if the exhalation is disrupted or inhibited, the voice is also.

Anytime we silence or strongly limit part of ourselves we are creating tension in our bodies and our psyches as we try to hold that part of ourselves quiet and out of sight. It is like holding an inflatable beach ball underwater. Even though the ball is out of sight, it takes a great deal of energy to hold it under the surface. Holding part of ourselves in uses up energy that we could be using for other more important things like honest expression and healthy development and living. It also puts us under constant tension, never able to relax fully, or act spontaneously, because we might lose our grip if we do anything out of the ordinary. We carry this tension in our psyche and in our bodies and it will show up in our singing voices, possibly as a held or pushed quality or, in my case, as a very tight throat that held the breath and allowed only a thin sound out. The beach ball of banished needs and feelings usually succeeds in eluding our control once in a while and then it erupts out of the water with a splash of overwhelming energy, making an even more embarrassing scene than if we had allowed it to float freely on the surface. The fear of these explosions causes us to tighten our grip even further, physically and emotionally. The fear of re-living those deep experiences or having that shameful part of us exposed keeps us holding them "under our breath." This costs us in physical tension and lack of emotional, physical, and vocal freedom.

Voice teacher Wormhoudt (1992) claims, "Breath control is ninety percent courage" (p.10). He could have been referring to the courage needed to use air freely while exhaling, not compromising the tone quality by conserving air to make sure you can get to the end of a phrase. However, I believe that the courage necessary to inhale expansively and exhale freely for singing is the courage of re-connecting with one's body and feelings and facing whatever is being held below the surface of one's psyche.

Transition to Chapter Five

Breathing is the foundation of singing. We have discovered that getting deep enough in the breath and body requires opening up to new experiences and sensations, and can bring one in touch with buried emotions. Freeing the breath and releasing vocal and emotional inhibitions are processes of change involving several steps. In Chapter Five we examine the process of moving towards freedom of self and voice, and further analyze and synthesize the themes that emerged from the student interviews, Annika's life, my voice lesson, and the master classes and lessons.

CHAPTER FIVE

SYNTHESIS

Moving Towards Freedom

Flying in the Air: Singing on the Air

> *"If I get stuck in who I am now, I will never blossom into who I might yet become. Today's identity is tomorrow's prison. I need to practice the gentle art of surrendering and letting go"* (Keen, 1999, p.16).

As I climbed and looked up, the thirty-one feet to the top of the rig seemed a long way. By the time I reached the platform and looked down at the net and the floor beneath, the distance had doubled and words like *abyss, chasm, void* came to mind. The primal fear of high places began to take me over... My hands began to sweat and adrenaline flooded my system... He handed me the trapeze, told me to stand tall, lift as high as I could, bend my knees, and ease my feet off the platform... I dove into the ocean of emptiness. My arms snapped like a bow that had suddenly broken a string, but the pain was brief and I was quickly lost in the pleasure of swinging. (Keen, 1999, p.12)

Sam Keen (1999), former professor of the Philosophy of Religion at Louisville Presbyterian Seminary, and former Consulting Editor of *Psychology Today*, decided at the age of 61 to pursue a childhood dream of learning to fly trapeze. In his book *Learning to Fly: Reflections on Fear, Trust, and the Joy of Letting Go,* Keen "traces his life journey that led him to respond to the lure of the trapeze... and shares what his five years of intensive practice taught him about living" (book jacket). Keen faces his fears while flying through the air. He learns to let go of the trapeze and be caught by another flyer. The external physical pursuit of trapeze flying is a vivid metaphor for the risks, fears, and letting go—and the resulting freedom—experienced on the more internal journey of a singer learning to free her voice. I will refer to Keen's insights and "trapeze wisdom" as a metaphorical guide throughout the following discussion of control, letting go, trust, and vulnerability as they pertain to freeing the voice.

Why Do We Sing?

Annika, Maureen, the accompanist of the master class, and I were discussing what drove singers to take the emotional and vocal risks they do to free their voices. Maureen talked about a number of deep issues that she had recently resolved, and joked:

Maureen: I don't have to sing any more because I've resolved the issues. So often I think we sing because there are things that need resolution around the parts of us that sing or the emotional things that make us sing.

Joan: Singing is the reason that you're trying to keep resolving all this stuff, to get totally free?

M: Yes, that's right. We [herself and Annika] are both seekers, inveterate seekers.

J: And singing is the vehicle?

M: Right.

Accompanist: People do it in different ways—visual arts, or buying and selling companies.

Annika: But [singing] is much more real because it's in your body… you can mask things while painting that you can't mask singing.

J: So it goes both ways. You had to resolve these things because you had an internal need to keep singing, and you sing to resolve these things.

A: It's the inner desire, the determination to move forward in my path whatever that is. And some peoples' determination to move forward in their path is much less than others for various reasons. Their fear takes over and they're not driven.

Master class student, Lisa, came to the realization during our interview that singing was the one place that she experienced "joy and peace" and the avenue that allowed her to cultivate more of that in her life. She explained, "Why else would I do this at this age? I still want to learn and figure [singing] out, because I get this huge emotional benefit when I do. It's like flying; it's like this pure joy. When you get it right it's just fabulous."

Carolyn, another student, described singing as, "It's like an addiction… Sometimes when I really hit a sweet spot, like when everything's free and working properly, it's like you are able to just let everything go and it feels just so good to have the energy flowing in the right direction."

Maureen's pithy summary of the meaning of singing in her life was, "Singing is the way we have chosen to work out our lives." Ironically, Keen (1999) experienced the art of trapeze in a similar way. "Sometimes the practice of trapeze peeled away the outer layers of my psyche and allowed me to look more deeply into my self than I had been enabled to do by either philosophy or psychotherapy… The trapeze… showed me what lies beneath my surface" (p.117). Trapeze flying, singing, buying and selling companies, painting—these are quite diverse activities. The similarity is that they can become a means to self-discovery and growth, which is the same process whether one is flying through the air or singing on the air. It is a process of facing fears, feeling vulnerable, trusting enough to let go of control, and landing in a freer place that is one step closer to being "home" with ourselves.

Facing Ourselves

As I look back over Annika's vocal journey, the students' stories, and my own experience of attempting to free the voice, I see that all of us had to face ourselves as we worked towards vocal freedom. As we re-connected with our bodies through the breath, and sought to release various tensions, we were re-introduced to parts of ourselves that we had hidden from ourselves, cut off from in shame, never considered worth developing, or of which we had been afraid. As these dis-integrated parts of ourselves were unearthed we were challenged to re-integrate them into ourselves if we wanted to move forward. Certainly there were technical challenges, but the core of the struggle, as many of us experienced it, was on an identity level.

Sandra learned to hide her personal power because of shaming messages from her family that to display it was "showing off." She did not say where this value came from in her family, but it is similar to the conservative religious view we examined that condemns pride and withholds praise from children to keep them humble. Unfortunately, it had the negative result of taking away Sandra's power and her joy in her abilities. "Being afraid that I might be showing off means I would not be pulling deeply from myself, I'd be covering who I really am... I'd be putting a barrier between me and the audience; I'd be creating a façade." Sandra has been facing this hidden part of self and claiming her power as she is concerned less and less with the opinions of others.

Julie had not fully come to grips with her identity as a black woman and strongly rejected the stereotype of a black gospel singer. The audible break between her rich low register and a very small head voice reflected her attempts to keep the resonance she associated with black gospel singers out of her voice. Her challenge was to fully embrace her identity as a black woman, and her inborn voice which naturally held the colour and depth common to voices of people from her ethnic origin. Perfectionism also made it difficult for Julie to take risks and try things she might not do perfectly. I don't know the origins of Julie's perfectionism, but it is likely connected to shame, based on her feelings of being exposed "like a nut that has no shell," and of seeing herself as being at the bottom of the class, not worthy to be there and needing to earn her place.

Shauna was very uncertain of her abilities and was always looking for external approval. She wanted a teacher to tell her for sure that she had a "fine instrument that will sing." When teachers did reassure her she said, "I still doubt them. I'll think, 'That's *right now*, but I'll do it tomorrow and it will be gone.'" Her strong need for external approval, and her inability to accept or believe the approval she received, speaks of a struggle with self-rejection, and most likely shame. Shauna wanted things to be "spot-on" to prove herself to Annika and Maureen. These perfectionistic expectations of herself frustrated her to the point of not being able to interact appropriately in master class. She had a lovely voice, but accepting that for herself and giving herself the approval she needed was difficult for her to do and was causing a lot of turmoil on her road to vocal freedom.

Lisa said she "didn't like to be asked to lose control" and admitted, "control is already an aspect of my personality." This need for control showed in her rigid posture, her tightly controlled sound, and her sensitivity to correction. As we will see in the following discussion of control, taking risks, and letting go, Lisa's need to stay in control is counter-productive to the process of freeing the voice physically, emotionally, and musically.

Carolyn had already come through a number of roadblocks on the road to vocal freedom, particularly facing fear and vulnerability that were amplified by post-traumatic stress syndrome following her first car accident. During the time she wasn't able to sing after her accident, she realized:

> I was very lost and depressed because I thought, "I can't sing, so I'm worthless." I felt terrible because I couldn't sing. Coming back to finding the joy in singing was finding other things that I can identify or create as an identity for myself. It's not just the singing.

Carolyn had to re-balance her identity to embrace more of herself than just her identity as a singer. She also had to face the grief she was still feeling about her mother's death two years earlier. She had a particularly emotional time during the week of master classes since it was the anniversary of her mother's death and Maureen reminded her of her mother. Fortunately, she didn't try to hold in these feelings. She allowed herself to let go and be vulnerable emotionally in conversation with Maureen, which also helped her let go vocally.

For me, the journey towards vocal freedom had awakened shame, pain, and perfectionism, and challenged me to re-integrate my sexuality and re-inhabit my body. My road, as a heterosexual woman, was a different road than Annika's, but we both had to re-connect with our bodies and accept our physical and sexual selves as part our journeys home. Annika also dealt with shame and guilt, and still battles feeling "not good enough" at times. She still fears rejection at auditions. But she has worked through the need to prove herself to or please others, and now sings to please herself. She has released some of her life dreams and has come to accept her vocal career in the way it is unfolding, which has resulted in a more consistent, centered sound, and the freedom to embrace teaching and encouraging the next generation of upcoming singers.

The process of coming to vocal freedom, as Reid (1983) describes it, begins with "challenging inhibition stemming from anxiety that contact is about to be made with deeper layers of feeling." Inhibition defends against anxiety and contracts us physically, which protects us from contacting the deeper feelings. Vocal progress, however, requires more expansive movements than our contracted body allows:

> Emotional inhibition is a common cause of serious vocal problems. If these self-imposed limitations are to be overcome, the singer must face the fears aroused because of expansive movement and risk the consequences. While to do so requires courage, for those who dare, the rewards are highly satisfying technically, artistically and personally. Those who prefer to remain bound by their inhibition, however, and can never learn to sing freely. (p.159)

Ristad (1982) says:

> It takes courage to leap into the unknown. It takes an act of will to become vulnerable enough to explore scary, unknown territory in our minds and bodies… It takes will power and courage to suffer the turmoil of change. As long as we return to our old habits/formulas we will not take the step into unfamiliar territory. (p.198-199)

In my early experience of voice lessons with Michael, an act of the will was not strong enough to break through the resistance my body had against going into the unknown. I wanted to learn to sing and showed up faithfully for voice lessons with my music prepared, yet I was frustrated that I wasn't making any progress. In Annika's words, "The 'fear took over' on a subconscious level and kept my throat shut and my breath tight. My body had a mind of its own, and in its own wisdom was protecting me from accessing unhealed wounds and deep feelings of shame."

Master class student, Carolyn, explained her experience of a similar unwillingness in her body as being "like something is holding. I think it's really even a deeper level of a conscious awareness, 'No I don't want to go there.' I don't think you're conscious of when your body just says, 'No, not today.' You know you're not ready for it."

Master class student, Julie, talked about her progress being blocked by the desire for perfection, because the desire to "do whatever she had to, in order to keep from cracking" tightened her control. Julie realized the more she controlled her voice to avoid cracking, the more she cracked. Yet it was a risk to loosen the control and she "wasn't by nature a risk taker… jumping into the pool or going down a ski slope—that's not me."

Learning to Fall

Voice instructor Ron de Jager, of Briercrest Bible College and Seminary, says one of the first things he does with voice students is push them to crack, to help break their fear of cracking and reduce their expectation that they must sing perfectly. It helps them learn that it isn't catastrophic to crack, and they can trust him not to judge them when they do (Personal interview, Oct. 8, 2003). In trapeze flying this is the equivalent of the principle that you have to learn to fall before you can learn to fly:

> In my premature enthusiasm to fly free, I had violated a fundamental principle. Learn to fall before the trick; prepare for the failure. From the moment when a fledgling accomplishes the first free fall, progress in flying and falling go hand in hand. I had come to the point where I could not risk flying higher until I had mastered the art of falling (p.108)… It is clear that the great flyers have always been great fallers…. Thomas Edison failed a thousand times before inventing the light bulb. If you aren't failing frequently it's because you are too timid or too stuck in your rut to try anything new and risky. (Keen, 1999, p.110)

A male master class student provided a great example of "learning to fall" when he attempted some high notes that were a big risk for him. Annika commented, "It takes tremendous courage to go there… this student went up there in class and he made all those cracks and awful sounds but he was going for it. His determination was way beyond his fear."

How fearful can it be to crack while singing, in comparison to flying high above the ground on a thin metal bar, then letting go and taking your chances that another flyer will catch you in mid-air with split-second timing? At first glance the physical danger of the trapeze appears far more worthy of body-gripping fear. However, with the way I felt trying to pry my voice open in front of Michael, and the struggle in which I saw some students engage in order to open to another level of freedom in their singing, I'm not sure the fear was so different. Keen (1999) says:

> Fear is an inevitable part of the human condition. Because we are all flying through time toward oblivion, we grasp and hold too tight, squeeze the life out of life. We conspire to avoid awareness of our primal fear, our anxiety about existence, by cultivating the illusion that we are exceptional, invulnerable, immortal, immune to the perils, sufferings, and tragedies that afflict lesser human beings... Each day befriend a single fear... We learn to fly not by becoming fearless, but by the daily practice of courage. (p.45)

The student who made "awful sounds and cracks" in class was engaging in the "daily practice of courage." He was traveling the only road there is to new freedom in his voice— straight through the vulnerable lack of perfection and the chance of looking and feeling out of control, so he could come to a freer way of singing. By the final concert of the week, only a few days after the master class, he had opened up a new place in his voice that gave him more power and resonance. This illustrated one of Annika's favorite maxims, "You must lose control to gain more control."

Lose Control to Gain Control

Annika and I discussed the meaning of this phrase:

> Joan: You've said a couple of times that "you have to lose control to gain it." Can you talk about that, and how it was that you discovered that to be true?
>
> Annika: We have certain holding patterns and things that are our safety nets. As one of the students said today, "It's like having a crutch that has supported me, it's been the thing that's held it all together." You are used to having certain ways of approaching singing, and then to let go of it is really, really scary. It's scary... when you haven't ever been there—you can only imagine it. You can sense it, you can sense it in other people, you can hear it in voices that are free so you sort of have a concept of it, but to actually know what it is like physically, for yourself, is really scary because you don't even know where you're going.

Alcantara (1997) describes the same struggle occurring in the practice of the Alexander Technique, of not knowing where you're going but having to let go and move towards it anyway. "Clearly there is a vicious cycle at work here. You cannot perform an act correctly until you have had the experience of performing it, and you cannot have the experience without performing the act" (p.43). Annika described the problem of wanting to hold onto control when what we really need to do is loosen control:

> A lot of the holding patterns happen because we hold our breath... You can take a nice deep breath into the body and then you go to make the sound and as soon as you start making the sound it's like, "I'm going to hang on." So that all of [a] sudden... it's a series of muscles that start compensating because what you've done is put the brakes on. It's like you want to hang on so that you can put your toe into the water first to see if it's going to be safe. And the only way that you can really ever find freedom is to absolutely let go of all those things. Sometimes there are a whole series of them. They happen sometimes in a row, but sometimes it takes a while because it's like layers, one thing goes and then there's yet another thing. To find that freedom... the potential of going wrong is huge, and yet the simplicity of it is so beautiful because it is so easy. It is the process of learning how to get out of our way and not hang on, and in that way losing control.

Keen (1999) flew by the same principle on the trapeze that Annika did on the voice with regard to control:

> Control in flying is mastered by giving up control. It is one of those perfect Zen meditations in motion. Giving up control is letting my body move with its own ease. My intellectual, analytical mind may know the biomechanics of movement, but it is too slow and calculating to direct it. My mind outlines the basic plan while I am still on the ground, but my body produces the movements in the air... To fly, the body must be guided by uninterrupted somatic wisdom. It is the grace of mind-body-emotion cooperation and union. (Lisa Hofsess, "A Somatic view of Flying," in *Somatics*, 1988 cited in Keen, 1999, p.146-147)

Trust and Letting Go

Keen gave up his mind control and trusted his somatic wisdom to know the way to move while in the air in much the same way Green (1987) in *The Inner Game of Music* describes letting go of control of the inner critic (self 1) and trusting the intuitive, body wisdom (self 2). Green (1987) explains that we feel more in control when we are listening to the critic and trying to do what it tells us, but we are bound with unnecessary criticism and instructions. When we are thinking about instructions we aren't completely free to be present to the music. When we give the control instead to self 2, the intuitive, body-wisdom self, it might feel out of control from the perspective of self 1, but we must trust self 2 to give a better performance. "We are not giving away our trust blindly; we are letting go of years of listening to music and practicing the physical movements involved... our body has stored away memories of every piece we've ever heard, and it responds directly through the nervous system, much faster than self 1" (p.98). Annika's trust in "body's wisdom," as we saw earlier in her description of breathing, is based on the same principle:

> There are so many blocks that get in the way... It does seem very simple really, just trusting that your body will respond, that your vocal cords will respond, that your breath will go where it needs to. It's a process of getting out of the way. If you keep

trying to get in there to help and interfere with it there is no way—it goes against the trust.

It's like the trapeze artist who has to let go of his bar and fly free for a few seconds before he knows for sure that he has been caught by the other flyer. This is what trust is made of— acting before we can see with certainty what the outcome will be, and trusting the rest of the universe (our body, the other trapeze flyer, God) to do their part. When I asked Annika exactly what she was trusting in and encouraging her students to trust in, she explained:

> Trust in the body and trust in the self is also trusting in God. It's even a bigger trust… Performance… is one of those places that it feels that heaven and earth connect because, when it feels right, it feels that all we are is vessels or channels. This whole thing of getting out of the way, of not being in the way, is allowing the Divine, God, whatever you perceive that to be, to connect to that Divine and out to the audience so that when that communication works—it's like a circle of love when that happens. It's like being a channel.

One can only be a "channel" of something bigger if one isn't pre-occupied with oneself. Hiding a shameful part of one's self, or being preoccupied with protecting against failure through perfectionism, or putting oneself forward in search of approval, are manifestations of some form of self injury that "gets in the way" of our bodies' and our selves' ability to be free to function naturally. It also gets in the way of being able to trust in other people or God to act with us, through us, or for us. It preoccupies us with ourselves and gets in the way of being completely present to the body, the voice, and the music. Letting go of these defense mechanisms opens us to the anxiety of being vulnerable to the things we are defending ourselves against—failing, being less than perfect, not receiving approval, or feeling our shame. These are the deeper layers of self that must be faced, accepted, and released to allow us to release the parts of our voice and bodies that are getting in the way of our freedom.

Freedom Feels Scary!

Maureen described an experience she had of loosening control and singing freely in performance:

> I felt like I was not doing anything… When it works for me, I'm in one way very present and in another hardly there… because I'm not controlling anything. It's a bit like being hypnotized, you're still conscious but not controlling. You get in the grip of the music and the flow of energy till you really are in the present moment and anything can happen with the music and your relationship to it and to yourself.

Carolyn also felt:

> Like I almost wasn't doing anything to make the sound. It was like I was just vomiting it out… it was just happening and there were no blockages… I mean obviously there was effort because I was doing things in order to make that happen,

but there was no effort to make the sound happen, there was effort to make the tension not happen... it was pretty exhilarating.

Julie also felt this sensation of "not trying to make it happen" when she "trusted and let it happen, just setting myself and my body up the right way, knowing and trusting that it would happen." She felt there was "a wind going through her," not that she was increasing breath support, just that she was letting it move. As she had feared, "It's scary sometimes to be that open because I need to keep a part of myself... I just don't want to give it all away... I try to keep certain emotions inside." She used the metaphor of a nut being shelled and the tender insides being exposed and vulnerable. This echoed the feelings of shame I felt when trying to open my voice with Michael.

Sandra also found the free sensation scary, "It's kind of scary because it's so free. It's a new sensation. My teacher told me that she's had students who've experienced that and actually ran out the door because they were so frightened by it... it was so alien to them, that really free feeling."

As we saw in the discussion about breathing, Sandra tried to control her musical experience by holding her breath. Her description of learning to "let go" of the breath was "kind of a funny balance. It's like you have to jump off the cliff and then your wings sprout, but you don't know that till you jump off the cliff—it's kind of scary!"

Shauna described the feeling of being in this process of letting go as being in the middle of a swimming pool, having left the safety of one side, not knowing if you will get to the other side, and having nothing to hang onto. I certainly felt the "nothing to hold onto" phenomenon in my voice lessons with Michael, and often held onto the back of a chair so I felt less unstable, less like I was floundering in the middle of the pool.

When Annika and I were listening to recordings of her singing from when she was in her early twenties, she made these comments about the fear in her body:

> You heard at the very end of the aria—which is very, very high—that I was pulling up out of my body. That anxiety never really came to me in the lower register... but it gets scary when it goes up there! As we've demonstrated so many times this week, the tension [you feel in these bodies] just all of the sudden, it's almost... incontrollable, sometimes it's so last minute, but that grabbing on, that holding on says, "No! I'm not going there!"

Letting Go—The Indirect Approach

So how do you get yourself or your student to go to that scary place of "losing control" with so much at stake, the place of so much fear and risk? I asked Annika if she ever told her students directly to let go of control:

> Annika: Yes, they say that it's very scary, that they are afraid of doing that. That has been their way of making their sound. They're going to have to find a different way which they don't know about.

Joan: How do you know they are holding?

A: Because I can hear it in the sound, and because I can see the physical manifestations, either the head coming forward, the neck tensing, the torso locking… there is no way that you can actually make it happen until you let go.

While interviewing Lisa I asked how she felt when asked to lose control:

I don't like being asked to lose control; I find it counter-productive… it comes as a criticism that you're a person who's uptight all the time… Control is already an aspect of my personality—a big thing for me… My best singing doesn't come when someone says you have to let go, it comes from saying "Think yourself into the song more." When Annika said, "You have to lose control to gain more control," it didn't bother me so much because it wasn't a command, she was speaking in more generalities and she said "You have to allow it to sing. You have to feel it." Maybe that feels like losing control but it's really gaining more control over the sound.

Thinking directly of "letting go" didn't help Lisa but focusing on something else like the song did. Similarly, Annika pointed out in the breathing discussion that many teachers don't want to discuss the anatomy of breathing or the vocal folds because focusing on it too directly and technically can cause more tension rather than relieve it. It's like when you're lying in bed not able to sleep; focusing on how much you should be asleep only keeps you awake longer. Michael tried to distract his students out of their tight control by asking them to write or walk while singing or catch things that he threw towards them. He also helped singers approach scary parts of their voices indirectly by playing vocal games such as attempting extremely high notes through giggling or making siren noises.

The title of Alcantara's (1997) book on the Alexander Technique, *Indirect Procedures,* speaks to the helpfulness in body work of an indirect approach. "The cause of wrong tension is most often the lack of right tension. In such cases it is fruitless to try to relax these wrong tensions directly; the solution lies in creating the right tensions, and letting relaxation come about on its own" (p.18).

Balancing Tensions

An indirect approach helps make relaxation possible, as does the balance of "the right tension." Annika and many others, including Keen (1999) in his role as the trapeze flyer, talk of "losing control" and "letting go," but by this they don't mean total relaxation of all control. A more accurate description is that of loosening control, or re-balancing the tensions within our control.

To use a sailing metaphor, losing control would be like having the rope yanked out of your hand by the wind while you trying to adjust the sails. This leaves you leaving you truly out of control and at the mercy of the wind and waves. If you are able to hang onto the rope and adjust the tension so that the sails are neither luffing loose in the wind, nor pulled so tight and angled that they catch too much wind and make you flip, then you are sailing "close to the wind." This is an in that exciting, playful place where you ride the wind at maximum power and maximum risk. If you set the sails in the morning as you take off from the dock and never adjust them after that, you will most likely be swimming before long, since neglecting to adjust for a lull or a gust will mean your sail is not set at the appropriate tension to counter the ever changing wind. One maintains a balance between the tension of the sail and the force of the wind through a supple strength and continual interaction and adjustment.

Keen (1999) expressed this concept of balancing tensions in trapeze flying as " the need to balance strength with strength... The Greeks understood this and made an ideal of *sophrosyne*—harmony or balance. The ability to grasp and hold firmly needs to be balanced by the ability to release and stretch" (p.66). Giovanni Battista Lamperti (1957) describes this concept applied to the voice:

> Relaxing a muscle is beneficial only to educate and discipline outermost muscles to do their part in the process. Otherwise it is weakening to the final output. It is co-action, not non-action, that causes controlled effort to feel effortless... Singing is accomplished by opposing motions and the measured balance between them. This causes the delusive appearance of rest and fixity—even of relaxation. The singing voice in reality is born of the clash of opposing principles, the tension of conflicting forces, brought to equilibrium. (Alacantara, 1997, p.18)

Being asked or told directly to "lose control" could be difficult for many people to respond to positively, not just because of the implications of being "uptight" that Lisa cited, but because people have developed control for good reasons. Vocal freedom is often hampered by the ways we hold our bodies under control in everyday life to protect ourselves, hide our inadequacies, drive ourselves to achieve, or make ourselves appear acceptable to the outside world. The struggle in learning something new, challenging a vocal block, or releasing tension is that we must change. Change involves going into the unknown, facing uncertainty, risking failure, and feeling fear. It tests one's sense of self. Is the self strong enough to endure losing the security of old habits? Is it resourceful enough to figure out new ways to adapt? Is it "good enough" to be acceptable even if this change is a failure? The risks involved seem great, but without risking and moving towards change, one's voice stays blocked and the potential of one's authentic self remains undeveloped, covered by protective mechanisms. Maureen's statement, "Singing is the way we have chosen to work out our lives," can be more fully understood in this light. Facing the fears that emerge through the process of freeing the voice leads us to face our selves. It is the self that needs to be freed and developed. The voice reflects that freedom while at the same time being the avenue to that freedom.

Annika said that, as a young child, her voice lesson was the one place she could "escape" from being the obedient child and truly be herself. Annika's road towards vocal freedom was a tough one, unearthing issues of sexual identity that affected family relationships and re-modeled her spiritual life and beliefs. She had much to lose, fear, and risk on this road, but said she gained the satisfaction of knowing she had been "true to herself." She continued down this road because "of an inner desire, the determination to move forward in my path whatever that is." She did not let her desire to grow towards freedom and fullness be overthrown by fear. "Change and growth take place when a person has risked himself and dares to become involved with experimenting with his own life" (H. Otto (1970), *Guide to Developing Your Potential*, p.8 cited in Emmons & Thomas, 1998, p.62).

Annika's "experiments with her own life" were driven by determination to move forward and they were supported by trust. We have seen, in her views on breathing and her descriptions of working with students who were blocked, that she returned repeatedly to trusting the breath, the body, and the self. She connected that trust to something larger—a trust in God or the Divine. "This whole thing of getting out of the way... is allowing the Divine, God, to connect to that divine, and out to the audience to complete the circle of love." Her partner, Maureen, had to work through yet another kind of trust - learning to trust the audience in order to complete the circle of love:

> It's taken me a long time to allow in the love from an audience to complete the circle ... For years I've felt overwhelmed by an audience energetically. It was massive, hundreds of people pressing against me, and I've had to learn ways of giving myself space. Once I learned how to give myself space, and in a sense protect myself from the onslaught of energy without cutting [the audience] off, then I could let their affection reach me. And, of course, part of it is the fear that it isn't affection that they have but judgment. That's also an aspect of trust... Each performance is at some level sort of life or death, and sometimes it has felt very keenly that way, I mean raw. In a good way I feel that it is the most important thing I'm doing and if I'm not going to give it my all, then why do it? But on the other hand... it has felt like it could just about kill me sometimes. It is often that vulnerable-making, that dangerous, that exposing.

Maureen is not alone in her feelings of sensing judgment from the audience. Sandgren (2002) discovered in her qualitative and quantitative study of opera singers that the psychological struggle most spontaneously mentioned by singers was how they related to the opinions of others about their performance. Along with struggling with the constant evaluation and judgments of others, and to some extent also with the accolades, "The audience was regarded as a whole, reacting unanimously to their performance, more in terms of being an enemy than an ally" (p.12).

Maureen's description of learning to trust an audience contained some of the key components of trust in any relationship. Taking the risk was vulnerable-making, dangerous, and exposing. She had to learn how to give herself space and maintain her sense of self, yet not cut off from the audience so that their affection could reach her. This issue of separation and boundaries is difficult for anyone who does not have a strong sense of themselves, but particularly for women who haven't been encouraged to individuate and have been conditioned to be "pleasers." Maureen had to trust that the energy the audience was sending towards her was affection, not judgment. This is difficult for those who carry shame or self-judgment, because they are much more prone to project their judgment outward and perceive it as coming from others. It is also difficult for a person who judges themselves critically to believe that others could see them any differently than they see themselves—worthy of harsh judgment instead of affection and acceptance.

The Effects of the Voice Teacher/Student Relationship

Trusting the audience in performance felt as "life and death" for Maureen as it was for Keen (1999) to trust the other trapeze flyer to catch him in mid-air. He believes:

> Faith, love and flying all depend on a relationship that can be created only by an act of trust that involves taking a risk of falling into the void. Before the fact, all risks are folly. It is only after a successful flight to the arms of the catcher that the risky decision to trust is seen as the essence of wisdom. (p.60)

A very successful solo trapeze artist was training one day with Keen:

> She was as fearful as any amateur and refused to go to the catcher. "No way," she said. "On the single swinging trapeze I'm in control. It's all me. I trust myself and know my own strengths and limitations but I don't have to depend on anyone else." Her observation about herself struck home with me. I don't trust easily nor am I eager to surrender control… Solitude may be lonely, but it's safe. (Keen, 1999, p. 58-59)

Solitude would be lonely in the vocal world as well, but it isn't an option if you are seriously pursuing vocal freedom. You must depend on others to reflect back to you how your voice sounds since you can never hear it accurately inside your own head (something several of the singers I interviewed commented on). This much-needed feedback about your sound typically comes from your private teacher, or sometimes from a coach who helps with diction and learning the music. Annika and Maureen, at their advanced level of singing, still see coaches and teachers from time to time, and they have the unique opportunity of being each other's objective ears.

Singers have a parallel process of vocal-image development to that of an infant developing a self-image. Just as a child needs the mirroring of her caregivers to know who it is, how it appears to others, and how to interpret its feelings, so a young singer is dependent on her teacher to reflect back to her what she sounds like and what certain sensations mean. Carolyn, Julie, and Sandra all said that they were scared when they let go of some of the tension, and that it was an unusual sensation because it was so new to them. With their teachers' reflections they could be reassured that those strange feelings weren't bad or to be avoided, but signs of progress. However, voice teachers, like parents, don't always give accurate reflections. They can't know exactly what the singer is sensing inside their body, and the language of describing physical sensations can be ambiguous. Voice teachers have their own personal tastes in what they like to hear in a voice, just as parents have values about how they want their children to be. These values will shape the reflections they give to the student. This, in turn, affects the vocal image a singer builds of herself in much the same way that the words of a parent affect a child's developing self-image. Therefore, it is crucial that a

152

singer trust her voice teacher, and that they hold similar vocal values. The teacher must be trustworthy in her reflections and her ability to put her own ego needs aside.

Pruett (1988) suggests that part of the role of the music teacher in a young person's life is to nurture the "we" position or attitude in the child:

> Lots of people are out there with the gifted child on stage—parents, teachers—all are part of a holding environment: a holding environment that traces its roots back to the healthy grandiosity of the second year of life in which the infant seems to feel his experiences are shared by *everyone*. That grandiosity provides the child with a sense of shared experience, a fundamental relatedness that preserves self-esteem even in the most adverse circumstances. (p. 74)

Even with the best intentions of supporting a student, problems can arise when a teacher perceives the student's voice one way and the student perceives it in another. Because the voice is so personal and tied to identity, the suggestion of change in tonal quality is easily perceived as a personal attack. Master class student Lisa said she "felt like she was being torn apart by a pack of wolves" when teachers corrected her too directly. She spoke of "needing more nurturing" and not having a "great big ego" that could withstand that kind of criticism. Bunch (1993) suggests "the student must learn the difficult art of separating him/herself as an individual from the voice as an instrument so that objective learning rather than subjective inhibitions will take place" (p.18).

Another difficulty that arises because of the strong link between identity and voice is the preconceived ideas a singer has regarding her sound which might differ from that of her teacher. Master class student Julie was a fascinating example of this. She was determined not to sound like a black gospel singer because she did not want to be associated with what that represented to her. In her efforts to avoid that sound and its meaning, she had cut off from a lot of her inborn resonance and her natural voice. Teachers previous to Annika and Maureen had heard Julie's vocal tensions and suggested ways for her to open to her natural voice, but she felt as if she was being pushed towards an identity she was not prepared to accept. Julie had been becoming more open to her identity as a black woman in the year previous to the master class, as seen in her experience of looking at a picture of herself and laughing as she realized who she was. That growing acceptance, coupled with Annika's gentle support and the encouragement to re-connect with her body through the breath, helped her explore the possibilities of her natural resonances without judging them as being part of an identity she couldn't own.

> Vocal quality changes which threaten the singer's self-concept have to be managed in an objective, positive and analytical manner that fosters a healthy singing technique (p.18) ... The voice teacher must deal with a human instrument and intangible sensations and emotions. Therefore it is important to honour the sensitivity and self-consciousness of the student. (Bunch, 1993, p.20)

Julie was beginning to accept a new self-concept and Annika and Maureen provided the supportive holding environment in which she could explore it without criticism. She was able to take a step towards freeing her voice and accepting herself as a black woman. Julie was a living example of Maureen's statement that "singing is the way we have chosen to work out our lives," as she discovered and began to embrace a part of her self from which she had previously been distant.

Master class student Carolyn talked about a different aspect of trust she struggled with when she was young and excited to have the opportunity to study with "someone really famous:"

> I implicitly trusted her, I trusted whatever she said as "the law." and I think I ran into some troubles there because I trusted too much almost… You have to understand that they are not the only person that has something to say… So you have to trust your teacher but you also have to trust your own instincts. You have to be able to say, "I'm not comfortable; that's not something I'm able to do."

This kind of giving oneself over to an external authority and negating one's internal wisdom is quite common with young students who idolize their teachers, and contributes to the power imbalance between teacher and student. As Carolyn learned, it was important to continue trusting herself and speaking up for her boundaries when she was uncomfortable. Ristad (1982) says, "We yield our wills and our imagination to experts, both visible and invisible, and pretend that only the experts have god-given powers of perception. We forget the legitimacy of our own knowing" (Ristad, 1982 cited in Bunch, 1993, p.21).

I asked Annika about her experience of students trusting her and she said she didn't know exactly what went on in their minds, but that she hadn't experienced a lack of trust as a problem with her students. It appeared from what I observed both in master class and in private lessons that Annika's students trusted her easily. I'm sure part of this stemmed from her genuine desires to see them succeed and to nurture them as whole people. She feels her main task as a teacher is "to help students to believe in themselves." She knows "so much of singing has to do with self confidence," which can be so easily crushed by too much criticism. This comes from her own experience of working with someone who gave little positive feedback and was predominantly analytical:

> I can feel myself—my own energy space, my own aura, and my whole body just starts shriveling and caving because my belief in self and my confidence gets crushed, because all I'm getting is criticism… Part of me is just longing [to hear], "That was really lovely, just great," to reinforce the good before working on something different. I'd like to think that I'm past that, but I still find myself feeling that way.

When Annika and Maureen teach together, as they did in the master classes I observed, they complement each other's teaching style. Maureen is, according to Annika, "incredibly analytical" and detailed in her work with students, "zeroing in on the things that need working on" without spending many words on encouragement. Annika is quite the opposite, always making very positive comments to the student before anything else, and then working with more general concepts rather than perfecting details. Annika says their team teaching "ends up being balanced. Maureen is aware of [being less encouraging], but she's being true to herself. It's how she works." Annika acknowledges the need for that kind of work and she sees her role in the teaching team as being the one who provides the encouragement.

> In my observation, people improve if you tell them, "That was really good." I think I probably go overboard sometimes, especially when I'm working with young kids. They can so easily be crushed by criticism… It's so precious, that belief in self. It's such a precarious balance of when you feel well in yourself and feeling you don't believe in yourself. And, of course, as soon as you do not believe in yourself it's pretty hard to sing, pretty near impossible. So very often I feel that my job is to make people believe in themselves. Once they start believing in themselves it's just so incredible what comes out.

Annika understands the need for this kind of support, not only from the negative effects of its absence but from the positive effects of its presence. She reflected on the effects of working with the teacher who was the first person she confided in about her lesbian relationship with Maureen:

> Had I not been able to talk to her about it I think I would have been really stuck. I'm not sure how I would have been able to resolve that without her incredible love and support… Who else would I have turned to? I wouldn't have known… She and her husband were very close to Maureen and me, like second parents… She was really on the extreme of being positive and supportive. She's been a huge influence on me. I would say her wall of positiveness did affect me hugely in my working with students… It's basically having somebody really believe in you.

Annika's teacher from her adolescence, who was the first to challenge her to get into her body rather than singing from her neck up, was also a huge influence on her. She was more blunt and critical, but clearly communicated her belief in Annika. They were, in Annika's words, "great buddies." Within this trusting context, Annika says, "I just found her a huge inspiration because she's amazing. She is incredibly blunt, but it is something I admire hugely because I'm not so good at being able to expose the bare truth sometimes… I'd rather cushion it with something that's really palatable." This was the same teacher that Lisa described as "a tiger" and "brutal." I asked Annika why she wasn't hurt by this teacher in the ways Lisa was. She said sometimes she was upset, but she knew this teacher was telling her the truth she needed to hear in order to keep progressing in voice, and she knew she was believed in.

Annika thought back over her experience with many teachers over the years:

> In my experience it has been the teachers who were willing to support me emotionally who were [the most important] because they were caring enough to understand. The other ones I felt, "Yeah, but you don't really understand, you don't really know where I'm coming from." I would say it is very much reflected in how I deal with my students.

I observed that this was Annika's way of being with students in lessons and master classes. There was none of the ego, or diva, or even the hierarchical perception that she was the teacher with the answers whom students should fear and obey. Rather, she was on an adventure with them, helping them discover their voices and themselves, and she was truly there to serve them and not herself. She and Maureen were very open about their own vocal and personal journeys, and open to listening, discussing, sensing, and supporting whatever the student brought into the studio.

As we saw from Julie's interview, she struggled with being afraid of letting go and showing vulnerability, yet she made some breakthroughs during the week of master classes. I asked her what helped her through the fear that had held her back from taking risks in the past. She responded, "Just having Annika there to remind me helped me go through. Annika is very loving and nurturing, and she has that very motherly quality. She makes me want to try to figure myself out."

At the end of the week of master classes, many of the students gave Annika and Maureen thank you cards. One of them read, "I'm so glad I had the opportunity to come under the influence of the singing Mommies." We saw in Shauna's interview that she viewed Annika and Maureen as her "Aunties," and they were very important role models and wise older friends. They helped her navigate through accepting her sexual identity and many other issues of growing up that she faced without her parents while she was away at boarding school. There were many hugs and tears between teachers and students at the end of the week of master classes, and a feeling that genuine, deep connections had been made.

Perhaps some of this closeness I observed was due to the unique, almost camp-like setting of the week of classes, and the intensive togetherness—all day every day, and in the evenings over dinner. However, Annika and Maureen also carry this attitude of love and support throughout the year for those they teach out of their home. They don't hesitate to get involved in the lives of their students. Annika describes a student whom she met at the voice class the previous summer:

> She's a friend. She's 27, so it's a different generation, but she's such a gift. We have so many youngsters in our lives who are friends. This woman is someone who has ended up being really very close to us. She moved over to Europe and it was a huge step, a pretty scary thing for her just to drop everything and move. She didn't know a soul and she's got health problems, so sometimes she would come out and stay overnight with us. She doesn't have any money so we've worked out an exchange whereby she works for us for a few hours in exchange for a lesson. It doesn't always turn out that way on the work side of it but sometimes she's there and hangs out for some time. It's a very precious relationship and we savor it. When I went up to another country for three weeks doing this very interesting project… I brought this 27-year-old student/friend over to do the lead [in an opera]… It was the first time that she had performed after the year working with us. It was so amazing to see her because it's a new thing for me. Having worked so intensely with her for the year, and sometimes banging our heads on the wall, and she'd get frustrated—it's an ongoing process. But she had such a huge breakthrough when she was doing these

performances. She just blossomed, and it was like all of [a] sudden it happened for her. And it was so tremendous to see and it gave me such joy, such incredible inner joy. The high I often feel after I perform—well this was almost tastier. It was at least as much of a joy to see her actually fulfill [herself].

This is the story of one of many students to whom Annika and Maureen opened their home and their hearts with excellent results. The fact that Annika is so overjoyed by the success of her students tells something about her journey with them towards freeing their voices, and about her emotional engagement and support. She told the story of another student who comes for lessons:

Annika: I have this guy who comes for lessons who is about my age… He comes from very upper class and… he's got all the money in the world, but all he wants to do is sing. What he really wants is approval from his Dad… that he would be loved by how he expresses himself by his voice, that is so vital to him. He tries so hard. When he first came it was just excruciating… his body language was so obvious.

Joan: How have you worked with him through this?

A: Very slowly. His lessons usually end up being two hours. I don't think we ever come away at less than two hours because some of it ends up being chat, but again, he is so judgmental of himself and he needs so much encouragement to move on… We laugh a lot and I tell him that I know he can do it. Once you give that layer of support and encouragement it is so amazing what can end up coming out. His issues have also been control issues. It is so hard for him to trust and let go. He hangs on and in his mind he really wants to live in his head so he's always trying to control everything instead of just letting it happen. I keep stopping him and telling him to keep riding the breath, just trust and keep going on the air stream.

J: When you say "just trust" what are you asking him to trust?

A: Asking him to trust his own voice, his own sound, trust the gift that he has. Because he actually has a fine instrument but it gets so covered up by him holding onto it that it's sometimes hard to see. But his determination is just huge. I mean he is by far the hardest working pupil I've ever had.

This is the kind of patient, encouraging, supportive work that people who don't feel "good enough" or are hungry for approval need in order to open their voices and accept themselves. As we saw in the section on the use of voice in music therapy, the issues that arise for singers in relationship with their teachers are the same as those that arise in the transference between music therapists and clients. A sensitive, supportive, aware teacher like Annika can provide a very healing, therapeutic experience for a voice student. Conversely, a driven, emotionally cut-off voice teacher can bring up negative transference in the student and contribute some of his or her own ego needs in the form of counter-transference, which could deepen the student's wounding. People who carry a lot of shame, perfectionism, and struggle to accept parts of their identity, need a very secure trust in their teachers to risk letting go. It takes conscious, patient work to develop that trust.

Dual Role Relationships

The issue of how close a voice teacher should get to her students, and of how much "counseling" or discussion of therapeutic issues the teacher engages in, is hotly debated. Within the field of pastoral counseling and psychotherapy, guidelines in the licensing board Code of Ethics clearly state that therapists should not see clients socially outside of the therapeutic setting, or be romantically involved with them, or engage in any kind of dual role relationship. The CAPPE Code of Ethics & Professional Conduct (2001) reads:

> We acknowledge the complexity of pastoral relationships, and do not abuse the trust and dependency of our clients. We avoid those dual relationships with clients (e.g., business or close personal relationships) which could impair our professional judgment, compromise the integrity of the counseling process and/or use the relationship for our own gain. (Section C.6)

The Canadian Code of Ethics for Psychologists (2001) states:

> Be acutely aware of the power relationship in therapy and, therefore, [do] not encourage or engage in sexual intimacy with therapy clients, neither during therapy, nor for that period of time following therapy during which the power relationship reasonably could be expected to influence the client's personal decision making (section II.27) ... [Do] not exploit any relationship established as a psychologist to further personal gain ... Avoid dual or multiple relationships (e.g., with clients, research participants, employees, supervisees, students, trainees) and other situations that might present a conflict of interest or that might reduce their ability to be objective and unbiased in their determinations of what might be in the best interests of others. (Section III.33)

The reason the Code of Ethics is so explicit about avoiding dual role relationships is because of the intrinsic power imbalance between therapist and client, the high risk of abuse, manipulation, and exploitation and, at lower levels, the risk of damaging boundary violations. Within the bounds of the code guidelines, a great diversity of interpretation exists from one therapist to another, and between therapeutic approaches. Some self-psychologists believe in using the transference and counter-transference that arises as a diagnostic and therapeutic tool (Cashdan, 1988). They allow their clients to become emotionally dependent on them for a time to provide a new experience of an attentive, mirroring selfobject to heal wounds from the client's original parental experience. Cognitive-behavioralists are much more likely to focus on altering behaviors and analyzing thought patterns, and might entirely avoid working with feelings and emotional attachments. Certain therapeutic approaches attract certain types of people but within any approach the therapist's level of awareness, individuation, and emotional health, not to mention his/her basic personality and life experience, will affect the level of emotional closeness that s/he allows and encourages with his/her clients.

As seen earlier in the discussion of the use of voice in music therapy, transference and counter-transference can emerge in the relationship between voice teacher and student, just as it does between music therapist and client. As I analyze my first experience of voice lessons with Michael, I realize that transference issues complicated our work together. I felt ambivalent about relating to him, sometimes being pulled towards him, and at other times feeling pushed away by shame and fear. My unmet mirroring needs from childhood surfaced, and I felt driven to present myself as perfect to gain his approval. Yet I felt like a constant failure because even if I did receive some approval, which was not that often, I couldn't trust it because of my own self-rejection. I can only speculate, but there seemed to be some counter-transference on Michael's part. His narcissistic wounding drove him to be demanding of himself and his students, and he seemed to be trying to meet his own mirroring needs through the adulation of his students. I felt myself falling into the familiar role of wanting to take care of his needs to earn my worth and his attention. The combination of both of our narcissistic needs and wounds, and of the transference and counter-transference issues floating around the voice studio, made for anything but a safe environment for my tentative, ashamed, authentic voice to emerge. Cameron (1998) says that finding our voice has a lot to do with finding our safety (p.156). In "Winnicottian" terms, this would be a "holding environment," where the exploration necessary to separate and find the voice of our own unique being can be supported. My voice was not safe in the context of that student/teacher relationship. My body knew it, and protected me by refusing to open.

Since voice work has the ability to unearth deep emotional and psychological issues, cause regression, and trigger transference and counter-transference between student and voice teacher, it seems only responsible for voice teachers to become aware and educated to some degree about what might be going on in their studios other than Mozart arias and Schubert Lieder. Without becoming therapists, voice teachers, like body-workers and massage therapists, should educate themselves to the possible side effects that come through breath work. They need to become aware that if they are meeting resistance, pushing harder musically is not necessarily the answer. They also need to avoid motivating with shame and competitive incentives. Above all, they need to turn their highly attuned ears towards hearing beyond the music—to listen to the self being revealed in the voice and support that self. Again, this does not mean the voice teacher has to become a therapist, but listening attentively will help the teacher know when the issues need to be taken out of the studio and to a therapist. It would be wise for voice teachers to familiarize themselves with the counseling services available in the community or the student services available on campus, so they will know where they can refer students for help. And they should not hesitate to do so, if necessary. Knowing yourself and your limits is part of being a responsible teacher. Trying to save a troubled student and getting caught in your own counter-transference issues could be the undoing of both of you.

Boundaries

In the profession of voice teaching there are no ethical guidelines formally delineated as in pastoral counseling or psychotherapy. But the same dangers exist, and elicit a wide range of opinions on how they should be handled. Annika believes in being friends with her students, having them in her home, listening to their personal problems, and offering some counsel. Not all the stories Annika told of her relationships with her students were as successful as the ones I have recorded here. However, her overall experience has been that personal involvement is an asset, both for the student and for her as the teacher. Annika was profoundly supported and encouraged in her vocal journey and in "coming home" to herself through friendship with her teachers. She bases her teaching style and boundaries on what was helpful to her as a student, and in turn many of her students benefit and thank her.

However, there are other views on the teacher/student relationship. Voice teacher Wormhoudt (1992) writes about the psychology of teaching voice, taking a strong stand on the role of the teacher:

> We are teachers, not therapists, and in cases of deep depression and certain other heavy emotional problems, we must take care not to overstep our teaching duties and abilities, trying to advise these people on how to feel and think. We are not trained for this, and we may do harm. (p.5)

Master class student, Shauna, expressed in her interview that she was struggling with the master class because she had been close friends with Annika and Maureen for several years and she didn't want to lose that friendship or have it altered because she became their student in the master class context. She felt extra pressure in performance, wanting to please and impress them as her friends and mentors. She was confused by their treatment of her in class which seemed more distant than the close personal attention she was used to in a private context. This illustrates the dilemma of dual roles in both the therapeutic context and the voice teacher/student relationship, and is part of the reason they are cautioned against in ethical codes.

Arman's (1999) approach is, "In my teaching… a relationship should be built with affections, caring and mutual respect combined with a great sense of professionalism. I can teach a friend of mine, but while I am teaching, I'm the teacher, not the friend—and there's a major difference" (p.132). Arman (1999) is displaying what I believe is a typical oversight on the part of teachers, and some therapists, who believe they can be involved in dual role relationships with their students or clients. Arman (1999) easily switches back and forth between the roles of teacher and friend depending on his view of the situation. Since he is in the power position he feels secure as both teacher and friend, and he controls when to switch from one to the other. However, the student (as in Shauna's case) can experience confusion as to when and why the switch is happening, since the friendship is turned off or on at the teacher's discretion. When the shift out of friendship into a more professional relationship occurs the student can feel powerlessness, rejected and insecure about the state of the friendship. Many teachers who are friends with their students are unaware of the power imbalance and don't intentionally use it in a controlling or hurtful manner. In fact, they feel that being friends with their students is an invitation towards equality and empowerment. It was a positive experience for Annika to be friends with her teachers, and the students I interviewed found her warmth and personal involvement a positive aspect of her teaching.

However, it is worth noting that it has dangers and that the power imbalance creates different problems for the students than for the teachers.

Outside of her relationship with Annika and Maureen, Shauna quite clearly stated that she didn't want her teachers to be her friends. It was important for her to feel she was being understood by her teachers, and that they were respectful of her emotional states in lessons, but she did not want to "waste" her lesson time chatting when she could be singing.

Sandra displayed a similar view, as seen in her experience of having an emotional breakdown in a lesson. She was glad the teacher allowed her to have her feelings, offered support, and ended the lesson early since she wasn't able to sing in that state, but she did not want a long counseling session. She appreciated the "professional and appropriate" way the teacher dealt with her, and saw that as the ideal in the teacher-student relationship.

When Carolyn had an emotional time in a lesson and realized that it was connected to the anniversary of her mother's death, she was glad to have a personal conversation about it with Maureen. Carolyn said that Maureen's supportive, understanding attitude helped her through the difficult time, and built trust between them. However, although she wanted a teacher to understand her and be "nurturing" of her singing, she was not looking for a friend in a long term voice teacher, and preferred to work out her personal problems with a close friend.

Each of these students said they didn't want a close friend in a teacher, and yet they set their boundaries and expectations of the relationship at different levels of closeness within what they defined as a professional student/teacher relationship. Even though Annika's boundaries are set yet closer, inviting friendship with students, she does have her limits. This is displayed in the following excerpt from the story she began earlier about the 27-year-old student who often stayed over at their house:

> Annika: She's been intense about a whole bunch of her own emotional issues. In this case we have actually sent her to somebody to have counseling. I mean we talk an awful lot, but it became clear to us that it needed to be someone else besides us to really help her through it, and so she's just been starting that. It will be interesting to see where that takes her.

> Joan: When you say she needs someone else other than you, did you ever run into problems with talking all the time rather than teaching?

> A: We do a lot anyway; lots of tears and lots of things come up. The issue was more that it was beyond our being able to handle it… it's really quite complex, what she's going through, and it just seemed that she needed to have an outside, completely objective person to be there for her because we can no longer be that kind of person.

Those who teach the Alexander Technique run into the same difficulties of knowing how personally involved to become with the emotional issues that surface for their clients. Alcantara (1997) outlines three possible stances a teacher can take. First, they can choose not to deal with students at all, to "create some distance—let us call it the pedagogical space— between herself and the pupils, and to make it clear to the pupil that he [sic] is there to learn the Alexander Technique, not to undergo psychotherapy" (p.83). It is thought that this approach is not damaging to the student if the teacher behaves with common sense and decency. Depending on the student, and on the way this distance is maintained, this could be communicated as being respectful but detached, or as I experienced with Michael, it could be communicated as being dismissive of emotions which felt damaging to me. Choosing not to deal with emotions at all is certainly the safest choice for the teacher, and depending on the teacher's comfort level with emotions, might be the best approach.

"The second choice is for the teacher to receive counseling training and combine her teaching of the Technique with actual counseling" (Alcantara, 1997, p.83). There are advantages and disadvantages to this approach. Many people who are good teachers are not necessarily good counselors. Even if they could be, it might not be possible to spend the time and money to receive counseling training. It also introduces a dual role relationship of teacher and therapist, which can invite unclear boundaries and role confusion for both parties. It breaches the limits of the pedagogical space and "risks losing sight of the actual goals of the Alexander Technique [or, in our case, vocal development], goals which may well diverge from those of psychotherapy" (p.83). However, because the emotions naturally emerge through the Alexander Technique and, in our case, voice lessons, it can be helpful to both the personal process and the vocal process for the teacher to be able to work through some of the emotions with the student so they are not holding back as I was with Michael. During my voice lessons with Kate I found it helpful to be consciously blending both processes—voice lessons and psychotherapy (as seen in my journal entries in the Introduction). However, I wasn't trying to work out both processes with one person, which allowed me that pedagogical space in the voice lesson.

The third choice is for the teacher to "encroach in the pupil's emotional life without having received professional training" (p.83). Alcantara (1997) suggests that this is always an unwise choice and should be avoided. "Encroaching" doesn't sound positive, however, Annika's approach of working with a student's emotional issues to a point and then recommending counseling seems to be quite successful and a responsible way of handling things. She is unusually sensitive, patient, and intuitive. Annika is also self-aware enough to know when to refer a student on to therapy. However, voice teachers without these qualities could become entangled in emotional issues and relational enmeshments that would be unhealthy and best avoided.

Every student is different and wants and needs something different from a voice teacher, just as different clients need different things from a therapist. Both therapists and voice teachers have places they are afraid to go themselves, and it is from going to these very places that they will hold their students back. Therefore, therapists and voice teachers owe it to their students, themselves, and the art of singing to work out their own healing and freedom, so they can be safe holding environments that facilitate the growth and freedom of their students.

I have hardly scratched the surface of this discussion, but think it is an important issue to raise, since the teacher/student relationship can be a significant factor in the student's journey towards vocal freedom, with the potential of being both damaging and healing. In my own vocal journey, I see that the relationship with Michael added to my vocal tightness and emotional confusion rather than pointing me towards freedom. I think of his exasperated comment, "You have to trust me!" and realize that since he had to tell me to trust him, there must have been reasons he had not yet gained my trust. Dale Throness, Voice Instructor at the University of British Columbia, told me in a personal interview that, "It is the challenge of the teacher to gain the student's trust. You can't force it on them. It takes time to build and they have to come to their own inner knowledge of it" (June 20, 2003). Michael was correct in realizing I didn't trust him, and that was part of what was holding me back vocally. However, just as Lisa reacted negatively to being told directly that she had to let go of control, being told to trust actually increased my inability to trust.

I had little knowledge at this point in my life that feelings are experienced and held in our bodies. Since I was fairly cut off from my body, I wasn't fully aware of myself or of my true feelings:

> Much of the sense of self is in bodily feeling ... Alienated from the inner self, we do not understand the body's message... The body gives us vital clues to what is going on. Inability to understand the body's messages keeps us from deep understanding of self. Thoughts set up bodily feelings although we do not feel the process. If we can't understand our bodily sensations, who or what are we? Only thought? (Golomb, 1992, p.158-159)

I thought I should be able to "mind over matter" my way through voice lessons, forcing my body to do what Michael was asking for, and what I had determined in my head was necessary to do (that is, to pry my voice open in whatever way possible to please him), even if my body rebelled. I had a similar attitude towards my body that Carmen Berry (1993) had about hers as illustrated in a conversation with her massage therapist in *The Body Never Lies*:

> "You are a walking head," my therapist said. "It seems like the only purpose you have for your body is to carry your brain around."
>
> "What other purpose could it have?" I smiled at her... I had to admit that [my body and I] were strangers. I was thoroughly cut off from any reason to have a body, except to help me accomplish my various career and intellectual goals.
>
> "Your body has a lot to teach you, if you will pay attention."
>
> I didn't want to pay attention to my body. I wanted my body to pay attention to me! After all, I knew what was best. My body was supposed to be my disciplined servant, ready and able to respond to my commands. (p.131)

I had no idea how to listen to or work with my body. I didn't want to have a body, or the feelings that it held, so I remained as distant from it as possible. When I began voice lessons I thought of singing as a musical, auditory, intellectual activity. I was anxious that I might sound horrible and be deemed a poor musician, but that anxiety paled in comparison to being asked to open my body to sing! To do that I would have had to acknowledge my body in front of another person, put my hands on various parts of my body as they observed how the breath was working and, in some cases (as in the lesson with Maureen) let another person touch my body and feel it at work. Imagining what another person saw and felt in my body, the body I wasn't "supposed" to have, felt so shameful to me that it constricted my throat and I was powerless to open it. Not only that, but the sound of my authentic voice, and the feeling of letting it move freely with vibrato and fullness seemed very connected to femaleness— something I desperately wanted to keep hidden. It felt threatening to have that part of my identity vulnerable and visible in front of a male teacher, particularly since as a child I was exposed to some of the dangers and powerlessness I might face as a woman. I had always been ashamed of my sexuality and thought it was the most ugly, sinful part of myself. I had done all I could to keep it covered. Trying to open my voice felt like taking off all my clothes and standing naked, with my body in full view.

Teaching Students To Stay Home To Sing

Fortunately, I had a very different experience trying to open my voice with Annika and Maureen. Even though I ran into some shame, fear, and a need to control, I found the gentle, attentiveness of these women, and their acceptance of me and my emotions, a much more trustable relationship. It allowed me to begin inching towards release. When I became anxious, tight, and tearful, Maureen said, "Just stay home to sing, you don't have to go to the scariest place." That was a great moment of release for me. I was allowed to welcome my feelings, my intuition, and my sexuality—all the banished parts of myself—home to be part of the vocal endeavor. I wasn't able to integrate everything immediately; in fact I'm still working on it. However, the invitation to stay home, to stay whole, to accept and partner myself through the fear, held possibility. With Michael I kept hitting the wall of fear and shame and bouncing off of it. With Maureen and Annika I saw a way through, not just to freeing my voice, but also to come home to my self.

Annika and Maureen provided a non-critical space where it was safe to unearth deep emotion, and gave me permission to be with my emotions and work through them. This was very different from what I experienced in voice lessons with Michael. There, deep emotion was sometimes unearthed through the breath work that re-connected me to my body. But if that emotion started to show, I did not feel I had permission to express it. When a student became emotional, Michael's philosophy was to direct the student to sing simple repetitive vocal exercises to "get the lesson moving again." However, it also served his purposes of providing a way for him to avoid the student's emotions. Emotions were one of the parts of my self that I learned to deny as a child, so I have always struggled with allowing myself to "come home" to them. Sensing Michael's avoidance of my emotions told me it wasn't safe to show them in front of him and that I should keep them under strict control. Yet at the same time he was asking me to breathe, let go of my tight control, and take risks with my voice, all of which put me in touch with my emotions quite intensely. There was no way I could breathe deeply into my body and let go of control while at the same time holding back my emotions. I chose to swallow my emotions by staying disconnected from my body. That made it impossible for me to free my voice.

Michael wasn't doing anything particularly unusual. In fact, he was teaching the way most male musicians, and some females from a particular era, personality type, and training, teach. As a flutist I had many experiences of being expected to cut off from myself, my body, and my feelings and "do whatever I had to, to perform." My university flute teacher told our master class regularly that he didn't care how tired or emotionally frazzled we were, when we came to a lesson or a concert we simply had to find the energy to put on a good performance. If you had to use the frustration of hitting a wrong note as a way of "cracking the whip" to make yourself do better in the next phrase, fine. Your "self" was worth sacrificing for the performance. The only way I knew how to do that was to be harsh with myself—cut off from my body, and my frightened, sensitive, authentic self.

"Staying home to sing" was quite a different experience, and there were many examples of its effectiveness throughout the master classes. The way Maureen dealt with Sandra, who was on the verge of tears right before her performance in class, was one such example. Maureen allowed Sandra to remain inward vocally and emotionally, and sing while sitting with her head in her hands, expressing her feelings through the music. This seemed to actually enhance the performance, and certainly helped Sandra explore a new interpretation of the song and hold onto herself in the process. Obviously there must be a balance between containing ourselves while performing, and letting everything show. The possibility of re-balancing my approach by staying home with myself, instead of cutting off in harshness and criticism, was empowering and freeing.

Coming home to herself was Annika's journey to a free voice, so she teaches "staying home" as foundational to the process of unlocking the voice. This essential difference between Michael's teaching and Annika and Maureen's was, in my experience, the difference between a brick wall of tightness and a path of possibility towards vocal freedom. Michael's approach reinforced my already self-critical banishment of my authentic self in the hope of gaining his approval. Annika and Maureen showed me a new way that was gentle, compassionate, and accepting of feelings—a way that encouraged me to stay home to sing.

My Spiritual Coming Home

My vocal experience with Maureen and Annika affected my approach to singing and showed me how to come home to myself on a deep spiritual level. As seen in my journal entries and personal analysis throughout this study, I carried deep shame and self-rejection which had never been released through talking therapy. It had been aggravated and intensified while working with Michael. Several years later, healing had begun through a combination of psychotherapy and voice lessons with Kate. However, in the lesson with Maureen and Annika these issues surfaced once more, clearly not yet healed, and once again I turned my eyes away in shame. Fortunately, the experience did not end there for me. Instead of staying frozen in my shame, beaten vocally and personally by my harsh self-criticism, I was given a model of a new way to treat myself through the compassionate tears in Maureen's eyes.

Spiritually, one of my longstanding struggles has been in this same area of not being able to see myself as truly loved and accepted by God. As seen in my journal entries in the introduction, I was ashamed of my body and my sexuality to the point that I believed God damned me for it. The emotional wounds in those areas never seemed to heal and I was convinced it was because they were my fault for simply being physical, female, and sexual. I cut off from those parts of myself and tried to hide and deny them, but could never completely get rid of them.

Carmen Berry (1993) who treated her body "as if it was only there to carry her brain around," came to healing through re-connecting to her body through massage and embracing her sexuality.

> The Christian church has erred by dividing body from spirit, then over eroticizing the body. Perhaps this division is due, in part, to the close link between spirituality and sexuality. Both are passionate expressions of intimacy, creativity and love. Both touch us deeply, and touch us on a visceral level. Sexual alienation and a sense of body-based shame are common experiences among spiritually wounded people. . . . As spiritually wounded people we believe that to please God we must deny, hide, avoid, mistrust and control our sexual feelings. Healing begins when we include our bodies in the spiritual journey. (p.122-123)

Including her body on the spiritual journey involved massage therapy, a "legitimate, healing spiritual discipline." She saw her body as a vehicle of communication with God that is "as valid as any traditional approach to spiritual growth, such as prayer or Bible reading" (p.xiii).

I doubted God's acceptance of me because of my shame and self-rejection and because I still carried a childhood image of God rooted in early selfobject relationships and conservative Christian teaching. That image of God was harsh, demanding, perfectionistic, dismissive of feelings, and concerned only with my usefulness to Him in ministry. I refer to God with a male pronoun throughout this section because my childhood image was, and still is, male. Theologically I realize God is both male and female, but my selfobject has not grown to embrace this yet.

As an adult I had tried to change this image, to discover a more loving and accepting God through theological studies and feeding my mind Biblical truths. I memorized scripture, (particularly Hebrews, chapters 2-4) about the compassionate brother Christ walking with us in our pain and struggle, having been made just like us in flesh and blood so he could truly understand us. This was helpful but, as with most of my attempts, it was a cognitive approach and a theological act of the will, motivated by the need to "get it right" once and for all. Unfortunately, this approach only reinforced my problem—seeing faith in God as a mental pursuit that didn't touch or account for my emotions, allowed me to remain disconnected from my body, and didn't connect me relationally to God or others.

166

As a musician and outdoors enthusiast, I began looking to the arts and my experiences in nature to help me create a new image of God. This was the beginning of healing for me, as I was able to experience a more gracious God while jogging in a west coast forest, or being gently supported as I floated in the ocean, or carried away on the waves of sound of a Beethoven symphony. When I was alone in the early morning mist at the beach, an intimate God full of hope and grace emerged and I had moments of feeling loved and accepted. I didn't know why at the time, but I now believe it was the combination of being physically involved, walking or jogging or swimming or feeling musical vibrations in my body, and having a new symbolic image of beauty, serenity, and energy that brought these holistic experiences of healing to me. I made it part of my daily spiritual practice to spend time outdoors being active, and also spent time in music or other arts. These moved me along in my journey home to an integrated self, loved by God. However, in the context of relationships, the childhood rejecting God returned sometimes, and the shame and inability to trust or feel loved takes over.

In my voice lesson with Maureen and Annika I ran into the old feelings of shame as I tried to open my voice. But this time, Maureen's eyes looking back at me were not judging and hard, but spontaneously filled with tears of compassion. I saw God looking back at me with acceptance, encouraging me to stay with myself and keep walking through to the other side of this wall of fear and rejection. It wasn't perfect and I felt uncomfortable at times. I struggled to trust Maureen's eyes, and tried to escape by darting my own eyes around the room. Eventually I settled into resting in her eyes and drawing strength from them. I felt Maureen was going to the scary places with me rather than against me. In that moment I experienced a new God, who was with me and not against me.

For about a month after this experience I felt very different inside. I was less cautious of people and felt freed to be more vulnerable with my feelings. I felt excited and hopeful about new possibilities in life that I had yet to discover and I had more strength to face difficult things. The newness of this feeling wore off in time but the change seems to have remained. I regularly return to those gracious eyes in my imagination and let myself feel the acceptance and compassion as a way of re-focusing my new image of God, and coming home to self-acceptance.

Transition to Chapter 6

We have explored the literature, the data, and a synthesis of the two. Now we turn to the conclusions we can draw from this study, and their applications for voice teachers and pastoral counselors.

CHAPTER SIX

CONCLUSIONS

The Breath, Body, Emotion Connection

"Breath is the life force that feeds the spiritual fire of the musical self. To breathe in is to inspire, bring in, open and receive. It is a respiriting from without. (Sokolov, 1987, p.357 cited in Oddy, 2002, p.70).

This study has been an exploration of the experience of a singer in the process of freeing her voice. A singer's body is her instrument; therefore her sense of identity is closely related to her voice. Thus the process of freeing the singing voice goes far deeper than learning vocal techniques, and can become a means of discovering and freeing the self. Freeing the voice is a journey home to oneself, and can involve peeling protective psychic layers, facing shame and fears, and re-integrating rejected parts of self. The catalyst for this freeing, reintegrating process is the breath.

Our breath connects us to our bodies, our emotions, and our spirits. "The way we breathe influences how we feel and what we feel has a direct effect on how we breathe" (Austin, 2001, p.24). It was the breath that carried Annika home to her body and herself. It was the breath that began unlocking my fearful body and exposing feelings of shame that had kept me cut off from my body. We saw in the music therapy literature related to the voice that, "The process of recovering one's true voice involves re-inhabiting the body" (Austin, 2001, p.23) the breath that helps us do that. Singing is, "a way to access one's deepest self... intimately connecting us to our breath, bodies, and our emotional lives. . . . The voice is like a bridge that we can connect the mind to the body and heal splits between thinking and feeling" (Austin, 1998, p.316).

North American culture and conservative Christian teaching (which has been influenced by Gnosticism) encourages this mind/body split by teaching us to live in our heads. The holistic unity of mind, body, and spirit, God's original design, is interrupted when we shame the body and exalt the mind. The ancient Greeks reflect this intended unity in their linguistic connections between breath, spirit, and psyche. *Pneuma* in Greek, means *spirit* and *wind*. It is the word used in John 3:8 "the wind blows where it chooses" describing the Holy Spirit's work of regeneration in a person's life (Dictionary of New Testament Theology, 1998). In Aristotle, *pneuma* was the formative power which produced a mature individual and then became the instrument whereby the soul controlled the body (Dictionary of New Testament Theology, 1998). "The Greek word *psyche*, meaning *soul*, has the same root as the word *psychein*, which means *to breathe*. . . .The Latin words *animus*, meaning *spirit*, and *anima*, meaning *soul*, come from the Greek *anemos*, which is another word for *wind*" (Newham, 1998, p.444). As reflected in the etymological roots of these words, our physical breath, psyche, and spirit are intertwined – a truth that has been honoured in other eras and civilizations, but which we have lost and need to recover.

The process of freeing the voice is one road to recovering this connection between body, psyche, and spirit. Another significant finding of the study is that shame can be a strong force of resistance against this reconnection. Shame is a feeling of exposure to the eyes of scrutiny, usually attributed to an external eye of judgment, when in fact, it is an inner eye of self-rejection. Shame can be built into a person's identity through insufficient or inaccurate mirroring and attunement from a selfobject, and/or the lack of a good selfobject to satisfy the need for merging with an ideal object. The individual experiences this lack as rejection of the need or part of herself that is unseen. In an attempt to protect herself from further rejection, she cuts off from that part of herself and maintains the cut off through self-rejection in the form of shame.

It makes sense that reconnecting to a cut off part of self through the breath while in the process of freeing the voice, would bring up feelings of shame. That part of self was originally cut off as a response to rejection and when it first reappears the desire will be to push it away again to avoid feeling its woundedness and to protect from further rejection. It is an emotional wound held in the body, as all emotions are, so when the singer re-connects to the body through the breath, she reconnects to the wound which prompts her to resist the process. The singer will have to open herself to re-experiencing the pain to release the wound. She has to loosen her control, risk exposing the cut off part of self to her teacher (or whoever is listening) and to herself, and hopefully this time it will be accepted more graciously and can be reintegrated. The physical loosening of control in this process can begin with the breath as she concentrates on not holding her breath, but exhaling freely.

In terms of self-psychology and object relations, the perspective through which we examined shame and its effects on the development of identity – that is, this process of relinquishing control of the cut off part of self -- is letting go of the false self and acting out of a more authentic self. The popular phrase "finding one's own voice" is a way of describing the process of embracing one's authentic self and speaking or singing from that self. If we stay in the false self, only letting ourselves feel and express the expected, acceptable qualities that we think will keep other people happy, we usually find ourselves paying the price in depression, or psycho-somatic illnesses – our body's way of asking us to stop betraying our true self, and listen to the needs of the cut off parts of self.

The process of freeing the voice led Annika towards the core of her authentic self. Her journey home to herself began with the realization that her strict religious upbringing taught her to cut off from her body which robbed her of the freedom and energetic breath needed to support a free voice. Coming home to her body involved many forms of release, beginning with the breath, and expanding to various forms of body work such as Alexander Technique, osteopathy, and cranioscaral work. She came home to her sexual body through her relationship with Maureen. This was a tumultuous leg of the journey fraught with shame, guilt, and fear. Her somatic response to these emotions, and the rejection of her parents was years of physical illness and depression, leading to an overall lack of confidence which affected her vocal career for a time. However, she is convinced that her relationship with Maureen further opened her body's resonances for singing, and brought her to a deeper place spiritually. In this place she let go of the rigid, rule driven God and began to construct an image of a relational God. She still struggles with shame in feelings of "being bad" at times but is gradually releasing this view of self and embracing the belief that there is the "good of God" within her, and that she is accepted and connected to the Divine.

Annika went through more release physically, emotionally, and vocally as she worked through the death of her father, and a measure of reconciliation with her mother. She finds herself in the freest and most centered state vocally in the last few years. This is due to coming home to self physically, emotionally, psychologically and spiritually through all the work she has done to free her voice. Releasing career expectations has also contributed to Annika's new vocal freedom. She no longer sings to please other people or prove herself, nor does she compare herself to the ideal career and judge herself a failure for not achieving it. She is still open to and pursuing more significant performing opportunities, but is letting her career be what it is, which at the moment includes a studio full of young singers learning from her vocal expertise and personal supportiveness.

Breathing low enough into the body, from the soft palate in the mouth to the pelvic floor, is a basic principle to which Annika returns often in her teaching. She understands the connection between the breath, emotions, identity, and soul of a person, and seeks to provide a safe, supportive environment for a student to access her authentic self as part of the process of freeing her voice. She believes in and supports her students as people, and doesn't hold back from becoming friends with them or listening to whatever emerges from their personal lives. Annika has found a way to manage this level of closeness with her students, however, teachers and counselors alike are cautioned against dual role relationships because of the potential for abusive or exploitive boundary crossings. As we saw from the music therapy literature, the potential for transference and counter-transference is very high between voice teacher and student because of the experiential and medial aspects of singing that facilitate unlocking emotions, regression, penetrating defenses, and accessing unconscious material.

We saw from Annika's teaching, as well as from the experience of the students and the help of our trapeze flying metaphor, that the process of freeing the voice is one of a number of possible vehicles people use to peel back their psychic layers and access their true selves. The process involves feeling the fear of trying something new and unfamiliar, taking the risk of jumping into the unknown, loosening control, and trusting the body's wisdom. The result of this leap of courage was landing in a new way of being which felt scary, vulnerable, free, and like it was running itself. This process was inhibited in different ways for different master class students. Each person spoke of personal feelings and struggles being part of their blocks, and the majority of them showed elements of shame, but all of them took courageous steps towards freedom during the week of classes.

Carolyn came to the master class with an advanced, fairly free sound. However, she experienced "just letting it happen" when she let go of an element of "faking it," her tendency to produce a pretty, easy sound that she wasn't emotionally connected to. She was quite aware that emotional issues were near the surface since it was the anniversary of the death of her mother that week, and Maureen reminded her of her mother. She allowed herself to let go and be vulnerable emotionally in conversation with Maureen, which also helped her let go vocally.

Julie was working out issues of her identity as a black woman and a resistance to sounding black which resulted in a distinctly different vocal quality at the top of her voice as compared to the bottom. She let go of some of the control of her upper range and allowed more of the rejected black characteristics. This brought more vocal freedom. Julie also struggled with a feeling of being "unworthy" to be part of the class since she saw herself as "at the bottom" of the students. She did not explain the origins of this feeling, however she expressed it in the language of shame – being lesser than, unworthy, feeling a need to be perfect, and feeling overly vulnerable when she sang which affected her ability to "let go" and try new things with the breath.

Sandra was hiding her personal power because of shaming messages from her family that told her she was a showoff when she performed. Sandra did not say where this value came from in her family, but it is similar to the conservative religious view we examined which condemned pride and withheld praise from children to keep them selfless and humble. Unfortunately, it had the negative result of taking away her power and joy in her abilities. But she was reclaiming her voice as she put less importance in the opinion of others.

Lisa admitted that by nature she needed a high level of control in her life and this resulted in tension in her posture and voice. She made huge strides in releasing this tension, not by addressing it directly, but by focusing on the music, and the joy of singing as a means of letting go. Lisa did not mention shame, however, her feelings of being attacked when corrected, her tendency towards perfectionism, and high degree of needing to remain in control would be in keeping with shame motivated behaviour.

Shauna also spoke the language of shame as she struggled with low-self esteem and was externally focused on finding approval and reassurance that her voice was "good enough to make it." She struggled with self-rejection and a strong critical voice which kept her from being able to absorb the approval she was given, and distracted her while performing in master class.

My own vocal experience is a clear example of shame and identity issues blocking vocal freedom. I have analyzed my experience throughout the study, much to my shame since it is easy to feel ashamed of one's shame! However, one of the most significant personal learnings of this study has been identifying my shame, tracing its roots to my own religious upbringing and involvement in conservative Christian communities, and beginning to release these old beliefs. Through my months of research, self-reflection, and writing, I have become far more able intellectually to have compassion on myself for being a physical, sexual, imperfect, and at times weak and vulnerable person. My body, emotions and spirit still need to experience the change and that will be the real test. However, the experience of being graciously accepted by Maureen and Annika, as they saw me in my shamed and vulnerable state through their tearful, understanding eyes, has already started me on the journey home to my own body. They provided a mirroring experience of being seen and accepted that released some of my shame and gave me a model of how to accept myself.

I remember telling a friend about this gracious experience during my voice lesson the day after it happened, and saying, "Maybe that is what God is like. Maybe He looks at me with tearful, compassionate eyes when He sees the vulnerable, shameful part of me." I was already thinking/feeling in self-psychological terms and an image of a new more gracious God image was emerging.

Contributions to Knowledge and the Literature

An interdisciplinary study such as this integrates knowledge from fields which might not normally come in contact with each other. Through this mingling of disciplines, information can be verified from more than one perspective. Knowledge from one field can illuminate mysteries not yet solved in another, and questions can emerge for further investigation.

For example, the ability of the breath to reconnect us with our physical and emotional selves is basic knowledge to a music therapist, but a pastoral counselor may never discover this truth on her own, or read or hear anything taught about it if she stays exclusively within the field of pastoral counseling. Voice teachers wanting to improve their teaching and puzzled by the emotional outbursts and tense relationships they experience with some students will find little help within the vocal pedagogy literature. Some of the most contemporary pedagogues acknowledge psychological blocks, inhibitions, stage fright, or lack of confidence, but don't go deeply enough into those issues to explain the true psychological problems, or give adequate suggestions of how to deal with these problems. There is plenty written about the importance of breathing for good vocal technique but the connection is not made that breath reconnects us with our bodies and emotions. This would explain a lot of the tears in the voice studio, or the resistance to letting go vocally to avoid the emotions.

Music therapy literature that deals directly with the voice comes much closer to answering these emotional, relational, and psychological questions of vocal pedagogues, since it acknowledges the effects of the breath on the body and emotions, and the ability of music to penetrate a person's defenses, in ways that talking therapy does not. There is only a small body of literature that deals specifically with the use of voice in music therapy; most of it is authored by Diane Austin (1991, 1993, 1998, 2001) and is quite new and exploratory. Her work is based on self psychology and Jungian archetypes and is deeper psychologically than most music therapy writings. This makes it more substantial than the more common anecdotal writings of many music therapists. Austin's (1991, 1993, 1998, 2001) work is based on two basic principles I have discovered through this study -- the connection between voice and identity, and the connection between breath, body and emotion. Her work explains the heightened transferential possibilities between voice teacher and student, and the experience of emotional regression that singers might feel as early attachment issues are stirred within the holding environment created by the musical experience. I see this study of freeing the voice as building on Austin's work. I deepen the understanding of identity issues affecting vocal freedom through the detailed examination of a single case (Annika), and the analysis of my own experience and that of the master class students. I also explore and integrate two new aspects of identity – the role of shame in shaping a false self that masks the authentic self, and the role conservative religious teaching can have in generating shame and keeping a person from being able to own or express a more authentic self

Patteson's (1999) unpublished masters thesis on the transformation of nine women through voice lessons also relates very closely to this study. It reinforces the finding that the breath is what reconnects a person to her body and sense of self, and that one's sense of self is reflected in the voice. However, instead of exploring the psychological and religious forces affecting women's voices as I have done, Patterson examines feminist theory in relation to music education and the general domination of women. Our studies are complementary of one another with enough overlap in findings that we verify each others work, particularly in the breath – body connection, but we apply our findings to different fields.

The other side of this interdisciplinary study is the psychological and theological literature. Self-psychology and object relations are immensely helpful perspectives through which to view identity and shame. They explain the transferential issues that arise between client and therapist in a way that is easily applied to the musical experience with another person. However, they are theories of 'explanation' and do not deal with or acknowledge anything regarding connection to the body and the emotions. They leave off where most psychological theories do - talking about the issues and perhaps the feelings, but not facilitating a way to experience and release them. Alice Miller (1981) says, "Problems cannot be solved with words, but only through experience. . . . Mere words, however skilled the interpretation, will leave unchanged or even deepen the split between intellectual speculation and the knowledge of the body, the split from which [we] already suffer"(p. 117). It is true that authors such as Cashdan (1988) and Kohut (1978) apply the theory to the relationship between the therapist and the client, suggesting that the therapist could become a good selfobject and a new experience of being more attentively mirrored, but that is where the theory stops. Austin's (1998) belief is that singing is "a way to access one's deepest self… intimately connecting us to our breath, bodies, and our emotional lives," and that the voice "is like a bridge that we can connect the mind to the body and heal splits between thinking and feeling" (p.316). Woodman & Mellick (1998) elaborate on our need to reconnect to our bodies:

Our bodies...are vast, often untapped sources of wisdom. Because most of us are in a culture that devalues the information our body gives us, we can fail to see, hear, taste, touch, and smell the subtle signals it sends us – in waking and sleeping- about our emotional states, spiritual well-being, physical health, and mental functioning...Research and experience indicate that mind and body are not separate but part of a seamless, intricate network of intelligence. From a more intuitive perspective, your body can be considered a reservoir of cellular memory, wisdom and guidance. (p.40)

Massage therapists, acupuncturists, Alexander Technique teachers, osteopaths – any therapists who deal directly with the body know that "problems can't just be solved with words," and need to be integrated into our bodies. However, their knowledge, and that of music therapists, has not been embraced strongly enough by pastoral counselors or psychologists in their work. Pastoral counselors in particular run the danger of being unaware of how much they are still influenced by conservative religious theology that contributes to the mind-body split, and how much they live with that split themselves. The theological literature on shame that I reviewed was written, for the most part, in the last five years. It cites the mind-body split as a current problem that conservative Christian teaching still endorses by continuing to shame the body for being a hindrance to one's spiritual life. People are still locked in shame through being taught to deny the self to avoid selfishness or pride, and to take on a passive, dependent, weak position before the image of a mighty, punishing God. Those views are changing, and the literature I reviewed reflected a shift towards a new theology which addresses shame healed by grace, and removes the emphasis on sin, guilt, and forgiveness. However, the "worm theology" and rejection of the body have such deep historical roots, and continue to be taught in conservative settings and carried in the theological biases written into the translations of the Bible in current use, that there is still plenty of shame found in most people with a strong religious upbringing.

This study brings together the mechanics of breathing from vocal pedagogy and the music therapy knowledge of the connection between the body, breath and emotions. It examines shame and identity through a self psychology and object relations perspective, which shed light on the types of psychological blocks a singer might encounter when re-connecting with her body and emotions through the breath. The study of self-psychology and object relations extends into the spiritual realm and offers a perspective on the relationship between a person's sense of identity and image God. This led to the exploration of a shifting emphasis in theology that recognizes the need for a gracious answer for the shame people experience instead of the focus on sin, guilt, and forgiveness. All of these areas of knowledge came together to help us understand the experience of a singer in the process of freeing her voice, as seen in Annika's journey, in the experience of the master class students, and in my own experience.

Topics for further study

As seen in the method chapter, when designing this study I was faced with the question of what would be lost if I interviewed only female singers. I decided to only interview women because I had to limit the study to be manageable, I had the opportunity to work with a particular singer who was a female, and I thought I would get more data about the emotional and psychological aspects of the experience of freeing the voice from women. I am satisfied that given the time and resources I had available for the study, this was a good decision. However, I do see a need for similar studies to be conducted with men, and with men and women compared in the same study. The small amount of research I found on male singers and what I was able to understand from personal interviews with male singers, showed me that their experience is very different from that of women. Studies of men in the process of freeing their voices could reveal useful information for male singers who are trying to understand their own process, just as I found this study useful for understanding my female experience. Voice teachers working with students of the opposite gender would benefit from understanding the different challenges and feelings their students experience. This new experience might allow them to teach more effectively, and avoid some communication and relational confusion.

Another area for future study is the use of breathing techniques and vocalizing in the context of pastoral counseling. As seen in the literature, therapists such as Paul Newham (1998, 1999) and Carolyn Braddock (1995) have developed therapeutic techniques based on vocalizing and the use of breath. It is unlikely that the majority of pastoral counselors will go as far afield from their theological and psychological training as required to use full fledged voicework. However, based on the principle of the breath connecting us to our bodies, emotions, and even our spirits, research could be done to explore the use of breathing and vocalizing that would be suitable for use by pastoral counselors who are not trained musicians, singers, or voice experts.

In my counseling practicum I have been experimenting informally with the breath and have begun seeing results. One of my clients is a very quiet, soft spoken, passive, 21-year-old woman. She is struggling to individuate from her parents but is very hesitant, wondering if that type of independence is disrespectful or will incite rejection. She questions whether or not she is strong enough to handle life on her own. In one session she was circling around what to do, not expressing her feelings and obviously holding a lot in. I asked her to take a couple of deep breaths and then choose a simple phrase that expressed one aspect of what she was feeling. She took a few breaths and then mumbled something that sounded like annoyance, something I had never heard this "sweet" Christian girl express before. I asked her to take a few more breaths and say it again a little louder so I could hear her. After a few more breaths, in a voice I didn't know she possessed, she came out with, "I wish they would just leave me alone!" I asked her to keep exploring that feeling as she spoke the phrase a few more times, breathing deeply all the while. She gained a physical connection to her body and her feelings through this exercise. In fact, after a few more breaths she began crying and expressing a deep sadness that she said she didn't know was in her. This very small physical intervention didn't involve any knowledge of music or even much about breathing, but it seemed to be extremely helpful in accessing this client's emotions, and showed me that the body and breath can be part of pastoral counseling in subtle, simple ways.

Applications for Voice Teachers and Singers

The central learning useful to both pastoral counseling and freeing the singing voice is the ability of the breath to put us in touch with our bodies, which, in turn, puts us in touch with our emotions and a deeper sense of self. For singers and voice teachers this goes beyond the already established technical aspect (of freeing the breath in support of the voice) to highlighting the emergence of emotions that accompany breath work. The music therapy literature reviewed has made it clear that singing can by-pass a person's defenses and cause regression, open emotional wounds, and trigger transference issues.

The issue of trust is crucial to the progress of a voice student, and can't be forced. It must be won -- proven over time as the voice teacher provides a safe, supportive relationship for the student to peel away her psychic layers in her movement towards vocal freedom. I believe this study's findings point to the need for voice teachers to do some of their own therapeutic work so they can be responsible teachers. This will help them avoid bringing their own countertransferential issues into the teacher/student relationship and enable them to deal in an accepting manner with the emotional issues of their students -- not necessarily trying to resolve them, but not causing further damage.

Every student is different. Each wants and needs something different from a voice teacher, just as therapy clients need different things from therapists. The places that both therapists and voice teachers are afraid to go themselves are the places they will hold their students back from going. Therefore, therapists and voice teachers alike owe it to their students, themselves, and the art of singing, to work out their own healing and freedom so they can be safe holding environments that facilitate the growth and freedom of their students. I also think teachers need to consider the issue of dual role relationships with their students and be intentional about setting boundaries that protect themselves and their students from emotional entanglement and exploitation.

The information on identity formation and shame can help singers understand the psychological roots of their vocal blocks. It could help them realize the need to address these issues through other types of therapy, such as Alexander Technique, and not expect the whole process of freeing the voice to take place in the voice studio.

Coming home to herself was Annika's journey to a free voice, so her approach of "staying home" is foundational to the process of unlocking the voice. In my own experience, and that of some of the master class students, the difference between being encouraged to stay home to sing, and being pushed to ignore my inner experience and cut off from myself, was the difference between beginning emotional healing and vocal release, and further shaming and vocal constriction. Therefore, I believe many students and teachers would benefit from standing back from their performance driven approach to voice and taking stock of the effects such attitudes have on the integrity of the self. Teachers should consider taking the approach that they are teaching people to sing, rather than teaching singing to people, and consider the well-being of the whole person. This approach might not be what every student is looking for or what all teachers are capable of. At a certain level of self- confidence and vocal experience, the student doesn't allow the teacher to affect her so deeply, nor does the level of emotional awareness and support matter as much. However, the voice teachers who work with young or inexperienced students, which is the majority of high school and university voice teachers, need to recognize how significant their role is in the development of the vocal self-image of the student. They need to be aware and take seriously the terrifying level of vulnerability required for some students to open their voices. They need to honour the shaky authentic self that might be exposed for the first time in front of another person, and respect that students are revealing a very vulnerable part of themselves.

Applications for Pastoral Counselors

There are multiple applications of the learnings from this study for pastoral counseling, from the material on shame and identity development, and from the material more directly related to the singing voice. Beginning with the shame related learnings, it is important for counselors to understand how shame is developed as part of a person's identity, and what a paralyzing force it can be. The clients who seem the most "together", who come from "good Christian families" may well be carrying the most shame. The "together" image a client presents could be a well developed false self she has created in response to being taught to be a "nice girl" – not proud, selfish, angry or jealous. She has learned to deny her authentic self and cut off from "negative emotions" – those feelings viewed as sinful, or at least not fitting for a "good selfless Christian." She might cling tenaciously to scripture and church teachings in her efforts to "improve", asking you to essentially help her find the self-discipline to keep the rules well enough so she can finally feel good about herself. As pastoral counselors we want to encourage the spiritual growth of a person, yet reinforcing this type of shame-based thinking will hamper her growth in all areas since it is based on the belief that the self is bad and shame is appropriate to use as a means of controlling the "sinful" self.

Listening to the client's view of herself through her Christian expectations of perfection and "should's" can be an indicator that the "perfect" Christian family she describes has caused her shame she may be unaware of. Also, listening for her image of God can help the counselor understand her internal object relations. Is she weak and dependent in the eyes of a powerful, punishing God? Her spiritual object relations will tell you something of how she experienced her early selfobjects, what mirroring needs were unmet, and how her view of herself is bound up in her view of God. In trying to help her to see herself differently she will also need to "update" her image of God. If she is unable to make headway on the view of herself, the entry point might be through working on her view of God. In doing this it will be important to listen to what her present images mean to her and not assume that a Biblical image is necessarily helpful just because it's Biblical. She might feel bound to try to see God through Biblical images that still hold a lot of judgment, even if that aspect of the image isn't obvious to her initially. She might need to purposely avoid Biblical images and teachings for a while because they have subtly (or sometimes not so subtly) been used to shame and control her in the past and will still carry those connotations for her. Encouraging her to attach to something else in her life that speaks of acceptance and grace might help her re-image God. This might come in the form of other good relational experiences in her life where she has had an experience of a good selfobject and has been more attentively mirrored. These gracious images might also be found in nature, the arts, working with her hands, gardening, or doing physical activities she enjoys that re-connect her with her body and feelings. The pastoral counselor should also seriously consider that the relationship she provides for the client could be a new experience of mirroring. Even if other interventions don't appear successful, the relationship itself can be an experience of grace and acceptance and is worth spending energy building.

In order to be able to offer attentive mirroring and a shame lessening relationship, a pastoral counselor must have dealt with her own shame. She must know what triggers her own descent into shame feelings, and what tempts her to want to shame others. As Alice Miller (1987) illustrated in her work on "poisonous pedagogy," parents who have been shamed themselves for certain feelings or needs will find it very hard to let their children have those feelings and needs. Their narcissistic wounding will come to the forefront when they see their children asking for what they themselves were denied as children. The temptation will be to shame their child as they were shamed, or be so cut off from their own needs that they are blind to the needs of their children. In the same way that a parent passes on her shame to her child, the therapist can pass on her shame to the client by avoiding certain issues, not letting her have and express her true feelings, and refusing to acknowledge when she has misunderstood the client or acted out her issues on her client. Shame is also passed on when the narcissistically wounded parent uses her child to fill her own mirroring needs. This is another danger for the narcissistically wounded counselor since the counseling relationship is a perfect situation for a "weak, needy" client to admire the "strong, all-knowing" therapist, thus filling some of the therapist's mirroring needs but further depleting the client as s/he tries to fill those needs.

In the literature review of the spiritual roots of shame, we examined an article by Thompson (1996) which explored the shame dynamics of the counseling relationship itself. It is important for pastoral counselors to realize that coming to counseling can be a shaming experience for clients, and counselors should work to lessen that shame as much as possible. Clients often feel shame that they require counseling, and then to be asked to disclose their shameful information to a stranger, exposing their weaknesses to the eye of a counselor who appears collected and in control, can increase their feelings of failure and inadequacy.

Counselors need to be very intentional about creating a safe holding environment and accept the client as he/she is. This is not only done through withholding judgmental comments or facial expressions, but doing enough personal work on her own shame and identity issues that she can genuinely offer acceptance to the client and see her as a fellow journeyer to be companioned and not judged.

Just as singers have to come to grips with the fact that their bodies are their instruments and therefore anything that happens to them also happens to their precious instruments, so the person of the pastoral counselor is the primary instrument in counseling. Whatever issues of shame, narcissistic injury, un-integrated parts of identity, or other personal struggles a pastoral counselor carries, they carry right into the therapeutic context. These aspects of their "instrument" show in the relationships they build with their clients, the countertransference that emerges, the impact the client's issues and emotions have on them personally, and the types of therapeutic interventions they will be comfortable using. This reinforces the need for counselors to practice good self care, work through their own issues as they arise, and have some form of regular supervision.

Pastoral counselors are not typically singing in session, but the quality of their speaking voices can reveal a lot about their moods, physical health, and identity, and can impact their clients deeply even if they are not consciously aware of it. Quite literally, the quality of the speaking voice –for example, harsh, gravelly, extremely quiet, or seductive -- will affect the client's feelings of safety and ability to join with the counselor. Music therapist and voice teacher, Susan Summers, demonstrated to me in a personal interview (Jan. 24, 2004) just how much power she had to control the depth of the conversation, the mood, the level of intimacy, and to some extent, my emotions by creating different environments with the use of her speaking voice. She changed the volume, emotional quality, timing of the words, breathiness or nasal quality of the tone. She had me close to tears one minute, feeling that she understood me personally, and wanting to shut her up the next, all by the use of her voice. She demonstrated mirroring the client's emotional states with the tone of her voice, something that might not be consciously recognized by the client, but is part of creating a safe and receptive environment.

However, the opposite can be true if we don't adjust our voices to mirror our clients, or if we are unaware of how our voices come across to other people. I will never forget an incident that occurred when I was teaching, before I had any experience in pastoral counseling. I had to take a very depressed and frightened student to a psychiatrist for the first time. He practically yelled from his chair behind his huge desk, "So you feel like killing yourself?" She buried her face in her hands and asked me to take her home. It wasn't just the words. It was the loud, non-compassionate, matter-of-fact yell this man let out that shut the student right down. He might have treated five other suicidal patients that morning and been ready for a coffee break, but to her it was a desperate moment that took all her energy to face, and his voice alone told her she wasn't going to be treated with understanding. It is important for pastoral counselors to consider the possibilities available to them in their speaking voices.

The goal is not to become manipulative, but to become aware of how to use the voice --the effect it has on people and how it can create the desired space in which therapeutic healing can occur.

Listening to how clients use their voices can be a source of information about their sense of identity and self-esteem, and their emotional state. Watching their breathing can tell you when they are holding back emotion, and tell you something about their relationships with their bodies. As seen in the music therapy literature, Austin (2001) observes her clients holding their breath when approaching an emotionally charged issue, controlling their feelings by restricting the intake and release of their breath. When she asks them to exhale fully "they often come in contact with a feeling they have been suppressing. Likewise, the inability to take in nurturing or other kinds of experiences and information is mirrored in restricted inhalation" (Austin, 2001, p.24). As seen in the earlier example of the timid student who discovered her true feelings through deep breathing and focusing on simple phrases expressing her emotions, simply encouraging clients to focus on the sensation of using their breath and voices, and helping them experiment outside of their normal parameters can be revelatory and therapeutic.

The very concept that emotions are felt in the body is not consciously known or relied upon as a source of wisdom by many clients who come to counseling. Neither is it known by many pastoral counselors, since we live in the same society in which Annika and I grew up, that teaches us to cut off from our bodies and live in our heads. Training for pastoral counseling doesn't stress this connection, or in many cases, even acknowledge it. A great deal of therapy is done from the "neck up," and is just as disconnected from the client's experience and emotions as Annika's singing before she came home to her body. Therapy that helps a client re-connect with cut off parts of self and heal emotional wounds has to be connected with the physical experience of feelings, and the breath can be the doorway to those experiences.

Recently I had an experience working with a client in which many aspects of the learning from this thesis informed my approach. The client struggles with depression and has a very flat affect. He speaks almost inaudibly and has what sounds like a perpetual tightness in his throat which he is forever trying to clear out of the way. He often talks about his church involvement and mentions Christian principles that "should" help him, but he seems to have no felt connection to God or much of anything. He was recently given something akin to a Christian pep talk by one of the men in his church who meant well, trying "get him back on track spiritually." I asked the client how he felt about the pep talk and he began giving me logical reasons why it should have been helpful to him, and why this particular person might have said these things with good intentions. I persisted in asking how he felt and he continued to skirt around the feelings until I told him that a "Christian" response of that kind to my depression would make me angry. He seemed to resonate with this comment, but expressed very little other than sighing heavily. I asked him who God was to him and he struggled to admit that he did not feel he had much of a connection to God.

I knew that his father had been an alcoholic and was not emotionally available to him as a child, so I asked if he felt any similarities between his feelings about his father and his God. He saw the connection intellectually but to help him begin to experience it emotionally I asked him to ask the little boy that still existed inside him what *he* felt and needed from his father. I also commented on his heavy sighing and asked him to consciously do some deep breathing to get in touch with his feelings as he re-visited the little boy. He closed his eyes, began breathing deeply. Feelings began to emerge as the little boy asked his father why he had treated him so badly. He asked to be comforted, held, and approved of. He became quite agitated saying that he wanted the pain to stop. I asked him to imagine that he was now breathing in God – the soothing touch of God that was healing the wound. As he consciously breathed in God he would become less agitated. Then another wave of pain would overwhelm him and he would express more of his childhood pain, disappointments, and needs to his father. When the pain was too great I would encourage him to breathe in God and he would release another layer of pain. I asked him if he had an image of God, and how he saw himself in relation to that image. He said he saw God dimly behind a thick layer of glass that he couldn't hear or feel through. Nearing the end of the session I asked him about the image again, and asked if it had changed at all. He said he could put his hand on the glass. He held up his hand as if against an imaginary pane of glass, and tried to breathe in God's hand being held against the other side of the glass.

This was the most I have seen this client engage with or express authentic feelings and it appeared to be the combination of connecting to his body and emotions through the breath, and the beginnings of re-imaging a new, gracious God that had facilitated this movement. This session showed me the power of the breath and the possibilities for understanding and working with a person's internal object relations through the images that already exist for them, and the possibility of opening up those images to be transformed in the direction of healing.

Parallels Between the Vocal Process and the Counseling Process

There are many parallels between the process of freeing the voice in a studio with teacher and student working together, and the process of freeing a self in an office with pastoral counselor and client. The process is very similar – both are intangible, internal, and not directly observable, at least not as the pianist's fingers on the keyboard are observable. The progress of the singer can only be inferred by changes in the sound, posture or facial expression. Similarly in the counseling process the client talks about how she feels different (the "sound" of her expression changes), she might carry herself differently (a more relaxed or energized posture), or she might show different facial expressions and begin to make different life choices. Both processes require the people to face fears, take risks, be vulnerable, trust beyond their own control, let go or loosen their conscious control, and let themselves be carried to a different place that is hopefully more free. As we saw, singers face psychological fears and emotions as they try to learn a new vocal technique. Counseling clients face the same kinds of psychological issues and emotions as they attempt to change. They discover the challenges, not in their voices, but rather in their families, relationships, or jobs.

In trying to teach, coach, or counsel clients or students towards change, both teachers and counselors struggle to balance the use of metaphor, theory, scientific knowledge, and personal experience to convey the internal changes being sought. The meaning of language in describing these internal, experiential happenings is regularly a source of confusion and miscommunication. Teachers and counselors both need a high level of empathic attunement to understand the world of the student or client, and to find a way of entering that world and being a positive force of change within it. Trust is crucial to both the teaching and counseling relationships, particularly since both deal with the core of a person's identity where shame lurks. Both are very intimate relationships which need to be taken seriously as significant factors in the process of change, and have the power to heal and free, or further shame and bind.

Personal Learnings

Writing this thesis has been a process of "coming home to myself" which has metaphorically been freeing my voice, (although I'm not singing full voice just yet). I learned a great deal about the breath connecting to the body and the emotions which shed light on the mystery of my extreme emotional reactions in my first voice lessons. I became much more aware of my shame and the parts of myself that had been cut off and silenced, and I have begun moving towards re-integrating them. I understand change now as a process involving fear, risk, letting go or loosening control, and trusting God and my body's wisdom to guide me towards a better balance as I relinquish control. I have taken a few such risks in my own life in writing this thesis and have learned how tempting it is to grab for control again when I become anxious. I am learning to stay more true to my own process, and stay home with myself more of the time. For me this means challenging the voice of my false self that wants to keep pleasing others to protect me from further shame and rejection. Staying home means companioning myself through difficulty rather than turning on myself in self-rejection and banishing a wayward part that isn't perfect. It means not pushing my feelings away as silly, or selfish, but listening to what they have to tell me and adding it to my way of knowing about myself and my environment. It means breathing deeply into wounded places in my life; breathing in the "respiriting life of God" and breathing out the pain as part of my healing process. When I stay home with myself in these ways I trust my own voice more, and feel more able to speak up, and sing out an audible expression of the self I am discovering and accepting. Godby (2003) says, "When a woman speaks with authentic voice, she is courageously communicating in that moment (whether in words or in actions) something of who she understands herself to genuinely *be*" (p.300).

There were times during the process of researching and writing this thesis that I was pressed by other "wiser" or just "louder" voices to abandon myself and my process and to doubt what my voice had to say. These were difficult voices for me to deal with, yet they were very important in strengthening my voice. I realized through the challenge of these other voices that I must resist my temptation to please, seek approval, or fall back into thinking that I have nothing to say and no self from which to say it. I can no longer passively allow myself to be overpowered by them. I must continue to listen to and believe in myself even when others can't see or hear that self, otherwise I am abandoning my self as much as they are. Marion Woodman & Jill Mellick (1998) describe the process that I and many people have gone through in finding their own voice:

> To find my own voice is to give truthful expression to how I experience myself and the world I live in. I might or might not be "right" by others' standards and measurements. But I can be truthful to my experience and to my way of expressing my experience. Such expression is unique to me and to this moment. Sometimes, we silence our beliefs in the face of self-doubt, self-criticism, fear of judgment, or lack of confidence in our capacity to express ourselves in the way that we believe others will respect and understand. While forces in the environment certainly push against our finding our own voice, all too often the force that silences comes from within. (p.88)

I am still "silenced from within" at times, and probably will continue to be on occasion throughout my life. But I am determined to continue challenging the shaming voices and encouraging the accepting voices. I will work towards being able to sing and speak from the authentic self with which God originally graced me.

"The voice is an instrument that echoes the soul
and it is the soul's energy that makes every sound unique."
(Rodenburg, 1992, p.118)

REFERENCES

Albers, Robert, H. (1995). *Shame: A Faith perspective.* New York: The Haworth Pastoral Press.

Aldridge, David. (1989). Phenomenological comparison of the organization of music and the self. *Arts in Psychotherapy, 16*, 91-97.

Andrews, M., & Schmidt, C. (1996). Case study of a first-year university voice major: disciplinary perspective. *Psychology of Music, 24* (2), 237-244.

Arman, Miriam J. (1999). *The Voice: A spiritual approach to singing, speaking, and communication.* USA: Library of Congress.

Armstrong, Frankie & Jenny (Eds.). (2000). *Well-tuned women: Growing strong through voice work.* London: The Women's Press.

Austin, Diane. (1991). The Musical mirror: Music therapy for the narcissistically injured. In K. Bruscia (Ed.). *Case Studies in Music Therapy* (p.291-307). Phoenixville, PA: Barcelona Publishers.

Austin, D. (1993). Resistance in individual music therapy. *The Arts in Psychotherapy, 20*, 423-429.

Austin, Dianne. (1998). When the psyche sings: Transference and countertransference in improvised singing with individual adults. In K. Bruscia (Ed.), *In The Dynamics of Music Psychotherapy* (p.315-330). Gilsum, NH: Barcelona Publishers.

Austin, D. (2001). In search of the self: the use of vocal holding techniques with adults traumatized as children. *Music Therapy Perspectives, 19*, 22-30.

Ayers, Mary. (2003). *Mother-infant attachment and psychoanalysis: The eyes of shame.* New York: Brunner-Routledge.

Barrett, Karen. (1995). A Functionalist approach to shame and guilt. In J.P. Tangney, & K.W. Fischer (Eds.), *Self conscious emotions: The Psychology of shame, guilt, embarrassment and pride* (p.25-63). New York: The Guilford Press.

Berecz, John, & Helm, Herbert Jr. (1998). Shame the underside of Christianity. *Journal of Psychology and Christianity, 17* (1), 5-14.

Berger, Dorita. (1999). *Toward the Zen of performance.* Ladysmith, Wisconsin: Flambeau Litho Corp.

Berry, Carmen Renee. (1993). *Your body never lies.* Berkley, California: PageMill Press.

Bollas, Christopher. (1987). *The Shadow of the object.* New York: Columbia University Press.

Braddock, Carolyn. (1995). *Body Voices.* Berkely: PageMill Press.

184

Bradshaw, John. (1988). *Healing shame that binds you.* Deerfield Beach, Florida: Health Communications, Inc.

Brennan, Richard. (1998). *Mind and body: Stress relief with the Alexander Technique.* Thorsons:London.

Brown, C. (1980). *The Dictionary of New Testament theology (vol.2).* Grand Rapids, Michigan: Zondervan.

Brown, William Earl. (1957).*Vocal wisdom: Maxims of Giovanni Battista Lamperti.* New York: Hudson Offset Company, Inc.

Bruscia, Kenneth. (1989). *Defining music therapy.* Phoenixville, Pennsylvania: Barcelona Publishers.

Bunch, Meribeth. (1993). *Dynamics of the singing voice.* Wien, Austria: Springer-Verlag.

Bunch, Meribeth. (2000). *A Handbook of the singing voice.* London: Meribeth Dayme.

Cameron, Julia. (1998). *The Right to write.* New York: Jeremy Tarcher/Putnam.

Campbell, Don. (2001). *The Mozart effect.* New York: Quill (Harper Collins Publishers)

Capps, Donald. (1993). *The Depleted self.* Minneapolis: The Fortress Press.

Cashdan, Sheldan. (1988). *Object Relations Therapy.* New York: W.W. Norton & Company.

Cresswell, John, W. (1998). *Qualitative inquiry and research design: Choosing among five traditions.* Thousand Oaks, CA: Sage Publications, Inc.

D'Angelo, James. (2000). *Healing with the voice.* London: Thorsons-Harper Collins Pub.

De Alcantara, Pedro. (1997). *Indirect Procedures: A Musician's Guide to the Alexander Technique.* New York: Oxford University Press.

Denzin, N.K., & Lincoln, Y.S. (Eds.). (1994). *Handbook of qualitative research.* Thousand Oaks, CA: Sage Publications.

Denzin, N, & Lincoln, Y. (Eds.). (2000). *The handbook of qualitative research.* Thousand Oaks, CA: Sage Publications.

Emmons, Shirlee, & Thomas, Alma. (1998). *Power performance for singers.* New York: Oxford University Press.

Gardner-Gordon, Joy. (1990). *The Healing voice: Traditional and contemporary toning, chanting, and singing.* Freedom, California: The Crossing Press.

Glesne, Corrine, & Peshkin, Alan. (1992). *Becoming qualitative researchers.* White Plains: New York: Longman.

Godby, Katherine. (2003). Courage in the development of self in women. *The Journal of Pastoral Care and Counseling, 57,* (3), 293-304.

Golomb, Elan. (1992). *Trapped in the mirror.* New York: Quill William Marrow.

Green, Barry, & Gallwey, Timothy. (1986). *The Inner game of music.* London: Pan Books.

Greenberg, Jay R., & Mitchell, Stephen A. (1983). *Object relations in psychoanalytic theory.* Cambridge, Maschusetts: Harvard University Press.

Holstein, James & Gubrium, Jaber. (1995). *An Active interview.* Thousand Oaks, California: Sage Publications, Inc.

Holstein, James & Gubrium, Jaber. (1997). Active interviewing. In D.Silverman (Ed.), *Qualitative research: Theory, method and practice.* Thousand Oaks, CA: Sage Publications.

Howard, Martin. (2003, Spring). On Singing and playing. *The Drumbeat, 3,* (2) 20.

Husler, Frederick, & Rodd-Marling, Yvonne. (1976). *Singing the physical nature of the vocal organ: A guide to the unlocking of the singing voice.* London: Hutchinson of London.

Jones, James. (1991). *Contemporary psychoanalysis and religion.* New Haven: Yale University Press.

Kaufman, Gershen. (1985). *Shame: the power of caring.* Rochester, Vermont: Schenkman Books Inc.

Kaufman, Gershem. (1996). *The Psychology of shame: Theory and treatment of shame based syndromes.* New York: Springer House.

Keen, Sam. (1999). *Learning to fly.* New York: Broadway.

Kohut, Heinz. (1978). *The Search for the self* (vol.1). Ornstein, Paul (Ed.), New York: International Universities Press Inc.

Leibowitz, Judith, & Connington, Bill (1990). *The Alexander Technique.* New York: Harper and Row.

Linklater, Kristin. (1976). *Freeing the natural voice.* New York: Drama Book Specialists.

Lynd, Helen Merrel. (1958). *On Shame and the search for identity.* New York: Science Edition.

Manheim, Carol, & Lavett, Diane. (1989). *Craniosacral therapy: and Somato-emotional release.* Thorofare, New Jersey: Slack Incorporated.

Martin, Sue Ann. (1996). I Voice, therefore I am. *Arts in Psychotherapy, 23* (3), 261-268.

Masters, Paul. (1988). *Osteopathy for everyone.* Penguin Books: London.

McCallion, Michael. (1988). *The Voice book.* New York: Theatre Arts Books.

McClintock, Karen. (2001). *Sexual shame: An urgent call to healing.* Minneapolis: Fortress Press.

Mertons, Donna. (1998). *Research methods in education and psychology: Integrating diversity with quantitative approaches.* Thousand Oaks, CA: Sage Publications.

Merriam, Sharan, B. (1988). *Case study research in education: a qualitative approach.* San Francisco, CA: Jossey-Bass Inc., Publishers.

Merriam, Sharan, B. (2001). *Qualitative research and case study applications* (2nd ed.). San Francisco: Jossey-Bass Inc., Publishers.

Merriam-Webster Online Dictionary. http://www.m-w.com/cgi-bin/dictionary (retrieved 02/16/2004)

Masters, Paul. (1988). *Osteopathy for Everyone.* London: Penguin Books.

Masterson, J. (1985). *The Real self.* New York: Brunner Mazel.

Meissner, W. (1984). *Psychoanalysis and religious experience.* New Haven: Yale University Press.

Miller, Alice. (1981). *The Drama of the gifted child: the search for the true self.* New York: Basic Books.

Miller, Alice. (1987). *For you own good.* London: Virago.

Miller, Richard. (1977). *English, French, German and Italian techniques of singing: A study in national tonal preferences and how they relate to functional efficiency.* Metuchen, New Jersey: The Scarecrow Press, Inc.

Miller, Richard. (1986). *The Structure of Singing: system and art in vocal technique.* New York: Schirmer Books.

Miller, Richard. (1993). *Training tenor voices.* New York: Schirmer Books.

Miller, Richard. (1996). *On the Art of Singing.* New York: Oxford University Press.

Moustakas, Clarke. (1990). *Heuristic Research.* Newbury Park, CA: Sage Publications.

The New Interpreter's Bible (Vol. 8). (1995). Nashville: Abingdon Press.

Newham, Paul. (1998). *Therapeutic voicework: Principles and practice for the use of singing as a therapy.* London: Jessica Kingsley Publishers.

Newham, Paul. (1999). *Using voice and song in therapy.* London: Jessica Kingsley Publishers.

Nouwen, Henri. (1992). *The Return of the prodigal son.* New York: Image Books, Doubleday.

Oddy, Nicola. (2002). Vocal improvisation – A pathway to deeper understanding of the self. *Proceedings of the 29th Annual Conference of the Canadian Association for Music Therapy.*

Pannenberg, Wolfhart. (1972). *The Apostles' creed in light of today's questions.* Philadelphia, Pennsylvania: The Westminster Press.

Patenaude-Yarnell, Joan. (2003, Nov.-Dec.). Sensations of singing: A look at time honored maxims, descriptions, and images. *Journal of Singing, 60* (2), 185-189.

Patteson, Ann. (1999). *Singing a woman's life: How singing lessons transformed the lives of nine women.* Unpublished master's thesis, Queen's University, Kingston, Ontario.

Pattison, Stephen. (2000). *Shame: Theory, therapy, theology.* Cambridge: Cambridge University Press.

Pruett, Kyle. (1988, June). Young narcissus at the music stand: Developmental perspectives from embarrassment to exhibitionism. *Medical Problems of Performing Artists,* 69-75.

Reid, Cornelius. (1983). *A Dictionary of vocal terminology.* New York: Joseph Patelson Music House Ltd.

Ristad, Eloise. (1982). *A Soprano on her head.* Moab, Utah: Real People Press.

Rizzuto, Anna-Maria. (1979). *The Birth of the living God: a psychoanalytic study.* Chicago, Illinois: The University of Chicago Press.

Rodenburg, Patsy. (1992). *The Right to speak: working with the voice.* London: Methuen Drama, Michelin House.

Rosenthal, Eleanor. (1987, June). The Alexander Technique – What it is and how it works. *Medical Problems of Performing Artists,* 53-57.

Rottschafer, Ronald. (1992). Grace and the importance of self. In L. Aden, & D.Benner,& H.Ellens (Eds.). *Christian perspectives on human development* (pp.145-156). Grand Rapids, Michigan: Baker Books House.

St. Claire, Michael. (2000). *Object relations and self psychology (3rd ed.).* Belmont, California: Wadsworth/Thomson Learning.

Sandgren, Maria. (2002, March). Voice, soma, and psyche: A qualitative and quantitative study of opera singers. *Medical Problems of Performing Artists, 11-22.*

Sirica, C. (Ed.). (1995). *Osteopathic medicine: Past, present, and future.* Dallas, Texas: Josiah Macy Jr. Foundation.

Smedes, Lewis B. (1993). *Shame and grace.* San Francisco: Zondervan Publishing.

Sprenkle, Douglas H.&, Moon, Sidney M. (1996). *Research methods in family therapy.* New York: The Guilford Press.

Stake, Robert. (1995). *The Art of case study research.* Thousand Oaks, CA: Sage Publications, Inc.

Stake, Robert E. (2000). Case Studies. In K. Denzin & Y. Lincoln (Eds.), *The handbook of qualitative research* (p.435-454). Thousand Oaks, CA: Sage Publications.

Stephens, Gillian. (1983). The Use of improvisation for developing relatedness in the adult client. *Music Therapy, 3* (1) 29-42.

Summers, Susan. (1999). *A Tapestry of voices: Community building with a geriatric choir reflected in a music therapy model of practice.* Unpublished Masters Thesis, Open University of British Columbia, Vancouver, British Columbia.

Taylor, Steven, & Bogdan, Robert (1998). *Introduction to qualitative research methods* (3rd ed.). Toronto: John Wiley & Sons, Inc.

Thompson, J. Earl. (1996). Shame in pastoral psychotherapy. *Pastoral Psychology, 44* (5), 311-321.

Titze, Ingo.(1994). *Principles of voice production.* Englewood Cliffs, New Jersey: Prentice Hall.

VandeCreek, Larry, & Bender, Hilary, & Jordan, Merle. (1994). *Research in pastoral care and counseling: Quantitative and qualitative approaches.* Decature, GA: Journal of Pastoral Care Publications, Inc.

Van Manen, Max. (1997). *Researching Lived Experience.* London, Ontario: The Althouse Press.

Vennard, William. (1967). *Singing the mechanism and the technic.* New York: Carl Fischer.

Whitehead, James, & Whitehead, Evelyn. (1995). *Shadows of the heart.* New York: Crossroad.

Winnicott, Donald W. (1971). *Playing and reality.* London: Tavistock Publications.

Wolf, Ernest S. (1988). *Treating the self.* New York: The Guilford Press.

Woodman, Marion, & Mellick, Jill. (1998). *Coming Home to Myself.* Berkely, CA: Canari Press.

Wormhoudt, Pearl Shinn. (1992, Dec.). On the psychology of singing and teaching of singing. *Journal of Research in Singing and Applied Vocal Pedagogy. 16*(1) 1-12.

Yin, Robert, K. (1984). *Case study research design and methods.* Thousand Oaks, CA: Sage Publications, Inc.

Yin, Robert K. (1994). *Case study research design and methods* (2nd ed.). Thousand Oaks, CA: Sage Publications, Inc.

Yin, Robert K. (2003). *Case study research design and methods* (3rd ed.). Thousand Oaks, CA: Sage Publications, Inc.

APPENDIX A

CONSENT FORMS

Consent Form for Co-researcher

Research Project Title: Coming Home to the Self through Freeing the Singing Voice.

Researcher: Joan Dosso (graduate student at St. Stephen's College)

Supervisor: Dr. Phil Carverhill* (306) 665-6242, carverhill@sask.usask.ca

This consent form will outline how you may be involved in this research project and the possible risks/benefits of participation. It will explain how confidentiality will be maintained and obtain your informed consent. Please read this form thoughtfully before signing and ask the researcher or advisor if you have any questions regarding the study or your participation.

Purpose of the Research

The purpose of this study is to explore the possible psychological, emotional, and physical experiences of a female singer in the process of freeing her voice. The study will be carried out as stated in this document without deceit. The data collected will be used in the researcher's graduate studies thesis.

Procedure

I (the researcher) will gather data through interviews with you (the participant) and through observing you singing and teaching singing. The interviews will involve open-ended questions inviting you to describe your experiences. The interviews could involve listening to recordings of you singing and teaching singing, and sharing journal entries or other documents (such as musical reviews) related to your experience of freeing the voice. There will be 3-4 interviews of one and a half hours each and 2-3 sessions of observation. I will tape record and transcribe the interviews and submit my analysis/interpretation to you within 5 months to check that I have accurately portrayed your experience.

Risks/Benefits

There are very few risks to you as a participant in this study. The one possibility I foresee is that painful or unresolved psychological or emotional issues could surface through the interviews. Therefore, you will be encouraged to be attentive to your feelings and are free to stop the interview or request a change in the direction of the interview at any time if you feel too uncomfortable. I will encourage you to use available therapy resources should the need arise from being involved in the study. You are free to cease participation in the study at any time without consequence and data from your participation to that point will be destroyed and not included in the study.

The personal benefit of being involved in this study is that it will give you the opportunity to reflect on and consolidate your experience of freeing the voice and come to a greater understanding of yourself. This could help you in your continuing journey towards vocal freedom, and in understanding the journeys of your students, and knowing how to work with them. Other singers, voice teachers, and therapists might also benefit through reading this study and understanding your process as a singer learning to free your voice.

Confidentiality

Tapes and transcripts of interviews and notes taken belong to me, the researcher, and I will keep them locked securely in a filing cabinet and show them only to my advisor. At the end of the study I will destroy tapes and consent forms, and erase names and identifying information from any remaining transcripts or notes. When the study is written in its final form, and if all or part of it is published or used in a presentation in the future, no names or identifying information will appear. A copy of the report will be available to you upon request.

Your signature on this form indicates that you understand what your participation in this study requires and are in agreement with its terms. It also gives permission for the researcher to utilize the data in future articles or presentations in which the same ethical provisions for handling data confidentially will be applied. Signing this form does not waive your legal rights, nor does it release the researcher, advisors, or involved institutions from their legal and professional responsibilities. You are free to withdraw from this study at any time without jeopardizing your relationship with the researcher. You are encouraged to ask questions throughout your participations so that your continued consent remains as informed as your initial consent.

If you have questions related to the research please contact:
Joan Dosso (780) 458-4741 jdosso@look.ca or
Dr. Phil Carverhill* (306) 665-6242 carverhill@sask.usask.ca

If you have questions concerning your rights as a participant in this research please contact Kristine Lund, Program Director of the Master of Arts in Pastoral Psychology and Counseling at St. Stephen's College (780) 439-7311.

_____	_____
Participant's Signature	Date
_____	_____
Researcher's Signature	Date

A copy of this consent form will be given to you to keep for your records and reference

*Dr. Phil Carverhill was the supervisor at the time the data was collected from the participants. Subsequently there was a change in supervisors and Deborah Barrett completed the supervision of the research.

<h1>Consent Form for Student Participant</h1>

Research Project Title: Coming Home to the Self through Freeing the Singing Voice.

Researcher: Joan Dosso (graduate student at St. Stephen's College)

Supervisor: Dr. Phil Carverhill* (306) 665-6242, carverhill@sask.usask.ca

This consent form will outline how you may be involved in this research project and the possible risks/benefits of participation. It will explain how confidentiality will be maintained and obtain your informed consent. Please read this form thoughtfully before signing and ask the researcher or advisor if you have any questions regarding the study or your participation.

Purpose of the Research

The purpose of this study is to explore the possible psychological, emotional, and physical experiences of a female singer in the process of freeing her voice. The study will be carried out as stated in this document without deceit. The data collected will be used in the researcher's graduate studies thesis.

Procedure

I (the researcher) will gather data through interviews with you (the participant) and through observing you singing in master class and private lessons. The interviews will involve open-ended questions regarding your experiences of learning to free your voice as well as how the interaction with your vocal coach/teacher affects your process of learning. There will be 1-2 interviews of one and a half hours each which I will tape record and transcribe. I will submit a copy of my analysis/interpretation of the data pertaining to your interview within 5 months to check that I have accurately portrayed your experience.

Risks/Benefits

There are very few risks to you as a participant in this study. The one possibility I foresee is that painful or unresolved psychological or emotional issues could surface through the interviews. Therefore, you will be encouraged to be attentive to your feelings and are free to stop the interview or request a change in the direction of the interview at any time if you feel too uncomfortable. I will encourage you to use available therapy resources should the need arise from being involved in the study. You are free to cease participation in the study at any time without consequence and data from your participation to that point will be destroyed and not included in the study.

The personal benefit of being involved in this study is that it will give you the opportunity to reflect on and consolidate your experience of freeing the voice and come to a greater understanding of yourself. This could help you in your continuing journey towards vocal freedom, and in understanding the journeys of your students, and knowing how to work with them. Other singers, voice teachers, and therapists might also benefit through reading this study and understanding your process as a singer learning to free your voice.

Confidentiality

Tapes and transcripts of interviews and notes taken belong to me, the researcher, and I will keep them locked securely in a filing cabinet and show them only to my advisor. At the end of the study I will destroy tapes and consent forms, and erase names and identifying information from any remaining transcripts or notes. When the study is written in its final form, and if all or part of it is published or used in a presentation in the future, no names or identifying information will appear. A copy of the report will be available to you upon request.

Your signature on this form indicates that you understand what your participation in this study requires and are in agreement with its terms. It also gives permission for the researcher to utilize the data in future articles or presentations in which the same ethical provisions for handling data confidentially will be applied. Signing this form does not waive your legal rights, nor does it release the researcher, advisors, or involved institutions from their legal and professional responsibilities. You are free to withdraw from this study at any time without jeopardizing your relationship with the researcher. You are encouraged to ask questions throughout your participations so that your continued consent remains as informed as your initial consent.

If you have questions related to the research please contact:
Joan Dosso (780) 458-4741 jdosso@look.ca or
Dr. Phil Carverhill* (306) 665-6242 carverhill@sask.usask.ca.

If you have questions concerning your rights as a participant in this research please contact Kristine Lund, Program Director of the Master of Arts in Pastoral Psychology and Counseling at St. Stephen's College (780) 439-7311.

Participant's Signature	Date

Researcher's Signature	Date

A copy of this consent form will be given to you to keep for your records and reference.

*Dr. Phil Carverhill was the supervisor at the time the data was collected from the participants. Subsequently there was a change in supervisors and Deborah Barrett completed the supervision of the research.

Consent Form for Subsidiary Co-researcher

Research Project Title: Coming Home to the Self through Freeing the Singing Voice.

Researcher: Joan Dosso (graduate student at St. Stephen's College)

Supervisor: Dr. Phil Carverhill* (306) 665-6242, carverhill@sask.usask.ca.

This consent form will outline how you may be involved in this research project and the possible risks/benefits of participation. It will explain how confidentiality will be maintained and obtain your informed consent. Please read this form thoughtfully before signing and ask the researcher or advisor if you have any questions regarding the study or your participation.

Purpose of the Research

The purpose of this study is to explore the possible psychological, emotional, and physical experiences of a female singer in the process of freeing her voice. The study will be carried out as stated in this document without deceit. The data collected will be used in the researcher's graduate studies thesis.

Procedure

I (the researcher) will gather data through interviews with you (the participant) on your observations of other female singers learning to free their voices (including the main participant of the case study). There will be 1-2 interviews of one and a half hours each which could involve a joint interview with the main participant of the case study. I will tape record and transcribe the interviews and submit my analysis/interpretation to you within 5 months to check if I have accurately portrayed the data pertaining to your experience. All participants will receive a copy of the analysis/interpretation of all interview data.

Risks/Benefits

There are very few risks to you as a participant in this study. The one possibility I foresee is that painful or unresolved psychological or emotional issues could surface through the interviews. Therefore, you will be encouraged to be attentive to your feelings and are free to stop the interview or request a change in the direction of the interview at any time if you feel too uncomfortable. I will encourage you to use available therapy resources should the need arise from being involved in the study. You are free to cease participation in the study at any time without consequence and data from your participation to that point will be destroyed and not included in the study.

The personal benefit of being involved in this study is that it will give you the opportunity to reflect on and consolidate your experience of freeing the voice and come to a greater understanding of yourself. This could help you in your continuing journey towards vocal freedom, and in understanding the journeys of your students, and knowing how to work with them. Other singers, voice teachers, and therapists might also benefit through reading this study and understanding your process as a singer learning to free your voice.

Confidentiality

Tapes and transcripts of interviews and notes taken belong to me, the researcher, and I will keep them locked securely in a filing cabinet and show them only to my advisor. At the end of the study I will destroy tapes and consent forms, and erase names and identifying information from any remaining transcripts or notes. When the study is written in its final form, and if all or part of it is published or used in a presentation in the future, no names or identifying information will appear. A copy of the report will be available to you upon request.

Your signature on this form indicates that you understand what your participation in this study requires and are in agreement with its terms. It also gives permission for the researcher to utilize the data in future articles or presentations in which the same ethical provisions for handling data confidentially will be applied. Signing this form does not waive your legal rights, nor does it release the researcher, advisors, or involved institutions from their legal and professional responsibilities. You are free to withdraw from this study at any time without jeopardizing your relationship with the researcher. You are encouraged to ask questions throughout your participations so that your continued consent remains as informed as your initial consent.

If you have questions related to the research please contact:
Joan Dosso (780) 458-4741 jdosso@look.ca or
Dr. Phil Carverhill* (306) 665-6242 carverhill@sask.usask.ca.

If you have questions concerning your rights as a participant in this research please contact Kristine Lund, Program Director of the Master of Arts in Pastoral Psychology and Counseling at St. Stephen's College (780) 439-7311.

_____   _____
Participant's Signature   Date

_____   _____
Researcher's Signature   Date

A copy of this consent form will be given to you to keep for your records and reference

*Dr. Phil Carverhill was the supervisor at the time the data was collected from the participants. Subsequently there was a change in supervisors and Deborah Barrett completed the supervision of the research.

APPENDIX B

INTERVIEW QUESTIONS

General/Psychological

1. What does the phrase, "the process of freeing your voice" mean to you?

2. When did you begin working on freeing your voice?

3. How did you begin working on freeing your voice?

4. What prompted you to begin the process at the time you did?

5. What thoughts and feelings did you experience in the early stages of your voice work?

6. What aspects of your voice needed freeing and developing? How did you know what needed work? Did you feel it physically? Did you hear it? Were you told by someone (i.e. a teacher or colleague)?

7. Describe an experience of encountering a block while trying to free your voice.
    a. What did you feel physically?
    b. What did you feel emotionally?
    c. What thoughts did you have?
    d. How did you work with the block?
    e. What were the results of that work?(physically, psychologically, spiritually, musically)
    f. Could others (such as teachers or audience) sense the difference? How?

8. Describe an experience of a student of yours encountering a block while working to free her voice.
    a. How did you know she was encountering a block?
    b. How did she describe what she was experiencing?
    c. How did you work with her and with the block?
    d. What were the results of your work?
    e. Was there a noticeable difference to you? To her? To an audience?
    f. If there was a difference, in what way was it noticeable?

9. What types of thoughts and feelings affect your ability to sing freely, either by enhancing or inhibiting it? (For example; anxiety, nervousness, excitement, confidence, pleasure in the music).

10. What situations or factors trigger these thoughts and feelings?

11. Describe a significant life event or circumstance that affected your vocal freedom.

12. How would you describe the relationship between your voice and your sense of identity?

Experience of Vocal Techniques

1. Describe your physical and psychological experience of working with the breath in the context of singing.

2. Describe your physical and psychological experience of working with your posture in the context of singing.

3. Describe your thoughts, feelings, and physical sensations when you were in the process of loosening the control of some aspect of your voice (i.e. vibrato, articulation of individual pitches).

4. If you have had the experience of feeling that you were loosing control vocally, describe what thoughts, feelings, and physical sensations accompanied this experience.

Wissenschaftlicher Buchverlag bietet

kostenfreie

Publikation

von

wissenschaftlichen Arbeiten

Diplomarbeiten, Magisterarbeiten, Master und Bachelor Theses
sowie Dissertationen, Habilitationen und wissenschaftliche Monographien

Sie verfügen über eine wissenschaftliche Abschlußarbeit zu aktuellen oder zeitlosen
Fragestellungen, die hohen inhaltlichen und formalen Ansprüchen genügt,
und haben **Interesse an einer honorarvergüteten Publikation**?

Dann senden Sie bitte erste Informationen über Ihre Arbeit per Email
an info@vdm-verlag.de. Unser Außenlektorat meldet sich umgehend bei Ihnen.

VDM Verlag Dr. Müller Aktiengesellschaft & Co. KG
Dudweiler Landstraße 125a
D - 66123 Saarbrücken

www.vdm-verlag.de